HOW TO RUN BETTER MEETINGS

How to Run

BETTER MEETINGS

by EDWARD J. HEGARTY

McGRAW-HILL BOOK COMPANY, INC.

1957   New York, Toronto, London

How Much Time Do You Spend in Meetings?

The other evening I was speaking at a meeting. The chairman asked, "How much time does the average man spend in meetings, Mr. Hegarty?"

The business man would answer, "Too much." The professional man will say, "There are too many." The ladies will agree, not because the master has spoken, but because they feel that way too. But the meetings go on, you and I attend, and they eat up valuable time.

And that time is the most important tool we have to work with. To do our work, our good deeds, to think, to play, there are only so many hours in the day. How often have you said, "Oh, if only I could spare the time"? And here we are spending so much time in meetings.

It's the purpose of this book to help save some of that time. For perhaps if our meetings were run better, if the minutes were used more effectively, some of that valuable time could be saved.

EDWARD J. HEGARTY

Who Is the Author?

Ed Hegarty has been called "Mr. Meetings Himself." A recent article said, "He's been responsible for a million better meetings." That well may be true, for he has been a meeting manager and crusader for better meetings for over forty years.

He has put on meetings, planned meetings for others to put on, written about meetings, and has been the guest speaker at thousands of them. He is an author of seven books and hundreds of trade-paper articles on speaking and running meetings. An engineer by education, he has been a salesman, sales executive, training authority, speaker, and writer. He is much in demand as a speaker before sales organizations, sales executives, and trade associations. His articles have appeared in business, professional, and popular magazines. He has spent forty years in the electric appliance business with Westinghouse and other companies.

The suggestions he gives in this book are out of his experience in managing meetings and in speaking at them.

To Meeting Managers

You girls and lads who put on meetings:

I'm giving you a new title, "Meeting Manager."

Maybe you never thought of yourself as a meeting manager. But let's say you are the one in the office the boss calls in and says, "Joe, I want to tell all the people in the office about our new ABC plan. We'll have Pete tell them about A, Ken or Tommy can tell about B, and I'll handle the C. But you organize it all. Let's get together at 3:00 this afternoon to discuss it."

O.K., who's managing that meeting? You are, aren't you?

Then let's say you are the president or secretary of a club. You have a meeting planned for next month. You know that if the meeting is to be organized, you had better do most of the work. And so you get the speaker, plan the notice, get it in the mail, arrange for the meeting room, take care of the other details, take the criticism if everything doesn't go right. O.K., who is managing that meeting? You are, aren't you?

Perhaps it's our nth freedom—the right to hold meetings. We Americans must hold a few million every week. Recently I read that one company was making a survey to determine the value of the meetings held by the company personnel. How were they making the survey? By a series of meetings, of course.

Before you laugh ask yourself, "How could they do it better?"

Since all of us show by our actions that we like to go to meetings, there are a lot of meeting managers just like you who must put these shows on the stage.

And so it is for you, you girls and lads who put on those million or more meetings every week, that these suggestions, thoughts, and ideas are brought together. Read on and when you find one that might fit your group, try it. If it works, great. If it doesn't work, mark yourself "A" for effort. But don't discourage easily, try another, and another. In no time at all you'll learn to select the ones made to measure for your group.

The group will like your meetings and you'll get a reputation as a Meeting Manager who knows his stuff. There's no thrill like the one you feel when the member says, "Joe, you put on a good show."

Is This Your Club?

No matter what kind of club you run, those members are a pain.

> They won't read the notices.
> They won't send back the return cards to say that they are coming.
> They won't arrive on time.
> They won't take the front seats.
> They won't ask questions.
> They'll shut the windows when you need the air, shut off the fans when you need the air circulation.
> They won't take part.
> But they will complain about this, about that, about everything.

To run a club you must love your fellow men, for you meet so many that are difficult to love. But since you are running the club, you are perhaps smarter than these members who won't do this and that. And it is the hope of the author that some of the suggestions given here might help smarten you up enough so that you will be able to get more of these members to help make your job easier.

Contents

xiv   *Contents*

HOW TO RUN BETTER MEETINGS

1 / A Meeting, a Meeting, Hurray, Hurray!

NOTE TO READER: The following describes a Service Club luncheon meeting. In putting it on the chairman and the guest speaker make a number of mistakes. See how many you can detect.

Dunkin Hazzel hurried across the street just as the traffic light was changing. He pushed open the door of the hotel, rushed up the stairs to the lobby. He was taking off his top-coat as he continued up the steps to the ballroom. The club fined you twenty-five cents if you were even seconds late for the weekly meeting of Service, Inc., and in his fourteen years as a member Dunk had never paid out a single two bits.

"Old Dunk's under the wire again," laughed Crunch Cooper, who was holding the watch this day.

"How many seconds?" Dunk asked.

"Three more steps and you wouldn't have made it," Crunch said.

Dunk saw Will Anderson sitting at one of the tables and started toward him. Towfrey Booter, president of the club, met him halfway and shook hands with him. "Gotta be chairman today," Booter said. "Art's the program chairman, but he's up in Cleveland to see the ice show. Excuse me."

Pete Peterson, the secretary, had called Booter. Pete was talking to a stranger up near the head table. "Art does a good job, but that guy—" Will Anderson said.

Hazzel looked at the stranger, probably the guest speaker. Booter was giving the stranger the works—smile, personality, all of it. Booter was president, but popularity hadn't got the job for him. He had come into town less than ten years ago, but he had married money. Hazzel couldn't remember who had brought him into the club. John King had said of Booter, "He's a phony, but he's a pompous phony. There's a difference. He probably won't hurt the club too much."

Booter hadn't. Any club had to have a president. Booter looked like one, anyway. The tables were filling and the men were taking their seats. Hazzel talked Will Anderson into moving to one close up under the speaker's lectern. He wondered why he tried to get close to the speaker. So many of them couldn't talk for sour apples. "It's a courtesy to fill up the near tables," he had preached when he had been president. While he had talked himself hoarse pleading to fill up those near tables, the listeners had not bought the idea.

Booter asked Paul Peterson to give the thanks. They all stood with bowed heads for the minute. Then he asked Joel Lange to lead in the singing. Hazzel couldn't carry a note, but he tried on the two numbers. Now the girls were bringing on the food. "Veal chops again," one of the brothers at the table said.

"I never get them at home," said another.

"This time, no peas," said a third.

"It's not the food alone you pay for," the first man said. "It's the guest speaker."

"Who is the guy and what's he talking about?" asked the fat man that Hazzel couldn't remember ever having seen before.

Nobody at the table seemed to know. "I got the notice and I read it," Hazzel admitted, "but I can't recall."

The girls were bringing on the dessert when Booter rapped the gavel. "While you good people are finishing your dessert," he said, "I have a few announcements to read. You just go right on eating."

As if anybody could stop them, Hazzel thought. The crust of the pie was the usual plastic, but the apples inside looked good. Hazzel tried one of them.

Booter looked at the paper in his hand, studied it. The audience with mouths full saw that he was lost. He walked down to the end of the table still studying the paper. He showed it to Pete Peterson, the club secretary. A minute of conversation, then Booter—still studying the paper, holding it at arm's length—went back to the center of the table. He rapped the gavel again. "I'm sorry for the delay, please excuse it," he said. "I couldn't make out this announcement. Now you continue your lunch," he advised. He started the announcement, but that reminded him of a story. It was the one about the mule that the trainer hit between the eyes with a two-by-four—the gag line, "That's just to get his attention." Hazzel had heard the story at least four times in the last week. Even Booter's garbled version was recognizable. Booter repeated the gag line, "That's just to get his attention." There was a smattering of applause that Booter's laugh almost drowned.

"Is this microphone working?" Booter asked. He tapped

it with a pencil, he snapped his fingers. He said, "Testing, testing."

The brothers told him it was not working.

"Joe Sobol," Booter called, "will you take two minutes while we send for the electrician and tell us about the plans for the ladies' night? Let's give Joe a hand."

Joe was glad to oblige. He took the two minutes and ten more to explain that the committee had moved the party from the hotel to the country club.

"Is this microphone working?"

"Why did they move it to the country club?" one member asked.

"Drinks will be seventy-five cents out there," another put in.

"There'll be some liquor in them, though," a third said.

Hazzel glanced at the guest speaker; the man looked sad. This rhubarb was cutting into his time.

"I realize there are certain members of this club that have an interest in building the revenue of the country club," said the man who had mentioned the seventy-five-cent drinks.

Hazzel was one of the governors of the country club.

He wondered how he could diplomatically tell them that
the country club didn't want them, that the seventy-five-
cent drinks were priced to discourage them. Instead,
he listened quietly. Why does a man come to these luncheons anyway? he asked himself.

Now old Forrest Ring was on his feet. "Mr. Chairman,
I object to moving this party to the country club. It's always
been held in this hotel. Why move it?"

"It was thought the membership would like the atmos-
phere of the club," Sobol answered.

"And those seventy-five-cent drinks," Ring went on.

Ring and Sobol were competitors. This went on every
time one of them proposed anything.

"But the committee has voted for it," Sobol protested.

"The help out there will high-hat us, and the drinks
will cost seventy-five cents," Ring went on.

Booter pounded the gavel. "We've taken too much of
the speaker's time, already," he said. "The affair will be at
the country club. Thanks to you and your committee, Mr.
Sobol."

But Sobol was not finished. "Get in your reservations
this week," he shouted, "this week."

Booter took off his spectacles to look at the Ladies' Night
Chairman. But Sobol was taking his seat. The electrician
came to fix the microphone. He made some adjustments
and asked Booter to try it. Booter called, "Testing, testing."
The group indicated that the mike was on. Hazzel wondered why the fuss over the mike. The room wasn't large
enough to warrant its use. Booter adjusted the mike until
it was at the right height. Now he looked at the announcements in his hand. "I'll make these later," he promised. He
stuffed the notes in his pocket, then said, "We have with
us today—" It seemed the head of the Psychology Depart-

ment at the state university had been the scheduled speaker, but he had been tied up with important university business and had sent his assistant. Booter apologized for the misleading announcement that had been mailed. "But we are fortunate at that," he went on, "to have with us his assistant, Professor Carius. I have been talking to Professor Carius, and in my opinion he will do just as well as his boss would have done." Hazzel was fascinated by the way Booter used his spectacles; he waved them at the audience, he scratched his ear with them, he took them off to offer an idea, he put them on to read about the schools and the degrees.

Booter read from a typed page of the professor's experience and education. He stumbled a few times in his reading and gave the impression that he had not seen the paper before. When he finished the reading, he turned the paper to see if there was more information on the reverse side. When he saw there was none, he said, "Without further ado, I give you Professor Jackson R. Carius."

Professor Carius arose with applause. He reached behind him for a set of charts he was to use. He tried to move a chair so that he could get the charts where he wanted them. The charts tilted and Booter was on his feet trying to help. He touched a spring and the charts collapsed. The audience laughed while the speaker set up the chart stand. In two minutes he was ready to go. He said, "Gentlemen—" Booter left his seat. He looked back at the first chart. Hazzel's eyes wandered from the first chart to watch Booter go out of the room. What did the chairman say about us being lucky to get a chance to hear this speaker? he thought. He looked back at the first chart. The type was difficult to make out—too small, and there was a lot of it. The speaker's voice was uninteresting; he gave the impression that he knew his subject but did not have any enthusiasm for it. Out the window Hazzel could see the blonde stenographer in the office across the street. He tried to figure whether it was the second or third floor and whose office it was. The blonde was making the type-writer talk, maybe two hundred words a minute. Must be a personal letter, couldn't be working that fast for her boss, he thought. He watched her take the sheet out of the machine, arrange some papers, and put them in the en-velope. He watched her put on her coat and hat. Then she was gone.

Hazzel's eyes went back to the speaker. The professor was still enmeshed in his statistics, still on that first chart. Hazzel looked at it again, then rubbed his eyes. He felt drowsy, statistics always did that to him. Why didn't these service club speakers ever learn?

A red hat in the hotel lobby caught his eye. It was that young Mrs. Kurston, the girl from Columbus that had married Fred. Nice dish; Fred must be twice her age. Hazzel watched her join a group of women. Probably a bridge club having a bite of lunch before the hostivities started.

His eyes went back to the head table. Booter was back now in an earnest conversation with Pete Peterson, the club secretary. Hazzel looked at the other men at the head table. Wes Cairnes, the oldest member of Service, Inc., was fast asleep. Hazzel bet Wes would be the first to congratulate the speaker on the excellent speech. Well, why not, it had put him to sleep, hadn't it? Doc Haynes, a vice president, had his pencil out and was drawing pictures on the table cloth. Allie Schentz, a director, was listening intently; but Allie was a University man—maybe he thought he should. Oggie Munch, another director, down at the end of the table was picking his nose. A head table sure helps a speaker, Hazzel thought.

Hazzel looked at the speaker. He was looking back through the charts trying to find the one that would better explain his point. "I had it here a minute ago," he said. Booter moved as if he might get up to help the professor, but the professor found the chart he was looking for. "This doesn't explain the point too well," he said, "but I believe—"

Hazzel looked longingly at the door. He wondered how much disturbance he would create if he got up and went out. He had always argued with those fellows who sat back by the door, but now—. He glanced back and saw that a number of them had gone.

At last the speaker finished. Booter was on his feet asking if there were any questions.

"Yes, I have one," a voice said.

Hazzel groaned. You could always depend on Butch Melistrup for a question. But it wasn't a question. It was a speech, a minute and one-half at least.

The speaker, who had sat down, started to his feet, but Booter beat him to it. "I think Mr. Melistrup's point is well taken," he said, "I believe—"

"Repeat the question," someone called.

The audience roared. Nobody could repeat the question, not even Melistrup.

Booter glared at the voice, he took off his spectacles and glared.

Now the professor moved in. He held up his hand and repeated the gist of Melistrup's question in ten words. "Was that your question?" he asked. Melistrup agreed that it was. The group applauded.

The professor bowed his thanks and answered the question. Smart guy, Hazzel thought.

Booter pushed up to the mike. "I beg to differ with the speaker," he announced.

Hazzel groaned. The door didn't look so far away now. He pushed his chair back, stood up, and walked resolutely out of the room.

Hazzel didn't stay to the finish, but so far in this short account of the meeting of Service, Inc., there had been twenty-eight mistakes that cut the effectiveness of this Service Club meeting. Some were the fault of the chairman, some of the speaker, but there was little reason for any of them. What were those twenty-eight mistakes? Well, here is a run down. How many of them did you detect?

One, Booter couldn't read that first note. He should have figured it out beforehand, don't you think?

Two, he broke into the announcement to tell that story. Should the chairman tell a story here? It may be one the speaker is planning to tell later.

Three, he repeated the gag line and laughed at it louder than the audience. O.K., so he is president.

Four, he checked the microphone at this time. Couldn't he have checked it before?

Five, he asked Joe Sobol to take two minutes to tell about the ladies' night. Why mention the two minutes before the audience? Get Joe aside beforehand and tell him his neck will be broken if he takes more than the two minutes.

Six, Joe took more than his two minutes. He started a rhubarb.

Seven, Booter took off his spectacles and put them on again.

Eight, the electrician and Booter caused a disturbance by testing the mike. It should have been done before the program started.

Nine, Booter promised to cover the balance of the announcements later. He shouldn't have promised to do anything later. The audience wants to go home later.

Ten, the chairman apologized for the misleading announcement about the guest speaker. How do you think that made the substitute feel?

Eleven, he stumbled in his reading of the data on the professor.

Twelve, Booter is active with his spectacles again, off and on, off and on.

Thirteen, the professor reached behind him for the charts he brought along. He should have had them set up beforehand.

Fourteen, Carius knocked over the charts.

Fifteen, Booter attempted to help him set them up. He should have allowed the speaker to straighten them out. All he could do was add to the confusion. He did.

Sixteen, Booter left the head table as soon as the speaker started and went out of the room. After telling the group how good the speaker was, he should have stayed to hear the talk, shouldn't he?

Seventeen, Carius' first chart had too much data on it, the type was too small to see.

Eighteen, the room was set up so Hazzel could look out the window and see the blonde in the office across the street. The audience shouldn't look toward the windows.

Nineteen, the room was set up so that Hazzel could look out into the lobby.

Twenty, the professor talked too long on that first chart.

Twenty-one, Booter talked club business with the secretary while he sat at the head table behind the speaker.

Twenty-two, the notables at the head table kept their seats where they could steal attention from the speaker. They always do, but they shouldn't.

Twenty-three, the speaker hunted back through his charts for an illustration that would help him explain a point. It shouldn't be done. A speaker is fumbling when he starts to hunt for something, anything.

Twenty-four, Booter started up to help the professor hunt.

Twenty-five, Melistrup made a speech instead of asking a question.

Twenty-six, nobody repeated the question so that the whole audience could hear it.

Twenty-seven, Booter started to comment on the question. Maybe he did have an idea, but it was the speaker's job to comment on it.

Twenty-eight, Booter started an argument with the speaker. He is there to protect the speaker from the wise guys, not to start arguments.

ONLY TWENTY-EIGHT SLIPS

"Twenty-eight slips—all details," you say. "What's so different about that? Those things happen at our club every week."

That's true, they do, and what's more they happen at most clubs, but that doesn't make them right.

"But they're details," you say.

I agree. But it is such details that make or break a meeting.

And are such mistakes confined to club meetings? They are not. Sit in on this meeting in a business office and see how many mistakes these men make.

2 / Do You Think the Business Meeting Is Different?

NOTE TO READER: In this description of a meeting in the office there are more mistakes. See how many you can find.

Foolish boy! foolish girl! They aren't. Just sit through this one and you'll see.

Jacque Aron took his seat about halfway back in the meeting room. He was there to observe and report. This was a meeting called by the boss to explain the new union contract to the supervisors. The meeting was called for ten o'clock and now a few minutes before ten the group started to drift in. But the first comers seemed to prefer the back seats. Aron thought that he might be up front by himself. The early birds seemed to take two chairs, one for the sitting and one for their feet. That soon brought the late comers up to Aron and even in front of him. Aron tried to move his chair so the light from the tall windows wouldn't shine in his eyes. The chairs were too close together; that one for the feet wasn't such a bad idea if a man wanted room enough to breathe. Now, with his chair turned, he had to move a bit to get out from behind the post that might block his view. He looked over the room. Yes, it might have been set up the other way so that the audience would not face the windows, and if it had been arranged that way the posts wouldn't have been hazards.

He glanced at his watch and asked the man next to him, "I thought this was to start at ten o'clock."

"It was," the fellow said, "but those guys from the service department are always late so we never get started on time."

A group came in and Aron assumed that they were the boys from the service department.

The boss vaulted up on the stage. He didn't need a bell or gavel. He was the boss and the room quieted. He started, "Fellows, this meeting is called to explain to you the new union contract terms. I want you to pay strict attention while the boys from Industrial Relations explain the new pay scale, the new benefits—hospital, vacations, pensions, and such things as that. But before they start I want to tell you that we have an expert on meetings with us today. He's here to observe and report. Mr. Aron will sit through the meeting and he will report to me on what we do right and what can be improved. While we want to improve always, I'd like to tell Mr. Aron that in my opinion, if I do say it myself, we run pretty good meetings around here. Will you stand up, Mr. Aron? I'd like to have our gang meet you."

Aron stood up. "Give him a hand now, fellows; we're paying him enough money for this report."

The group applauded. Aron looked sad as he sat down. He knew the group thought he had an easy way of making a living. Sitting in meetings and reporting. But the boss was saying, "Mr. Please, our Industrial Relations Manager, will act as chairman today, so without further ado I give you Charlie Please."

Mr. Please arose. He had a great sheaf of papers in his hands. He walked to the lectern in front of the stage and placed his papers on the stand. He seemed to spend an inconsiderately long time arranging his notes. He looked at the audience, cleared his throat, and started, "Fellows, I wish that some of you would come up and fill in these front seats."

"Without further ado—"

The audience looked at him but nobody moved. Again he said, "Come on now, fill up these front seats, please."

Two men did move now. Aron thought they might work in the Industrial Relations Department. Charlie said, "Aw, come on, please."

Nobody moved and he shrugged. He hugged the lectern so he could lean on it comfortably. "Okay, we're going to make this fast." He explained the purpose of the meeting. "So that I'll be sure you get these explanatory forms, I'm going to have some sheets passed out," he said. "Will you, Dick, and you, Joe, pass out these envelopes?" Joe and Dick went up front to get the envelopes. Please talked on. The boss who had come to sit beside Aron raised his hand for Charlie to talk louder. Joe and Dick were passing out the envelopes, Joe working one side of the room, Dick the other. As the men in the audience got the envelopes they opened them and started taking out the pieces. Please talked on, not noticing the rustling papers. Then he stopped talking and said, "I'm not ready for you to look at those papers yet; please put them back in the envelopes and I'll tell you when to look at them."

There was more confusion while the group put the papers back but Please got back on his script again. He glanced up and saw some men taking notes. "You don't need to take notes, fellows," he said. "I'm going to give you a copy of this script when I am done."

Please was a short, fat man with a shiny, bald head. Every now and then he moved away from the lectern and all Aron could see was the top of his head. That's why soap boxes were invented, Aron thought.

"The program is going to run like this," Please announced. He shuffled through the papers in front of him, looking for the program. "I thought it was right here," he said. He turned to a table behind him. "Ah, here it is," he announced. He looked at the paper. "First, Tom Galls is going to tell you about the money end—anybody here not interested in that?" (Some laughter.) "Then Dick Good will tell you about the benefits, fringe and otherwise— we got him some slides from headquarters to help him in that. Since we got a full program here, we got to keep this moving. I hope each speaker will remember that. So without further ado, I give you Tom Galls."

Tom had a set of charts. He moved them up beside the lectern. He looked at the charts, then at the audience. He cleared his throat, then said, "Fellows—" He reached for the chart stand and started to adjust it. The screw he was adjusting slipped from his hand and fell to the floor. While he held the charts to keep them from falling, a man in the second row found the screw and handed it back to him. Tom adjusted the charts and started again. A man from the rear came up front to adjust a spotlight that Tom wanted on the charts. "Can you get that so it is on the charts and not in my eyes?" Tom asked.

The fellow tried to make the adjustment.

"There are some chalk marks on the floor there," Tom said.

"It's in the chalk marks," the man said.

Tom waited until the lights were adjusted. "Fellows, I'm going to read the script that goes with these charts," he said. "I'm not too familiar with the new plan; I don't want to be misquoted; and if those reasons aren't enough, the boss says I have to or else." He turned the first chart. "This chart is supposed to show—" he said.

Aron looked at the chart. He noted that, even with the spotlight on it, he had trouble reading some of the figures. Then from where he sat about half of it was hidden by the lectern.

Galls read the first line of the chart and started to talk about the point covered. Aron read the balance of the data on the chart. Please was sitting behind the speaker, a nervous Nell, Aron thought. Aron watched him light a cigarette and look at his watch, make some pencil notes, look at his watch. Aron shaded his eyes from the light from the big windows behind the speaker. Now Please was off the stage talking to a man in the front row. He would say a few words, then look at his watch as if he had to hurry back.

Galls turned to the third chart. "This chart is supposed to show—" he started. Then he stopped and studied the chart as if he had never seen it before. He looked at his script, turned a page, then another. "This chart must be in the wrong place," he said. He turned to the next chart and said, "This chart is supposed to show—"

Aron noted that Galls had notes on the charts scribbled in pencil but, standing behind the lectern, he could not get into position to see the notes.

When Galls tried to show the fourth chart, he tore the paper. "This paper's not too good," he said, "this austerity program—or they're paying you guys too much—can't afford tough paper." The crack didn't get the laugh he expected. He struggled on with the script, looking at the chart as if he were speaking to it and not to the audience.

"I'm going to read this because I don't want to be misquoted."

As he turned the next chart without accident, he said, "Better paper in this one. They handled my complaint but fast, didn't they?" He read a paragraph of script on chart five, then said, "Wait a minute, there was a point I meant to emphasize on that last chart." He turned back to the chart ahead, tearing the paper a bit more. He made the point. Unimportant, Aron thought; then Galls turned back to chart five. "I think the type on this chart is too small," he said. "What do you guys think? Can you see it?" They said they could and he went on. He was thinking about his time now. Aron caught him sneaking a glance at his watch. Galls speeded up his reading. He seemed absorbed in that printed page, he stumbled over one difficult-to-pronounce word, then another. Like most men reading a speech, he had a tendency to speed up, particularly with

Please, his boss, signaling to him that he was running short on time.

The speedy reading tended to hit a monotone. There was no hint of enthusiasm for the new pay plan in the speaker's voice. Aron thought the plan was liberal. A little more punch in the voice might have convinced these supervisors that they had a plan they could sell to their help. Galls was giving them the words to say, but he was not putting any conviction in them.

Aron looked at the haze of smoke in the light that flooded the charts. There wasn't much air in the room. He felt a bit drowsy. He saw that a window near the front of the room was open. That meant some air was coming in. But as he noted the window, the fire engines went by on the street below. The wail of the sirens didn't seem to bother Galls. He was hurrying to get finished. In a few minutes the fire engines came back. That fire-eater sure loved to lean on that siren. "Please close that window," Galls said. Somebody closed the window.

Galls announced, "This is my last chart." The audience moved restlessly. Aron looked at the chart. It was a summation; the type was small and crowded.

Galls finished and Please was draped over the lectern again. "Now, fellows, we got a problem here," he said. "We had a recess scheduled at this point, but if we skip it and hurry on we can finish on time. What do you say?"

They wanted the recess and they wanted the meeting finished. People in meetings always do. But nobody was too much in favor of one or the other to make much noise about it.

"Go right on," the boss said. He was feeling no discomfort.

"O.K., we'll get going then," Please said. "Now you got

the dope on the pay schedule, Bill Rood is going to give you the dope on the other benefits. He's got some glass slides that Headquarters has sent over, so without further ado, Bill, you take over."

Rood placed his script on the lectern, pushed the other papers out of the way, and said, "Gentlemen, I'll give you the background on this while the boys set up my screen and projector. Some of you may have to move a bit. I'm sorry to have to use these slides, but Headquarters says we must." Joe and Dick were on the job again, setting up the projector and screen. They asked a few men to move and there was some good-natured confusion. But Bill was paying no attention to the disturbance. He was talking, he had the opening rehearsed, and he went on with it while the screen and projector were set up and focused. He finished a paragraph and asked, "You ready now?" The boys said they were.

"O.K., turn off the lights and give me the first slide, please."

The lights went off and the first slide was on the screen. Bill started to explain a point. "Can't you put that screen a bit higher?" a voice called.

"I don't know, let's see," Bill agreed. Joe and Dick came back and the screen was raised and the picture focused.

"That better?" Bill asked.

"Much better," the voice agreed.

Bill explained the slide and called, "Next slide, please."

"I don't think you need the lights off for those slides," a voice called.

"O.K., let's have the lights on."

Someone tripped over a table hunting for the light switch. There was a bit of profanity, then the lights came on.

"See that?" Bill asked. The group agreed that it could.

Bill talked about slide two, finished, and said, "Next slide, please."

The slide came on for an instant, then disappeared. "I kicked the cord, sorry," a voice said. The plug was put back into the outlet and the slide came on the screen. Bill read the script on the slide and called, "Next, please."

This slide came on the screen upside down. Bill said, "Everything happens to me." The operator righted the slide but Tom said, "That's not the next one."

"How about this?" the operator called.

"That's not it either," Bill answered.

The third slide was it, and Tom went on with his reading. After a while he said, "There are five slides coming up now that I'm going to run through quickly. They don't help explain too much, and I don't think you'll miss them. Run them through, Jack, but fast."

Jack tried to run them too fast and jammed the machine. The screen had two half-slides on for a minute or two, then Jack got it working again. Aron noted the slides carefully. They seemed to be a part of the pitch to him. He wondered who told the speaker to give them the rush.

"I got three slides more to show," Bill said. When he finished with the first of the three, he added, "Bear with me, boys, there's only two more." He talked for a minute on the slide on the screen, then said, "Here it is, gentlemen, the moment you've been waiting for—the last slide." The slide showed the company slogan, nothing more. The group applauded. Bill sat down.

Please was up hugging the lectern. "Now those boys did a fine job, both of them, but just in case everything isn't clear, I'm going to open this rhubarb for questions. Has anybody got a question?"

The group looked at him as if they hadn't heard. He looked back at them, glanced at his watch. He seemed pleased. He said, "Well, the boys covered the subject better than I thought. Did it so well, there are no questions." He was smiling at his own cleverness now. But the boss crossed him up.

"I know you guys got some questions," he said. "Junior, haven't you got one?"

The fellow called Junior, who was up in the front, got to his feet. "Yeah, I got one," he agreed looking back at the boss. He took a card out of his shirt pocket and started to read a question. He stumbled over the pronunciation of the word annuity.

"Tom, you take that one," Please directed.

Galls stood and started to answer.

"Repeat the question," a voice called.

Aron thought the next question seemed involved. Galls, who tried to answer it, stumbled over the answer.

The boss was now on his feet. He asked the man who asked the question, "Jenks, can you answer that question?"

Jenks said that he could.

"O.K., you answer it," the boss said. "And we don't want any more wise-guy questions." Aron shook his head. Jenks answered the question.

"I thought you knew the answer," the boss said. "Now listen, fellows, we're running short on time. We want questions, legitimate ones, but not wise-guy." He glared at Jenks and sat down.

A man in the back row started to ask a question. Before he had said ten words, Galls started to answer. Aron looked back and saw that three or four hands were up. Galls said, "O.K., John." A voice asked a question that Aron did not hear. "What kind of a question is that?" Please asked. But Galls started to answer it.

"What's the question?" the man next to Aron asked. Galls repeated the question and then answered it. But the answer made him think of another angle. He talked about the new angle for about six minutes.

Aron looked at Please with amusement. It was apparent that the time taken by the questions was killing him. Poor fellow, ever since the meeting had started his ulcers had been churning overtime. But the men were getting information that the presentations had not given. The hands raised indicated that.

Now the boss's voice boomed out. "Somebody taking down these questions?" he asked.

Nobody was. "O.K., let's start now," he said. "You, Pete, you get them—you know shorthand."

"What about the ones already asked?" Pete asked.

"Check the guys that asked them after," the boss said.

The questions went on. Rood was getting most of them now. He remembered to repeat each question, to tell the man that it was a good question, and every now and then he asked, "Does that answer your question?"

Aron looked at his watch. It was twelve-thirty. The questions were thinning out; some were repetitions of ones asked earlier. Please moved in. He said, "Well, fellows, that's about all for today. Let's give these boys a hand." The applause came. "Boss, did you have anything else?"

The boss didn't answer. He had been called to take a long-distance call.

"O.K.," Please said, "meeting adjourned."

Aron looked at his notes. He riffled the pages in the small book. Quite a number. He started to count at the first page. He was in the thirties when Please asked him, "How'd you think it went?"

So you thought that business meetings were run much more efficiently, did you? It isn't so. In this little meeting there were just seventy mistakes. Two hours, seventy mistakes. What were they? Well, let's review them.

THE SEVENTY GOOFS

One, there was no arrangement to get the early birds to take the front seats. Better tend to that or the front seats will get little wear.

Two, the room was set up so that the audience faced the windows. Perhaps the boss did not like to face the light when he talked, but it's murder to ask an audience to do it. They are the ones supposed to get something out of the meeting.

Three, the chairs were too close together. Think of a man's width when you place the chairs.

Four, the room had posts in it. Maybe that couldn't be helped, but the room might have been set up so that the posts were not a hazard.

Five, the meeting did not start on time. The fellow next to Aron said that they never did; the men from the service department were always late. Start without them once and they'll pay some attention to the time.

Six, the boss asked the audience to pay strict attention. That's ancient stuff. Nobody can be ordered to pay attention. You have to show them what paying attention can mean to them. Nobody is asleep when they're drawing for door prizes.

Seven, not much, just that "without further ado."

Eight, Please carried a big sheaf of notes to the lectern.

The audience felt this guy would be talking till noon. Don't let the audience see your notes. It's a good idea to get them placed beforehand.

Nine, Please fumbled with his notes, arranging them before he started to speak. He must have known what he was going to say to start.

Ten, Please had a Casper Milquetoast approach to getting the fellows to fill in the front seats. If you want an audience to move, you have to go at it as if you mean it. A suggestion to try is given in Chapter 8.

Eleven, Please hugged the lectern and leaned on it. You can't make much of an impression on an audience leaning on anything.

Twelve, he mentioned time. He said, "We're going to make this fast." What's important—showing the supervisors how to explain this new contract to their employees, or the time it takes to do it properly?

Thirteen, Please asked the boys to pass out the envelopes filled with explanatory matter.

Fourteen, he talked on while the boys were passing out the literature. He should have stopped until the job was done. Ever see an audience pay any attention to a speaker while somebody was passing out something? He can't say anything that holds their interest when they want to find out what is in the envelope.

Fifteen, Please did not tell the group that they were not to open the envelopes. If he wanted them to hold the envelope-opening for later, he should have told them. Since he never mentioned the envelopes again in the meeting, he probably wanted them to take this material back and read it. He should have told them that.

Sixteen, he told the men that they did not need to take notes. This is poor meeting practice. If some of the group want to takes notes, let them. Usually such people get more out of a meeting when they take notes.

Seventeen, Please should have been up on a platform. The boss used the stage; why didn't Please set his lectern up on the stage? The audience gets more out of a meeting when it sees the speaker.

Eighteen, he couldn't find his program when he wanted to talk about it. With such a simple program why did he need to read it? When he saw the paper was not handy, he should have acted as if he had no such paper to lose.

Nineteen, he found the paper on a table behind him. A speaker should never put his notes behind him. When he turns to get them his back is to the audience. There is danger in that.

Twenty, he mentioned time again and reminded each speaker that he had to hurry to finish on time. He also said, "Without further ado"; I'm not counting it this time.

Twenty-one, Galls started to speak, then set out to adjust his charts. Why didn't he do that adjusting before the meeting started? Get everything ready—that's one of the first rules.

Twenty-two, the charts came apart on him.

Twenty-three, the charts and the spotlight could have been set up and checked before the meeting started. Galls was the first speaker to use exhibits, and his charts and spotlight would not have bothered Please.

Twenty-four, he apologized for reading the script. If you're stuck with a script that you have to read, do the best you can with it; don't discuss it with the audience.

Twenty-five, he used the introduction, "This chart is supposed to show—" Such introductions are seldom necessary.

Twenty-six, Galls' first chart had too much on it. The type wasn't large enough to be seen from where Aron sat.

Twenty-seven, Galls started to talk about the chart after he read the first line. The experienced speaker reads everything on a chart when he first shows it. Then he comes back and talks about each point in order. He has found that he better do this because the audience reads everything on the chart when he first shows it. When he reads it all he is going along with them. If he reads only the first line and then talks about that point, the audience is reading the following lines and is not listening to him.

Twenty-eight, Please was sitting behind the speaker. After a chairman introduces a speaker, it is good practice to take a seat in the front row and let the speaker have the spotlight alone.

Twenty-nine, Please moved about, talking to men in the audience, thus stealing attention from the speaker.

Thirty, Galls studied a chart as if he had never seen it before. It might have been Uncle Louie from St. Louis, the one he hadn't seen for twenty years.

Thirty-one, he said the chart must be in the wrong place. He should have checked that beforehand.

Thirty-two, he had notes scribbled on his charts but he couldn't see the notes. Again he should have checked beforehand.

Thirty-three, he tore the chart in turning it. Shouldn't he have practiced turning the charts so that he would not tear one?

Thirty-four, he talked to the charts, not the audience.

Thirty-five, he told the audience that he had forgotten a point. When a speaker forgets a point, he should not mention it. The listeners will not know. He turned back to find a chart that he had covered.

Thirty-six, he apologized for the size of the type on the chart.

Thirty-seven, he read his script too fast. All speech readers tend to speed up as they read on. He stumbled over the pronunciation of some words. He should have checked those words, learned to pronounce them, or substituted words he could pronounce.

Thirty-eight, Please was signaling for the speaker to hurry in a way that was apparent to the audience.

Thirty-nine, Galls was reading in a monotone.

Forty, he was showing no enthusiasm for the plan.

Forty-one, the ventilation in the room was poor.

Forty-two, Galls talked on while the fire engines drowned out his words.

"I know you can't see these figures."

Forty-three, the speaker asked to have the window closed. That cut off all fresh air to the audience.

Forty-four, Galls announced that he had come to his last chart.

Forty-five, the final chart had too much on it; it was difficult to make out.

Forty-six, Please asked the audience whether or not to skip the recess. In a meeting in which new material is explained, a recess never should be skipped. And the man running the meeting should make such decisions. He is running the meeting.

Forty-seven, the boss decided that there should be no

recess. Any group needs a recess after one hour of listening.

Forty-eight, "without further ado—" again. The new speaker fumbled with the papers on the lectern before he started. He scared the listeners with his notes.

Forty-nine, Rood asked the boys to set up his screen and projector while he tried to speak to the group. It's hopeless to try to hold attention while somebody does something in the audience. What the assistants are doing is much more interesting than any yak-yak.

Fifty, Rood said, "Give me the first slide." He should have arranged for some kind of signal.

Fifty-one, the screen was set too low. This could have been checked before the meeting started.

Fifty-two, "next slide" again. This will go on through the presentation.

Fifty-three, a member of the audience had to tell the speaker that the lights did not need to be turned off.

Fifty-four, the light switch was not found quickly. There is little excuse for this in a business office meeting room.

Fifty-five, the cord to the projector was placed so that a member of the audience could kick it out of the outlet.

Fifty-six, a slide came onto the screen upside down. Why does everybody laugh at this?

Fifty-seven, the wrong slide came up twice.

Fifty-eight, the speaker announced that he had five slides that weren't very important and that he was going to run through them quickly. A speaker should not belittle his visuals.

Fifty-nine, the operator jammed the machine by trying to run the slides through too fast.

Sixty, Bill announced that he had but three more slides to show.

Sixty-one, Please asked for questions in a way that discouraged anyone from asking the first question.

Sixty-two, the boss had apparently planted some questions without telling Please about it.

Sixty-three, Junior read the question that he was supposed to ask, or else. When the boss planted those questions, he should have told the men not to read the questions.

Sixty-four, Please tried to get the question answered without repeating the question.

Sixty-five, the boss jumped on a man who asked a question; a sure-fire way to stop questions.

Sixty-six, the boss mentioned time.

Sixty-seven, Galls started to answer a question before the man had finished asking it. Psychic, is he?

Sixty-eight, Galls answered a question and then talked about an idea of his for six minutes. That meant less questions.

Sixty-nine, Please was letting the audience know that the time taken by the questions was killing him.

Seventy, when a few questions had been asked, the boss thought about taking them down. It would have been nice to plan that before.

MAYBE THERE WERE MORE

That's quite a lot of goofs, isn't it, in two hours of meeting? But it is happening every day. Maybe you wouldn't call all of them important. In fact, some say they are not important at all. But when you are running a meeting, you have some objective. Here the boss wanted those supervisors to understand this new plan and to be able to tell their employees about it and perhaps sell them on the fact that it was a good plan. Did the goofs help in attaining that objective? I say they did not, and I further say—

3 / Details Make the Meeting

Sam thought Joe was handling it, Joe thought Bill was, Bill thought Sam was—

That's the alibi when something goes wrong in a meeting. But alibis don't help. When somebody goofs, the meeting does not go as well as it should.

If you are to have a good meeting,

1. You plan it.
2. You organize—get the interested parties together and agree on what you'll do.
3. You delegate—assign each the job he is to do.
4. You check—to see that each is doing his job.

The plan is a detail, isn't it? Overlook it and where are you?

The organization is a detail too, a lot of details.

The assignments all cover details, each individual has to handle one or more.

The checking—what are you checking? Details, aren't you? Has Joe started moving on this? What is Sam doing on that?

"Ed, you keep telling us to watch these little things," men who run meetings have protested time and again. Just the other day a friend asked, "What's more important—the objective or the details? A meeting is called for some purpose; if you worry too much about details, you may not accomplish your purpose."

That is my friend's idea, and I respect it. But I have put on thousands of meetings, and I have sat in a few thousand more. I've made notes in those meetings I attended, and each week I become more and more convinced that if you take care of the details, you will come closer to accomplishing your purpose.

The other evening I arrived in a town, scheduled to speak the next day. A committee of four members of the club met me at the station. I said in a joking way, "I am accustomed to being met by six men. Where are the others?" Most clubs don't meet the speaker at all. That was a detail, wasn't it, meeting me at the train? It would make any speaker feel good, wouldn't it?

On the way over to the hotel the chairman said, "Ed, we have your book and we're running this meeting according to the suggestions you made."

"Why do that?" I asked.

"Well, this is our tenth all-day meeting," the chairman said. "Those suggestions you give helped us run our past meetings like clockwork. Wait until tomorrow, you'll see."

I waited and I saw. The meeting went off with a minimum of goofs. There were a few, of course, but most of them were directly chargeable to the speakers. They hadn't read the book. The chairman and the committee handling properties made few mistakes.

Yet that book the man referred to was the forerunner of this one. It covered details. I said in it, just as I say in this, "Do this" and "Don't do that."

Most of the meetings you run are put on to sell some

idea. If I wanted to sell you a plan face to face, I'd organize my story so that it showed you what the plan meant to you, how you would gain if you followed the plan. I may know many details about that plan, but in my story to you I would use only those details that might appeal to you.

Let's say that I call on you in your office to sell you on being a captain in a fund drive. I start to tell you about it, I get your attention and arouse some interest, and then I ask, "Would you mind if I took off my overcoat?"

You don't mind, of course, but the thread of my story is lost. Now you too are thinking of my overcoat. That's what you do in a meeting when you goof on a detail.

Recently I was in a meeting. The speaker had asked for a blackboard and the hotel help had brought the blackboard without any chalk. The speaker saw the blackboard and assumed the chalk. When he got to the place in his speech where he wanted to use the blackboard, he turned to it and could not find any chalk. He appealed to the chairman. The chairman appealed to the secretary. The secretary went looking for the hotel manager. But because nobody had checked, the meeting ran into a snarl. You'd call that piece of chalk a detail, wouldn't you? At the time it was a mighty important detail.

Last month at a meeting of a club I belong to, the president came hurrying in just as the group was about to close the bar and sit down to eat. "Have you seen the guest speaker?" he asked.

Nobody had seen the speaker. "Maybe he's down in the bar getting fortified," one of the members suggested.

But a search of the bar did not produce a speaker. A telephone call to the man's home in a distant town called him away from a favorite TV program. He had the dates wrong, and the club was without a speaker.

Somebody had goofed on a detail there, hadn't he? A meeting built around a guest speaker—and no speaker. Is that a detail? Big one, I'd say.

At a meeting at which I was a guest speaker, the president said, "I can't figure this small attendance." They had told me they would have about one hundred, and they had barely twenty. I'm accustomed to exaggeration, but not quite that much.

"I'm sorry the notices didn't get mailed, but we all know our meetings are on the second Tuesday."

"I didn't get a notice," one of the members said.

A check showed that the notices had not gone out. What could we do but shrug it off? Somebody had goofed on a detail. Back in Chapter 2 Tom Galls, looking back through those charts, was goofing up his presentation, wasn't he? While he hunts, everybody in the audience is trying to help him. He had changed the group from listeners to hunters.

In that same meeting the boss bawling out the fellow who asked a question was goofing, wasn't he? What employee was going to ask a question if he thought that the boss might jump all over him? A detail of a different kind, but still a detail.

All of these goofs might easily have been avoided. But they weren't, and the meetings weren't as effective as they might have been. How do you stay away from these goofs? Well, I was the guest speaker at a meeting not long ago, and I noticed that the president had a small card that he referred to from time to time. "That the notes for your talk?" I asked.

"No, it's a list of points I check for each meeting," he

said. He handed me the card. It was a printed piece. "How is it you have it printed?" I asked.

"I'm in the printing business," he said. He turned the card over and showed me the advertisement. "I passed them out to the head men of all the service clubs in towns nearby." His was a service club that met once each week with a guest speaker as the main attraction. Here's what was on the card:

TO CHECK

Speaker	Microphone	Speaker's aids
Introducer	Song leader	Announcements
Tables	Prayer	Piano player
Head table	Badges	Guests

The man had an idea, didn't he? A similar list should help any chairman have a better meeting.

Recently a meeting chairman said to me, "After your speech, Mr. Hegarty, we will throw the meeting open for questions. Is that all right for you?"

I agreed that it was. "Do you have the quiz organized?" I asked.

"No, what organization do you need with a quiz?" the man asked.

At the moment I didn't have time to explain, but I could answer, "Plenty." For instance:

Does the speaker want questions?

If he does, what questions does he want?

Why not ask him for a few questions and pass them out to start the quiz?

That would handle a quiz, wouldn't it? The assigned questions would be asked, then others would follow, and there would be an adequate quiz session. But skip that one detail and the quiz session might flop. Surely one of the men you had assigned to ask a question would stand up and read it from that card you gave him. So you have to tell him not to read it, to say it in his own words. That would be doing about as well as you could, but in putting the question in his own words, he might come up with a question that would confuse the speaker. I had that happen once. The speaker listened to the revised question, and asked, "Would you please elaborate on that?"

The man who asked the question said, "Wait until I look at this card again."

Details, aren't they? The fellow running the meeting just can't win. But why does one group run a meeting well, and another kick things around? I've seen both kinds, and the difference is mainly in how the details are handled.

The other day a club member said to me, "Al always runs a good meeting."

That day I watched Al run a meeting from breakfast through dinner, and I agreed with what the club member said. Al did run a good meeting. Al looked after the details.

The chapters that follow give suggestions to all of you Als who run meetings. Perhaps you may feel that there is a lot of fuss about details. But details make your meeting. Perhaps the first is getting out the crowd. Let's discuss that one, for if you don't have the crowd, you don't have the first requirement of a good meeting.

4 / Getting Out the Crowd

You can't have a meeting without an audience.

Not long ago a friend who had attended a meeting at which I was the guest speaker, wrote, "Ed, you had them sitting on the window sills."

They were. The club had had to set up an overflow room to feed the members and guests that came out. But while Hegarty as an attraction may have had something to do with the size of that crowd, some brother in that club deserved most of the credit. He was the one who got out the publicity. That same Hegarty, a month later, with that same talk, heard the president of a similar club apologize for the slim attendance. "The man who handles publicity is vacationing in Florida, Ed," he explained. A pinch hitter had been assigned to fill in, but he did not get out the notices on time.

In the town where they were sitting on the window sills, the promoter had done another thing. He had sold his attraction. Somehow he had convinced the members that this fellow Hegarty had a message that would be of help to them. The average club member has to be sold. He gave up his noon hour last week, and the speaker was a disappointment. This week he feels he might just as well go out with the boys from the office. The meeting notice has to talk him out of that notion. And most notices are not good enough to talk anybody out of anything.

Just this week, a club chairman sent out a notice that said, "This fellow Hegarty gets up to $1,500 when he makes a speech. All it costs you is $1.65 for your lunch." I don't have to tell you that the luncheon was a sell-out. All through the meeting, the hotel people were setting up tables. Now, I don't advise such journeys into the realm of fiction, particularly on the speaker's fee, but the man did have the idea. He was selling his attraction.

As I travel about over the country, I ask the chairmen, "What do you do to promote attendance?"

They say, "Ed, it's pretty tough these days with the TV."

I ask, "What are you doing now that you weren't doing before TV?"

They say, "What can we do?"

I imagine I am much like most club members.

I get a notice that is the same month after month.

Same size, same color, same paper, same method of reproduction.

It looks exactly like the one I got last month.

The copy is about the same. All the printer does is to substitute the name of the new speaker. There is little sell on the attraction. There is no list of reasons why I should attend. There isn't any mention of what I can gain if I show up.

O.K., so I look at the notice and I lay it aside.

Now, I know it's not easy to make your meeting notice different each month or each week. But some clubs are doing it. And they are getting more of the brothers out, too.

So give some thought to getting variety into that notice. Of course certain details must be included.

WHAT SHOULD THAT NOTICE COVER?

1. *Why the Meeting?* If it is a regular club shindig you may not have to explain, but if you have a guest speaker, you had better tell a bit about him and about his subject. Why are you having a meeting on this subject? If I am to listen to a talk on this subject you better tell me what I will gain by listening to it.

2. *Why Is the Subject Important?* At first glance the subject may cause the average club member to say, "They found a guy who could speak on this subject—so what?" Tell the members that "what" in your notice. Tell them why they are interested.

3. *Why This Speaker?* Who is this fellow, what has he ever done? They won't come out just because he was a classmate of Charlie Whosis. Give them more than that. Is he a story teller? We all like stories. Is he humorous? We like to laugh. Is he inspirational? We all know we need a shot in the arm. What has he done to make him an attraction? If you dig on this point, you will come up with facts to show why this is not just another session. Even if the speaker is a nationally known authority, don't assume that they know it. Tell them who he is, what he has done, why he thinks

The boss sure can get the laughs.

every good American should be interested, and why you agree.

4. *Now the Details.* Now—the date, time, place, price, and all the other details. Make sure that you cover all of them. Even if you meet at the same hotel every time, mention the meeting place. Recently I spoke before a club that held regular meetings. At the time for the meeting to start, there were but a handful of the brothers on hand. Then one of the officers said, "Hey, I bet they went over to the other hotel." A quick telephone check showed that the notice had not mentioned the change in hotels, and the members had gone to the regular place. We got them at our meeting eventually, but the meeting started about fifteen minutes late. It pays to print such details in the notice. That wouldn't happen often, but it did this once.

SOME SUGGESTIONS ON THE NOTICE

Since I speak at so many different kinds of meetings, I get samples of all kinds of notices sent out by hopeful committees. The luncheon club pieces are usually a one-sheet mimeographed piece. They tell the story of what is to happen.

Another type of function I speak at is the sales rally. This is a session run by sales executives or retail merchants' associations. All of the salesmen in the town are brought into an auditorium and two or three speakers try to give the group some helpful ideas. Such a meeting calls for a printed piece for there is a ticket-selling activity in connection with it. These printed pieces (there may be more than one) are usually well done because to get out a crowd, the group has to sell tickets.

Some clubs have a regular publication. This may be a simple news sheet or a sixteen-page printed piece. In such a news sheet the club can give news of its members, sell advertising space to help pay the costs, but it still needs the plug for the program to get the member out to the next meeting.

No matter what type of notice your club has, there are ways it can be made more effective. Here are some suggestions.

1. *The Postcard.* The two-cent government post card is about the least expensive type of notice that can be mailed to club members. I belong to one club that uses it. Recently I asked the secretary why he used these cards. "It's cost, Ed," he answered. "They're dull, I know, but when I tried to get the board to go for a letter, they wouldn't agree."

"Why couldn't you take one batch, run a red border around the message side of the card, green on another batch, and blue on a third? It wouldn't cost much, but you might get a little more notice for the cards."

The secretary thanked me and I noticed that the next card had a splash of red on it. I don't know whether or not it increased the response, but I am sure that it increased attention.

2. *Fit to the Job.* Last month I received a post card from a club suggesting I take advantage of a golfing breakfast that the club was setting up on Sunday morning. I can't play golf on Sunday morning early for I'm not out of eight o'clock mass before nine. This golfing breakfast was a new idea to the club, and I believe that it would take more than a post card to sell it. Consider the job your mailing has to do before you send anything out. If I were promoting that golfers' breakfast, I would at least use a letter, and perhaps I'd use a return post card to find out how many were interested. Then if the club did not have a rule that I had to cover all members with the mailing, I might do a little work

on the list, culling out the ones who taught Sunday School, the ones who had to go to mass, etc. Get the idea? If I had that job, I would probably wind up with a selected list, a letter and post card, and then a follow-up post card canvass. You may say, "I don't have ideas like that to sell." O.K., let's say you have a special big-time speaker. Perhaps he is worth a letter rather than the post card you usually send out. Perhaps he is worth a telephone canvass of a special few. You can tell about your big-time speaker on your post card. But if you want the group out, go a little further.

3. *More of the Same.* A newly elected secretary of a club that holds meetings once each month told me, not long ago, "Instead of sending one notice, Ed, I think we'd do better if we sent two or three." I believe he is right. If I wanted to get a group of retailers out to a meeting, I would not depend on one notice. You may say, "This is a club and it's different." It is a club. But for some reason those brothers stay away, don't they? You might try this repeat mailing idea.

4. *Decorate the Piece.* I suggested that on the post cards, but it can be done, no matter what type of mailing piece is sent out. You might do the letters on different colored paper each month. If you use mimeograph, multilith, or multigraph, you might use illustrations, cartoon drawings, or other decoration to help get interest. If you print the piece, there are many stock cuts that the printer can get for you to help you decorate it.

5. *The Personal Note.* This is a great puller. Even though your notice is a single mimeographed sheet, you can write a personal note to the member on it, and so make the notice seem more important. I suggested that idea to a friend of mine who was having trouble with getting out attendance at a club of his. "Nobody reads those mimeographed no-

tices," he told me. "Why don't you personalize them?" I asked. He was open to suggestion, so I said, "Get a big red pencil and write something personal to Joe on the notice, do the same for Pete and Jim. It will take a bit of work, but it may help you get out more of the brothers." Since he had a club with fifty members, the task would not be too great. When I saw him later, he told me, "We had been getting 18 to 20 to the meeting; now we're getting 25 to 30 —it works." The same idea can be worked with a scribbled note enclosed with the notice.

6. *The Personal Letter.* I once ran a club with about four hundred names on the membership list. I knew personally about fifty of these. I'd send out the regular notice of the meeting each month, on a government post card. Then to these fifty, I'd write a personal note on my stationery, reminding them of the meeting and urging them to come. The note might say, "Dear Pete: The meeting Monday will be good. Come and bring Joe with you." There might be a few extra words, but the idea is expressed in the few I've written. The Joe mentioned would be a neighbor. As I got to know more of the members, I enlarged my list. When I gave up the job, I had about one hundred names on my personal list. I had those letters produced by a letter house and they cost me, including postage, about ten cents. Friends told me that many of the brothers on the list asked, "Does he write all of those letters personally?" I didn't, but the letters worked. From getting out a handful of the faithful to those meetings, the club grew until over half the membership attended every meeting. I feel that the personal letter had much to do with it.

7. *The Ticket of Admission.* For certain kinds of meetings this is helpful as a reminder, even though there is no

pay for the ticket. I've seen it used where each member is sent two tickets and told that is all he can have, that there will be an overflow and this is the only fair way to distribute the tickets. The tickets can be numbered and tied in with the door-prize drawing. A ticket of admission somehow indicates a privilege that this member has, and that others do not have. For that reason he will use it. I'm sure that you have asked friends about the time of a meeting or some other detail, and they have taken a ticket out of their pocket and checked for you. Even though you don't use tickets of admission regularly, it might be well to try them at one of your big affairs. But if you use tickets, be sure to pick them up. At a meeting not long ago the secretary of the club went around picking up tickets. "What're these for?" one of the members asked. The secretary didn't answer, just looked wise. I felt that the ticket might have been part of the at- tendance-building program. You might think up ways to use the ticket to help bring out a few more members to the meetings.

8. *Use the Telephone.* You get a "yes" or "no" quickly when you use the telephone. One club I know gives each member three names to telephone. Three calls do not seem like much and the calls are likely to be made. Not long ago, I heard a woman say, "They gave me three names to call and then another woman telephoned me." That's check and double check. Another club passes around the tele- phone chore. The trouble with this plan is that some of the members never seem to get around to telephoning the names. I've run clubs in which a captain was responsible for four members and he was supposed to telephone them. If you have this plan you may want a report from the captains. The telephone can be used as the only announcement of a

meeting, a follow-up on the printed notice, or as a last-minute reminder. I've used it all three ways and it works well. Don't leave it out of your plans.

9. *Publicity.* The newspaper and the local radio station will help you get out the crowds for your meeting. If you have a guest speaker coming, get a photograph and some material from him and give it to the newspaper editor. The newsman on the radio won't want the photo but he will use the written material. If there is someone in your club who knows how to prepare material for newspaper use, appoint him publicity chairman. Some clubs hire one of the reporters on the newspaper at a small cost and use him as publicity chairman. The young man is glad to make the extra money, and the club gets the publicity it wants. You might invite the editor of the newspaper to the meeting, and the newsman of the radio station. If any of the newspaper or radio station employees belong to your club, get them interested in this publicity problem. The space your club gets in the newspapers helps give the town the impression that your club is alive.

10. *The Neighbor Idea.* You might split up the club membership by the neighborhoods in which they live. Then make one member the captain for his neighborhood. He is supposed to contact Joe and Pete and Bill, or Millie, Angie, and Bess, who live nearby and can be contacted easily. He sees them out in the drive or mowing the lawn, riding the same bus, or using the same car pool. You have to arrange your membership list in neighborhoods to get this idea going, but it is worth the effort. If Jack asks me to go with him, I'm more inclined to go than if I have to go on my own initiative. In many clubs the members don't venture out alone because they are not sure that they will know anybody. You have had that feeling, I'm sure, about clubs that

you have belonged to. But if you knew that Joe was going and he asked you to go with him, it is easier, isn't it?

11. *Bad Timing Can Cut Attendance.* In setting the meeting date, watch for holidays or competing affairs that might take the play from your meeting. I've had chairmen excuse a small attendance by saying, "There are three or four other affairs in town tonight." I was invited to one town by a committee of four men. They made quite a thing out of it—called it "The Committee of Four to Get Ed Hegarty." I had telephone calls from each of the men, I had letters from each of them, and when I arrived at the meeting hall, not a one of the four was there. "Their wives made them go to the opera opening tonight, Ed," the chairman told me. Next morning the newspaper was full of pictures of the opera opening. Two of my committee members were shown in the pictures. While we had a fine attendance at our meeting, picking the night of the opera opening was bad planning. The meeting could have been held on the next night. So watch holidays, holy days, and other affairs that might take away from your attendance.

12. *When You Want Outsiders.* There may be times when you want to bring some outsiders to your club meeting. Our local Sales Executives Club was putting on a Sales Managers Clinic. A sales expert was to spend one day with club members discussing sales management problems. This was the type of affair that could be of help to all sales managers in the town, whether they belonged to the club or not. The plan used for promoting that affair was a personal letter to the presidents of all the leading companies in the area. With the letter went a circular describing the clinic and the expert who was running it. The letter was brief. It told the president, "No doubt someone in your company will be interested in this." The president referred the circular

and letter to the proper parties, and all of the seats were sold. The admission for the day was fifteen dollars, including lunch and some books the expert had written. When you want outsiders, make a list of the ones you want and work out a personalized approach to them.

13. *Sell the Attraction.* The letter to the presidents did that for the circular on the expert, and his clinic showed the sales manager what he would get out of it. But you don't always have a circular. Perhaps, then, if the attraction needs selling, you might tell the story in two or three mimeographed pages, and attach this to a short letter. If you can write those pages about your attraction, the man who gets the letter feels that this meeting is going to be good. In the piece tell what the man will gain by coming to the meeting. If you can quote men who have been to the meeting, do that. Show the member what he is going to get out of this meeting, and he will want to come.

14. *Split the List.* I've belonged to clubs where the list was split up among a number of members and each man was supposed to write letters to the ten names assigned to him. These letters can be all of the mail promotion, or the regular notice can be sent out and these personal letters used as a follow-up. If the list assigned to any one man is small enough, he does not feel that it is much work to get out the letters. In one club the men assigned lists all had secretaries. The fellow dictated a short letter, and the girl wrote it to the ten names as she found time. Nobody did much work, but the club got the promotion it needed.

15. *Do Something Different.* A member tires of the same kind of notice over and over again. I belong to one club that sends out its notices on the same kind of government post card. The notice is inexpensive, I know, but I wonder how effective it is. The other day I got three in the same

mail, all from different groups, all for different affairs, but all pretty much alike. I believe that a club would get better attendance at its affairs if it would mix a few letters and perhaps some printed cards in with those post cards. It would cost more, of course, but the added patronage of the club would more than make up for the extra money spent.

16. *The Letter to the Wife.* I belong to a club that has a ladies' night once each year. The club sends me a notice of that meeting, but it also goes all out on a notice to Mrs. Hegarty. When I come home that evening, she asks me if we are going. I tell her we are, and I don't have a chance to forget that date. The idea can be used on meetings that are not ladies' night. You might ask Min to remind Andy of a certain date. A good promoter can think of many ideas that can bring in the wife of the member. A variation of this idea is to send a notice to the member's secretary asking her to put it on the big man's calendar. It works.

17. *Send Notice to Both Home and Office.* This is an idea that gets two women on the job for you. The wife reminds him at home, and the secretary at the office. Many of the members who do not come to the meeting fail to come because they forget that tonight's the night. Many times the loving wife has told me, "You're going to be out for dinner on Tuesday night." "I am?" I ask, "Why?" She then tells me about the shindig. She is figuring that she will not have to plan a dinner for me on that night. Perhaps she'll have the girls in for bridge.

18. *More and More.* Recently I was speaking to a newly

"The door prizes make it worthwhile."

elected secretary of a club and I told him that one notice on the monthly meeting of his group was not enough. "You're right, Ed," he said. "Next year we are going to hit them with two, three, and perhaps four." You don't let that member forget when you send him more than one notice. You can work this same idea by sending first the notice, then the personal letter, then the telephone call. But if it is your job to promote attendance, don't feel that a notice of the meeting is all that you need. Members have other things to worry about. It may be work for you to get out the one notice, but to that member it is only another piece of mail. So do all the mail promotion you can.

19. *The Raffle.* One of our local clubs, in an effort to get a return post card from the member, works a raffle with the cards that come back. If your acceptance is received before a certain time, your card is thrown into a hat and a drawing determines the winner of a fifth of cheer. The members of that club are more inclined to get those cards back. This is an idea you might try if you need a count of heads. Your type of club might not go for the fifth, but some kind of door prize can be offered. Most clubs have trouble getting members to send in acceptances. A secretary told me recently, "I got forty-eight cards back, and there are almost one hundred here. What can get them to send cards back?" But the card isn't important to the member. He notes that the meeting is on Tuesday night, and he tosses the card aside. But if there is a chance to win something, he'll send in that card as soon as he knows he can make the meeting.

20. *Bring Joe with You.* This is akin to the neighbor idea. You and Joe are buddies and when I ask you to bring Joe, or ask Joe to bring you, I'm suggesting that the two of you talk it over. Just today one of my associates asked me, "You thinking about going to that meeting in Columbus?" I told

him I was, and we talked about who would drive. The notice of the meeting did not suggest that I bring him, or he bring me. But because he spoke to me, both of us were much nearer to going. Figure out how you can work this team idea into your attendance promotion. Think how many times you have passed up meetings because you had no one to go with.

21. *Look for Tie-ins.* Perhaps your meeting is one that might call for a tie-in with some local group. Let's say you have a banker as your speaker. Why not invite the local bankers to hear what he has to say? If he is a prominent retail merchant, you might invite the men who run the stores in your town. You could have members bring these men as guests or let them come on a pay-for-yourself basis. I have had strangers telephone me, when they read in the newspapers of a meeting I was running, to ask if they could come. Most people won't go to that trouble, but they might come if they were invited. If your club is looking for members, you might get a few out of such activities.

22. *Joint Meetings.* Many clubs use the joint meeting idea. I have spoken to combined meetings of the Rotary and Kiwanis. Such meetings get a larger attendance, and one club is relieved of the job of getting one speaker. My Sales Executives Club meets with similar clubs of Credit Men, Purchasing Agents, Advertising Men. When your club has a special speaker with a subject of interest to both groups, the meeting can turn out well. Your members get a kick out of meeting with the men from the other clubs.

23. *Paid Advertising.* For some kinds of meetings you might want to use paid advertising. A small notice in the newspaper, or a number of spot announcements on the radio might help swell the crowd. One of my clubs brought a group of lecturers to our town. The speakers' talks were

of general interest. The club advertised in the newspaper
and on the radio and filled the high school auditorium at a
one-dollar admission charge. The club was doing this as a
public service. The admission money did not cover expenses, but it allowed the club to finance the affairs at a
cost it could afford. The resultant publicity brought a number of new members into the club. Even though your club
has been operating in the town for years, perhaps there are
eligible prospective members who do not know there is
such a club. Every now and then I meet a sales manager
who does not know about our Sales Executives Club. We
have been running for at least five years, staging many civic
projects with much newspaper publicity, yet prospective
members do not know we are in existence.

24. *Sell, Sell, Sell.* In using any of these ideas, remember
that getting out the crowd to your meeting is a selling job.
Most club members would rather stay home. Perhaps you
don't feel that way, but most of your members do. You may
feel that attending your meeting is the most important thing
the member can do on this evening, but he doesn't feel that
way. He may be convinced that he will feel a lot better the
next day if he goes home and to bed right after dinner. Perhaps he joined the club because Joe Whosis pressured him
into signing the application, and he wasn't too much interested at the start. But at best he's indifferent to your problem of getting him out to the meeting. For instance, how
many of your past presidents are regular attendants at your
meetings? The board of directors of the club may say,
"With the TV these days, you have a tough time getting
them out." But you can't blame the difficulty on TV. That
is a factor, yes, but if you canvassed your members on what
TV programs they watched on meeting nights, you'd find

that some of them didn't watch any. It has always been difficult to get members out to club meetings. There are so many other things that they would like to do. And so, if you want this Joe to come to your meeting, you had better give him all the reasons you can for coming. It is not easy to do that on a government post card. You better do a little more than that.

PICTURE HIM AND THAT MAIL OF HIS

When you plan this announcement of your meeting, picture this member of yours. He gets lots of mail. One fellow is trying to sell him a book, another tulip bulbs, a third a new issue of bonds, a magazine, a security-analysis service. Then there are people who have selected him for the honor of membership in some exclusive group if he can see his way clear to put up a few bucks. There is the worthy charity that could use a small check. Some of this mail is on the best type of stationery, other pieces are printed in four colors; then mixed with it is a colorless communication from you about this meeting of yours. You meet the member on the street and ask, "Will you be at the meeting on Tuesday night?" He asks, "What meeting?" You think he doesn't read his mail, and you ask, "You got the notice, didn't you?" He says, "I don't remember it." And he doesn't.

But don't blame him. It's your fault.

You haven't even started to sell that fellow, have you? He doesn't even know there is a meeting.

Thank goodness all of your members are not like that Joe. But if you could imagine all of them just like him and you directed your effort to get him out, you'd do better with attendance, wouldn't you?

You can't run a meeting without an audience. And as the

meeting manager, you should realize you have to go all out to sell them on coming. What do I mean all out? Well, how about this:

First, mail the regular notice, that drab letter, or the government post card.

Second, follow key members with a personal letter. Tell the recipient to bring Joe with him.

Third, telephone each member. Give a number of your members the names of five or six other members to call.

Fourth, try this plan on your next meeting and see how it works.

That four-step plan has worked well for me over and over again. If the fellow running the meeting goes to all that trouble to build attendance, the members feel that the meeting will be worthwhile. Remember, it is not the members' fault if they don't come, it's the fault of the man whose job it is to sell them. So remember to sell, sell, sell!

Now, let's explore the problem of getting the attraction that will bring out the members.

5 / Signing Up the Guest Speaker

The program makes the meeting.

As a guest speaker and as a man who runs meetings, I know that too often we invite a group to come to a meeting and we don't offer them enough to justify the time they are asked to spend with us.

I am always amused at the attitude the average club member takes toward the guest speaker. The speaker is introduced to the club member. Then the man making the introduction says, "Mr. Hegarty is the guest speaker."

The man acknowledging the introduction says, "Oh, that so?" He may add a word or two but from the minute that he knows you are the speaker, he is interested in getting away from you. He doesn't want any of the brothers to feel that he is in any way responsible for you.

I can't blame him much for that. I belong to clubs that have guest speakers and I wouldn't want to take the responsibility for some of the speakers we have. But if the club is one that depends on guest speakers for its meetings, you have to get them. And you want to get good ones, that's for sure.

53

Chairmen tell me, "Ed, we've been having some mighty fine speakers before this club."

He tells me the names of some of his speakers and, because I know those speakers, I know that he has had good programs. But too many of the speakers that appear before clubs do not give the club a good program. You know that from the clubs that you belong to. The other day I was talking to two service club men. They had just come from a meeting of their Service, Inc. "How was the meeting?" I asked.

"I wish you hadn't asked," one of them said.

Then the two started talking about the run of poor speakers that club had had. "Why do you go to the meetings?" I asked. "I wonder why so many Americans feel they have to get out to a meeting once each week to hear a speaker that doesn't interest them. Why is that?"

The men didn't have a good answer. "I think it's because they meet the other businessmen," one of them said.

"It certainly isn't the speeches," the other added.

It isn't, we know. But we all agree, I'm sure, that the best way to sell present members is with good programs. The member can eat at the Greasy Spoon for less. He can meet some mighty nice fellows there, too, and he won't have to listen to a poor speech, either. So that guest speaker is important. How do you get good ones? Well, here are some suggestions:

HOW TO GET GOOD SPEAKERS FOR YOUR CLUB

1. *Ask Far Enough Ahead.* Any speaker will sign up for a speech next September, if September is seven months away. But he will cancel out, too. Just last week I had a distress call from the chairman of a sales rally who had sold nine hundred tickets for a two-speaker sales rally, and both of

his speakers had canceled out on him. I couldn't help him either, for I was scheduled for that night. So ask far enough ahead.

2. *Sell on the Importance.* Usually the man who telephones tells me that there will be one thousand salesmen at this rally. These fellows looking for speakers seem to exaggerate on the size of the crowd. But many of them don't tell me what that group means to me. Most speakers want to know who is in that crowd. Can they sell these people anything? If the speaker is asked to speak to a group in his industry, he knows who they are and what benefit his company might get out of his appearance. If the group is out of his industry, he may need some explanation and plenty of sell. So try to figure out what the speaker can get out of doing the job.

3. *Use His Company Distribution.* If the speaker works for a company that distributes nationally, go after him through his local distribution. A retailer or distributor that belongs to your club may represent the company. For instance, if the speaker works for a company like General Motors, go after him through a local dealer for General Motors. Some company executives will not take invitations direct. They insist that the invitation come through the local distribution.

4. *If You Can Pay.* If you can pay the speaker, tell him that you can. Ask him what his fee is. Most pay speakers charge a fee and expenses. If his fee is too rich for your club, tell him what you can pay. He might take the assignment. Most times he won't, but he might.

5. *Tell Why You Want Him.* At times this is good. It has worked on me. The club asked me to be the first speaker on a four-man panel, and explained they wanted me for this because I would be able to keynote the meeting. "Key-

noter"—that sounded good. You couldn't ask just any speaker to be a keynoter. Most groups want me to wind up the meeting. I'm a hot-shot speaker with plenty of enthusiasm, and when they explain they want me to wind up, I know what they mean. If the meeting is sagging when I come on, I will pick it up. You can't use this one with all types of speakers, but with some it is good. "The boys heard you at Milwaukee," is another of these appeals. That is almost as good as getting asked back.

6. *The Old Pal.* A fellow is in the news. Let's say he has just been made president of a company, and you know that he went to school with Joe Whosis over at the Gas Company. You go to see Joe and ask him if he will invite the friend. Joe will usually be glad to oblige even though he doesn't belong to your group. Now that the friend is in the news, Joe would like to remind the big shot that Joe knew him when; and basking in the limelight is good bait, for you'll surely ask Joe to introduce the big man.

7. *The Boss.* Almost any club member will be glad to invite his boss to speak to the club. Maybe after the boss has talked to the club once, he will allow the member to put the club dues on the company expense account. This one, of course, has its dangers. Some bosses are not so good as speakers. But the possibilities are there. Almost everybody in the club has a boss.

8. *The Old Oil.* The guest speaker recognizes it for what it is, but he likes it just the same. Use the "nobody but you can do this job as it should be done." That line, "the whole committee voted for you," is one of the most popular. At times I glance over the committee list and I wonder when any of that group have heard me talk. But it's a nice line to believe, anyway. Recently I had a chairman tell me, "We want you or someone in your field to do this talk for us."

I am mighty sure that some of the chairmen who call me never had heard of me before my name was suggested. But they surely give off with the old oil when they speak to me. They call me Ed, they speak of my books, they talk about my reputation in the field. The other day one of them told me, "You're the top expert on sales training in the country, and we want the best." Of course, he couldn't make me mad with that, could he? I've had chairmen tell me, though,

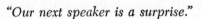

"Our next speaker is a surprise."

"I'm not very familiar with your work, Mr. Hegarty. Would you please fill in some details for me?" That's O.K. if the fellow planned to pay me for the talk. But this man was asking me to speak for free.

If you don't know this Joe you are inviting, talk to some people about him, get some scoop, and figure out how you can oil him up. It is productive.

9. *The Printed Program.* At times club managers have sent me printed programs and have said, "This is how our program will look if you accept." Since they have no commitment from me, I wonder about the other names on that list. I've had groups print up notices stating that I would appear when I had not been invited. This seems a bit dangerous to me, for there are few speakers that can guarantee a crowd. Then, if you bill a speaker and he doesn't show, the group may say, "He signed up and then ran out on them." Most speakers do not care for that kind of reputa-

tion. In the few thousand appearances I have made before groups, I've had only one occasion when I had to run out at the last minute. I was down with the flu in bed. Even then, I arranged for a substitute. The program listing is good if you say, "This is our proposed program, we haven't signed all of the speakers yet, but we have promises from the ones marked with the asterisk." There is little doubt that the list of your speakers can have an influence on the men you want on the program. But don't lie. These guest speakers may be as smart as you.

10. *Remember Approvals.* If you are asking a corporation representative to speak to your group, he may not have the authority to give you an approval. He may be able to tell you that the date is open, but he may have to get approval from his management before he can agree to make the talk. There have been times when I have had to get the approval of my boss, the manager of the department that sold merchandise to the group inviting me, and our field sales manager in the town in which the talk was to be made. Let's say you represent the Ajax Club in Salt Lake City. You write this company man and ask him to speak at your annual ladies' night banquet. He has never heard of the Ajax Club, of course. You tell him who you are and who will be there, but he has still never heard of you until your letter comes in. Now what is more natural than for him to write his sales representative in Salt Lake City and ask his advice? Usually he will ask, "Will it do you any good if I accept this date?" If the representative says that he has been trying to meet the men who belong to this club and that accepting the date would be a help, your speaker might accept your date. But getting this approval takes time, and you might be sitting around biting your fingernails and asking, "Why doesn't this guy answer

my letter?" He will answer it in time, but he has to check first. At times, the alert secretary of your invited speaker may write you and tell you that her boss is on an extended speaking trip and that he will answer your letter as soon as he gets back, but most times you will just have to wait. In writing this corporation man, think of the approvals he needs. He may be a big shot with a big title, and still can't accept unless he has the proper clearance.

11. *Use the Telephone.* It is more difficult for a speaker to turn down a man who calls him on the telephone. Recently I had a letter from a club asking me to speak at a big dinner. I sent it on to my boss, and he suggested that we turn down the invitation. I did that, and in a few days the club chairman telephoned me asking me to reconsider. I told him that management had turned it down. He asked for the name of my boss, and asked if I minded if he telephoned the boss. I told him I didn't. Later that day the boss called me in and said that Joe Wilks had called him and that I had better take that date. In explaining why he had changed his mind, he kept quoting Joe. Joe said this, Joe said that. "You and Joe are old friends, then?" I asked. "Well, I'm not sure, Ed; I can't place him. But he thinks it is pretty important." It was important because Joe had him on the telephone, and since Joe was a good telephone salesman he got the boss to change his mind. So use the telephone. If the man is dated up, you know it immediately. If the man is out of town, you can follow him over the country. Let's say you catch him in his hotel in Kansas City. By following him out there, you show that you want him, don't you? And when you are speaking to him, you have a better chance of selling him on accepting.

12. *Ask His Advice.* When you have the man on the phone and he cannot make the date, ask him to recommend

someone else. He might suggest a name that you haven't
thought of. Let's say he is an expert on some subject you
want covered. O.K., he should know some other experts on
that subject. Ask him, he may help.

13. *To Whom It May Concern.* As a prospective guest
speaker, I get a number of "To whom it may concern" letters. These usually state that the club meets on the second
Tuesday evening of each month and, if you are planning
to be in the vicinity, we'd like to have you as a guest
speaker. The letter obviously has been sent to a large number of speakers. I doubt that such a letter does anything
but allow the chairman to report that he has written a
number of speakers and feels assured of good programs,
especially later in the year.

14. *How Can We Get You?* The best authority on how
to get a certain speaker is the speaker himself. You might
write him and ask, "What do we have to do to get you for
one of these dates?" The speaker who works for pay will
tell you what his fee is, and will give you an estimate of
his expenses. The man who works for a corporation may
suggest that the best way to get him is to have the local
distribution invite him. At times I have given club chairmen the name of the man to see. Always I have advised,
"Don't tell the man that I suggested this. Tell him you
want me, and enlist his help in getting me." Usually the
local distributor or retailer will be glad to help. He wants
to share in the publicity, he feels that it will help him get
business, and he knows that you will invite him to sit at
the head table. I have had letters from field representatives,
saying, "Mr. A. T. Ajax has told me that you asked him to
have me invite you to speak before his group—" The chairman had told the local representative that I had explained
how to get my services as a speaker. Now let's say that I

had to get my appearances approved by my boss. I couldn't send him that letter, could I? It reads as if I am inviting myself. There is nothing wrong with that wording, if I could accept the invitation without approval of my boss, but I couldn't.

So when your speaker explains that he has to be invited through his local representative, enlist the help of that man in getting him. Give the local representative a big sell on what the appearance of the man before your club can mean to the representative locally. Most times you won't need that sell, for he will know. But if he seems cold to the deal, tell him why it will be a boost for him to have the speaker appear.

When making such a request, go call on the local representative. Don't handle it with a letter or telephone call. Work up a number of reasons why the local man will gain if the speaker appears. Call and give him the works. Get him enthused enough and he might telephone the speaker while you are with him. In most cases you will still have to write a letter, but by telephoning, you can clear the date. The man may have another engagement on that date.

When I need approvals for speeches I always ask the local man to write me a letter giving me all details. To make sure that I have it right, I asked him to have the chairman of the meeting write me, too. The letter can be routed into the boss's office. If you want a local man to help, write out all the details of the meeting so that when he agrees to help, you can say, "This piece I have written here gives you all the details. You might want to make it a part of your letter."

Recently I had a telephone call from one of our district managers asking if I could talk to a club in his territory. He knew the name of the club and the date, but he did not have any of the details. Now if the chairman had given him a memo with all of the details, he could have read them off to me while making that telephone call. I told him I couldn't take such talks without approval and suggested that he write me the invitation and have the chairman write me the details.

COVER THESE POINTS IN YOUR INVITATION

(*a*) Sell the guest speaker or his representative on why he will gain.

(*b*) Give him all details.

(*c*) Offer to help him, meet him, make hotel reservations, etc.

WHAT TO TELL THE GUEST SPEAKER

Here is a list of some of the things you should tell the guest speaker to help him make a better speech to your group.

1. *The Date and Time of Day.* The date alone is not enough; the time of day is important. A speech made to a luncheon club at noon has a time urgency that may not be important at the dinner meeting. At noon the brothers are anxious to finish to get back to the stores and offices. At evening they are recovering from the conviviality of the social hour and they may need some loosening up before the main speech starts. The time of day is important, too, because of transportation. I have had invitations that told me the date but not the time of day. There are times when a speaker might make a luncheon talk in one town and a dinner speech in another. So include both the day and the time.

2. *The Place.* Tell him that it is going to be in the grand ballroom of the local hotel and he can picture the setting.

If it is to be in the local high school or other auditorium, he can picture that, too. He might want to get his suit pressed before he walks out on that stage. Standing behind the head table, he might get by with yesterday's suit. The place may make a difference in the visuals he will use.

3. *The Program.* If there are to be other speakers on the program, the names of the speakers and subjects assigned might help. There have been times when I have exchanged notes on what I would cover with another speaker be-

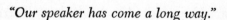

"Our speaker has come a long way."

cause we were assigned similar subjects. Many clubs send me the program for the year before, to show the kind of program planned. The chairman explains that the program for this year is not printed, but that this will show me the kind of program they put on. Many programs have a slogan or theme. If the speaker knows about this theme, there may be some way he can tie in.

4. *Time Allotted.* Tell the speaker how much time he will have. If it is a luncheon meeting and you adjourn at a certain time, tell him that. I have had clubs invite me to travel hundreds of miles to make a twenty-minute

speech. That time arrangement seems to be a little silly. Perhaps someone in the club has read that any speaker should be able to tell all he knows in twenty minutes, but don't ask a man to spend two days traveling and one hundred dollars in expenses to speak to your club for twenty minutes. Some speakers may be willing to do it, but most of them won't. Allotting a man thirty-five to forty-five minutes is about right for most speeches. It's courtesy to ask the speaker to tell you how much time he wants. Usually he will not ask for more than one hour. It's seldom that you can't squeeze in that amount of time. If you pay your speakers you can, of course, have them speak for any length of time, but remember ten minutes will cost you as much as an hour.

5. *Type of Speech.* I have had many suggestions from chairmen on this. One said, "Our club doesn't like speakers who read their speeches." No club does. But some readers do such a good job at it, that the members do like them. Other chairmen write, "You can use any of your stories before our group for there will be no ladies present." I don't happen to use that kind of story, *because I am there.* But the suggestion does tell me that I can change my way of life. Other chairmen tell me that their club likes some humor mixed in with the serious. That too is universal.

There are, however, suggestions that might help the speaker. You might suggest, "Why not make it as much 'how to' as possible?" or "Can you cover the psychological aspects of it?" or "What do you think of covering just the tax phase of it?" You will do better if you suggest.

Think of any such suggestions as being of help to the speaker. Don't say, "Our club likes this—" Say instead, "You'll make a big hit with our group if—" Recently a

chairman told me, "You can be as commercial as you like."
That was helpful because I have heard speakers criticized
for mentioning their company and its policies. The company had paid a few hundred dollars to send the speaker
one thousand miles to speak to the group, and the club
secretary was criticizing him for getting commercial. The
chairman who suggested that I could go commercial probably knew that I would make a better speech for his group
if I talked about a subject in which I was interested.

The chairman might name some of the speakers that the
club liked. If the speaker knows the men, he will know
the type of speech that goes over well with the group.
When you discuss the speaker's subject, try to give him
information that will help him. If you try to tell him what
to speak about, and how to cover the subject, you might
scare him away.

6. *The Subject.* There are times when you fail to get the
speaker because of the subject you assign him. Most good
speakers have one good speech. They care little what
speech title you put on the program. They will accept it
without argument. They might even mention your subject,
but they will not speak for more than a few minutes before
they get onto the standard speech. I have speeches on five
subjects. You tell me you want me to speak on training and
I give you the training speech. Not long ago a group
wanted me to speak on motivation. I asked about the program and found that they had signed up another speaker
to talk on meetings. Now, I have two books on meetings,
I'm a recognized authority in that field, so I asked the man,
"Why didn't you assign me that meeting subject?"

"That's right, we should have, shouldn't we?" he agreed.
"But we got you down here for motivation."

Of course I could speak on motivation, but I would have had to work up a speech on that. I have done this meeting talk hundreds of times. It's a classic, and the meeting would have been better if I had talked on meetings and some other speaker on motivation. In inviting a speaker, ask him what subject he would like to cover. Any chairman asks too much when he asks a speaker to prepare a speech especially for his group. Of course I'm speaking of the speaker that comes for free. The one you pay may speak on the subject you select, but even then he should charge you more for asking him to do the new speech.

Recently, I was asked to do a talk on handling employees. The group was a management group. When I arrived I found that I was down on the program for "What's Ahead for the Coming Year." I reminded the chairman that I was to speak on handling employees. He said, "Don't worry about that, Ed, the title ties in with the meeting theme." I made the talk on handling employees, and I don't believe that many of the audience knew that I never said one word about the subject assigned. Most chairmen don't stray that far afield from the speaker's assigned subject, but they do assign titles that are difficult to reconcile with what the speaker says.

7. *Program Strategy.* There may be times when discussing the program strategy with the speaker may help. When you do, be sure that you are right. Recently a club secretary asked me to speak at his big sales rally. He had all the merchants and salespeople from miles around coming. "I want you to open the meeting, Ed," he said. "Then we'll follow you with a hot-shot speaker to wind it up."

I asked if he had the hot-shot speaker signed up. He had and he told me the man's name.

"You want me to start it, and he'll wind up?" I asked.

"Yeah, that's it," he said. "He'll do a great job, won't he?"

I knew the man, and as a hot-shot speaker, he was no dice. He was a good man at presenting facts and figures. He knew his subject, but he was rather on the uninteresting side.

"You have heard this man speak?" I asked.

"No, but they tell me he is great," he said. As a program builder I knew that the man had the program turned around. He should have started with the other fellow and let me follow. I knew that the other speaker would have trouble following me, and so I did not accept the invitation.

I have had chairman tell me, "Ed, this is what we are trying to do. This is our theme, and you could do your selling talk in this spot, right at the close of the afternoon session. What do you think?" The information on the meeting objective was helpful, and I was glad to try to help. Usually the speaker wants to help, and he'll appreciate any information on how he can best help. But don't ask a high-pressure speaker to do a low-pressure job for you. Suggest the man fill a spot he knows he can fill, and he will work with you to fill it.

FINDING PROSPECTIVE GUEST SPEAKERS

This is a job for anyone running a club. There seem to be millions of them, but not when you want one. The man in charge of getting speakers for a club has a full-time job. He has to be thinking of it every day. If he has to produce a speaker for a luncheon every week, he's got a major job. If he has to produce one for a meeting each month, his subjects are perhaps limited because of the nature of the club, and that is a job too. The size of the town and its distance from the larger towns puts another limitation on the speakers available. Yet the brothers come up with speakers. How do they do it? Well, here are some suggestions:

1. *The Other Clubs.* Keep track of who is speaking at the other clubs. Ask a member who heard the speaker how he was. If he has come to your town once, he may find time to do it again. Then, too, he has a speech prepared. It is a compliment to be invited back.

2. *Watch the Newspapers.* If a new company comes to town or a national company opens an office, the newspapers will report it. Perhaps the head man of the new operation would welcome the opportunity to get acquainted with your group by speaking to your club. The newspapers also give you accounts of speakers at other clubs; they tell about natives who have returned from world trips. A meeting manager can get a large number of tips on programs if he reads his newspaper with speakers in mind.

3. *Your Own Club.* Don't overlook the talent you have in your own club. Many of your members could do a speech for you on some subject that is in the news. If yours is a service club, some of your members belong to groups in their professions, such as purchasing agents, advertising or sales executives, medical or legal groups. Check your club group for possibilities.

4. *The Hobbyists.* In every town there are hobbyists, some most unusual. At a service club recently I heard a speaker talk about the "do it yourself" craze and what that has meant to certain businesses. It was most interesting and the questions asked after the speech showed that it was a success with the audience. Of course, many of the hobbyists are not good speakers, and that is a chance you take, but the subject matter has interest. Talk to the man

who runs the local hobby shop and he may be able to suggest some prospects. He might do the job himself.

5. *The Businesses.* The utilities are usually good prospects. Telephone the manager of the electric light company, the gas company, the telephone company, and ask for suggestions. They know of programs that are available. The subjects may border on the commercial, but the three named have problems of educating the public, and your club members are a part of that public.

6. *The Big News.* The papers this week may be full of news about some phase of foreign affairs, of a flood in another part of the country. Perhaps your members would like more details on that news at a future meeting. Usually there is someone in your town who knows something about the subject and could give them a thirty-minute background that would be informative and interesting. How do you find these experts? Make a few inquiries and you'll be surprised at how many you can find. Maybe you have never had an interest in China, but there is someone in your town who has made an intensive study of China, and could make a good talk on the subject. Your job is to inquire, inquire, inquire.

7. *I Was There.* There are persons in your town who were present at almost every big event you could name. Not one person at all events, but one at each event. One club brings in a local fellow who goes to the World Series each year. He talks about the highlights and answers questions. It makes an interesting program. One of our local men was in a train wreck that got national publicity and he toured all of the local service clubs telling about his experience. Not long ago, at a service club luncheon, I heard a college student who had helped fight forest fires tell about his experiences. The brothers listen to such talks and they

ask questions, and those questions show they approve the
program. A chairman who is alert for such opportunities
gets some interesting programs for his club.

8. *Trade Association Members.* You read in the newspapers that one of the local citizens has been made a vice
president of a state or national trade association. Telephone
him and ask if his group has a message that he thinks would
be interesting to the club. An electrical man might answer,
"Yeah, we would like to talk about adequate home wiring."
Now most of your members live in homes, they have had
fuses blow when they turned on another appliance. They
might like to know what they could do about it. The talk
would tell them, and they would find it interesting and informative. These men might even get trade paper editors
from their fields to speak to you. At the meetings of the
associations they hear speakers that might be invited.

9. *The Causes.* Many of the associations in your town
have paid secretaries and these men can speak for you or
locate speakers. You may feel that such speakers may talk
too much about the group and its work, but you'll find that
your best speakers have an axe to grind. A speaker can do
well on a subject that means something to him. Organizations such as the Red Cross and the Scouts are good for
programs. Why not a special Scout program once each
year? If another club has that one, you might adopt another organization; your town has many of them. The program can be made interesting, and the members will feel
that your club is doing something worthwhile, that little
bit more than arranging for a speaker and ordering a veal
chop.

10. *The Special Weeks.* Why not get a list of the special
weeks that are set up by industry? Your local department
store advertising manager will loan you one long enough
to copy it. Perhaps there are three or four that you can tie

in with during the year. On these weeks the industry interested makes available a lot of material for use in towns
like yours. The department store man may be able to suggest how you can build a program around the activity. The
promoters of the week may have a special program worked
out for clubs like yours. You write the headquarters and
they will help you arrange the program.

11. *The Holidays.* Of course you'll have Christmas and
perhaps Easter programs, but what are you doing about
days like Ground Hog Day? You might find a number of
days like this that you can tie in with during the year. Let's
say you want to do something on Ground Hog Day. There
must be someone in town that could do a talk on how that

*"Our speaker was reluctant to
speak on this subject."*

legend began, what truth there is in it, and perhaps give
your group an interesting talk on it. It's timely, the boys
on the radio and TV are yakking about it. Why not build a
program on it? Try it, and do the same on some of the
similar days.

12. *The Sports.* I mentioned the local fellow who attends
the World Series as a prospect for a talk. The same goes for
the Kentucky Derby and a score of similar events. The
players and the coaches, they too are good prospects. The
officials, too—don't overlook them. You'd be amazed how

many questions the brothers will ask a big-league umpire. Perhaps you don't provide for questions at your meetings, but if you get any of these sports celebrities, provide the time. Don't let the group go home saying, "I'd like to have asked him a question, but there wasn't time."

13. *The Local Schools.* You have all kinds of specialists in your local schools and some of them may be willing to speak on their specialty. Recently I heard a speech by the school systems psychologist about aptitude tests for children. Most of the members of the service club did not know that the testing was being done, and knew little about the objective. If the school system is trying to sell an idea to the voters, you'll not have too much trouble getting the superintendent to assign somebody to talk on that project. You may be lucky and get a speech on a controversial subject. When Rudolf Flesch wrote his book *Why Johnny Can't Read,* a speech by one of the school officials on why he was right or wasn't right would have been great. Perhaps two speakers, one for and the other against, would have been better. But since you are figuring on getting speakers, you might have had the "for" man at one meeting, the "against" fellow at another. We're spending a lot of money on our school systems. Nobody is too much against the spending, but too few of our taxpayers know anything about the schools. You might get a few speakers each year by digging into this school field.

14. *The Government Agencies.* Here is another source: the local representatives of the Federal or State Governments can supply speakers for you. As an example, the members all drive cars. Do they know what the State Highway Department is doing? They see the State Highway trucks and workers as they drive through the country, but most of your members don't keep up with what's being

done. There is a change in a law that affects one of the
Federal Government Departments. Why not a speaker to
clarify the law? Then you have the armed services. Most
of the time they are working on a problem. Why not have
one of them come in and tell all about it? Again these
speakers may have an axe that needs sharpening, but remember that the man who is trying to sell an idea usually
makes a good speech. You might preface his speech with
the old standby, "The ideas expressed are wholly his own,
not the club's." Better, from the standpoint of producing
speakers, you might say, "Next week we'll have a speaker
on the other side of the question." Two speakers instead of
one.

15. *Mr. Big.* Every community has its Mr. Big. He may
be your representative in Congress, or your United States
Senator, a man prominent in a sport, an author, an artist.
He is your local light with a national reputation. Usually
such a man is good for one speech each year. You might
make it his day. Set up a tradition in your club that every
year, on his birthday, he speaks to your group. Get the
idea? He may not speak to you because he is Mr. Big, but
if you can work in some idea that makes it mean something
personal to him, he may fall for the idea.

16. *The Native Son.* This is the fellow who went away
to the big city and made good. Now he is a big corporation
executive or a prominent surgeon. You might stage an old
home week, collect a group of the boys that were in his
high school class, and perhaps have a joint meeting of two
or more clubs. Of course, if you have a big-league ball
player in the vicinity, you can have him once when the
season is over or in the spring when the season is starting.
Everybody in the old home town takes great pride in the
success of the native son. They all feel they knew him

when. His speech may not be too hot, but you'll have a successful meeting anyway. If you don't have the name of such a native son, telephone the editor of the newspaper or talk to some of the old timers in the town. They may give you names.

17. *The Trade Associations.* I was sitting at a speaker's table recently reading the notice for the speaker at the next meeting. I asked the chairman, "How did you get this fellow?" He was the secretary of a national trade association. "I wrote a letter to the trade association. Think he'll be any good?"

I had heard good reports of him. But the chairman, without connections, had written to the trade association and had come up with a program. One chairman told me that he had three trade association men scheduled for his programs this year. "I get them from the state associations," he said. Usually a trade association has some message to give the public. In most cases that story is well worked up, perhaps with visual aids so that members of the association can present the story to groups like yours. You invite the association to send a representative, and you have your program.

18. *Your Acquaintances.* You may say, "I don't know too many prospects." That may be true, but have you ever made a list of the men you know personally who might make a program for you? As I speak to chairmen who complain of the difficulty of getting speakers, I find that few of them have. This job of producing speakers is one that a man has to work at. Making up that list might be a start. I get many requests from my acquaintances. Some I can make, others I can't. But many times I speak to clubs because some old buddy asked me to.

19. *Local Associations.* The secretaries of your local Chamber of Commerce or Retail Merchants Association

might help you get speakers. At times they might provide speakers for you. Why shouldn't you have a program each year with a speech by the President of the C. of C., a sort of state-of-the-community speech? Perhaps you have a Sales Executives Club or an advertising club. Talk to the men who run such organizations; they get around to meetings over the state and hear many speakers you could use. Recently I ran into the secretary of the local Retail Merchants Association and he gave me the name of a speaker that he thought would be good for our Sales Executives Club. The secretary had heard the speaker at a meeting in Toledo. Getting speakers is a lot like canvassing. Ask enough people and you will get the names of enough prospects.

20. *Speakers' Bureaus.* Just about every association has a speakers' bureau. One chairman I met had made up a list of the speakers' bureaus in his state. You might start checking on this. I've suggested that you do it with trade associations, but why stop with those? Why not include all associations?

21. *Speakers' Agents.* If you can pay your speakers you no doubt are in touch with agents who can provide speakers for you. I met a chairman recently who had a number of such agents working for him. One chairman whose club hired one speaker per year for the annual ladies' night was dickering with three agents. He finally bought the speaker with the lowest fee. I don't advise that, for you probably get what you pay for, but I do suggest checking on available fee speakers close to your town. I say close because there is little sense in paying a speaker's fee of two hundred dollars and speaker's expenses of three hundred for transportation. In dealing with paid speakers, try to get an exact figure on the fee and an approximate estimate of the expenses.

22. *Club Publications.* Work up a deal with the other clubs in town to exchange club publications. Most clubs put out some kind of sheet. That sheet lists the speakers the club has. Let's say you can make this exchange set-up with six clubs. Think of the names you will get that way. If you read in a publication that Joe Whosis spoke at Rotary, telephone a friend in Rotary and ask if Joe was good. If your friend says Joe was, then find out who asked Joe. When you get in touch with Joe, he may say, "I'm not a public speaker, I'm not—" Break in and say, "Yeah, but you were mighty hot at Rotary." Now you got Joe on the hook.

23. *Local Officials.* The mayor, the city attorney, the traffic court judge, the sheriff, the prosecutor, the police chief, the fire chief—you may be able to use any of them. Most of the officials feel that the public knows little and cares less about how the town or county is run. I asked a chairman who was complaining about the dearth of speakers to write down the names of the elective offices in his town or county. He wrote twelve without stopping. "Why don't you have twelve prospects there?" I asked. I met one enterprising chairman who had scheduled a series of six talks on different phases of the city government. He got together with the mayor, laid out the talks, and got six programs for his club. His was a weekly luncheon club and he scheduled the talks on municipal government, one each month. I asked one of the members how he liked the series. "They're good, Ed," he said. "You know, we never pay too much attention to those things." You might try this one if the production of that weekly speaker is a problem.

24. *Check History.* Why not go back over the club programs of the past few years and ask for a repeat performance from some of the better speakers? It's a compliment to a speaker to be invited back. The second invitation

tells him most effectively that you liked him the first time.

25. *The Authors.* The other day I got a letter that said, "I have just finished reading your new book, and I hasten to write to invite you to address our fall meeting. If you can speak as well as you write, you are just what the doctor ordered for us." Nice man, wasn't he? Thousands of books are put out each year, many of them authored by men or women in your state. Why not step over to the library and see if you can get a list of authors in your state? You may have to read the man's book before you invite him, and I know that reading can cause you pain, but let's say you can produce two or more authors per year. If you like the subject of the book, ask the man to speak on that subject. Write him a note in the tone of the one I quoted and you'll probably sign him.

26. *The Directories of Speakers.* The National Sales Executives publish a directory listing speakers suitable for Sales Executives Clubs or sales organizations. The Chamber of Commerce of the United States also has such a directory of business speakers. There may be others but surely you will be able to find the two mentioned in your town. You might get in touch with the speakers listed from your state.

27. *Can You Suggest?* This has been mentioned before, but in inviting men to speak to your club, you will get many turndowns. When you get one of these, ask the

"We're extremely fortunate to have with us today—"

speaker, "Can you suggest anyone else?" If you have asked the man to speak on his subject, he will know other experts on that subject. What is more natural than for him to tell you of a few? This works better if you are asking the man by telephone. But when you get a mail turndown, why not write and thank him for considering your invitation, tell him you are sorry that he couldn't make it and ask for suggestions? If you get one of the men suggested, write the man, tell him of your success and thank him. Recently I could not accept an invitation to speak at a sales rally and the chairman asked me if I could suggest someone. I gave him three names. He signed up the first man he telephoned and then was good enough to telephone me back to report. "We'll be after you again," he promised. And I imagine he will.

IT ISN'T EASY, MISTER

When you read through all of these sources of speakers, you say, "Well, that should be easy." But it's work, no matter how you look at it. When you agreed to take on the job of producing speakers, you walked into something. But men are doing a grand job of producing speakers every day. I suggest these three rules to help:

(a) Be speaker-conscious.
(b) Make notes.
(c) Work at the job.

(a) *Be speaker-conscious.* Keep the need of speakers with you every waking hour. Talk about speakers to friends, customers, anybody. Inquire about every speaker that appears in your town.

(b) *Make notes.* Write down the names that appear in the paper. When you think of a subject, make a note. It won't help if all you can recall is, "There was a guy that

talked to some club—was it last week or the week before?"
Make a note of the name and the subject and you can work
on it later.

(c) *Work at the job.* This is no eight-hour-day project.
In assigning the job the president may have said, "All you
need to do is produce a speaker every week." He told the
truth, that's all—a speaker every week. But if you follow
these three rules you'll do better at it.

NOW THAT YOU'VE GOT HIM

Let's say you have that speaker's acceptance; he has
promised to speak at your club. Now how do you handle
him from there?

6 / How to Handle the Guest Speaker

I have been that guest speaker probably over one thousand times, and clubs have given me the works. Both ways! I have had every courtesy that a speaker could expect; and then I have been utterly ignored, perhaps like that relative you didn't exactly invite anyway.

Here's a description of one most unsuccessful appearance.

My plane rolled to a stop at the airport. I went down the steps hoping to recognize a smiling face looking for a fellow carrying a set of charts. The smiling face wasn't there. At the gate a taxi man asked, "Taxi, mister? Want to ride into town?"

I told him, "I'll see, but don't go off without checking me."

He said, "O.K."

I picked up my suitcase and charts and went into the waiting room. Nobody noticed a man with a set of charts. I was carrying the chart case, hoping. I stood for two minutes, examined the four people closely, but no sign.

The taxi fellow was a fine conversationalist—wife, four kids, farming four acres, driving this taxi, getting by.

At the hotel, the desk clerk could not find the reservation in my name. I showed him the letter from the club assuring me that they had taken care of the reservation. He couldn't find it but he had a room anyway.

"The club, it meets here?" I asked.

"Yeah, they meet here all right. They have cocktails up on the mezzanine at six o'clock, dinner at seven."

In my room, I lay down on the bed. I had been traveling since five o'clock in the morning. I had to get out that early to make plane connections. I was tired, and I hoped that the good brothers would give me thirty minutes for a nap before they called me. I must have been dead to the world for three hours, for when I did come to, it was six-thirty. I reached for the telephone. "Have there been any calls for me?" I asked.

"No, sir," the girl said.

"You haven't rung this room since three?" I went on.

"No, there have been no calls."

I washed up, put on my white shirt and the red tie I always use when I speak, picked up the chart case, and went down to the mezzanine. The bar was open in one end of the meeting room. The tables were set. I walked up to the head table and started to set up my charts. Apparently nobody noticed me. I finished with the charts and looked over the group. There were about forty men in the room, the bartender was busy, and I decided I would search out the bar downstairs and buy a drink for the guest speaker.

I started for the far door when one of the men called to me. "You're Mr. Hegarty, aren't you? I recognize you from your picture in the notice."

I admitted I was.

"I'd like to buy you a drink."

"That's the best offer I've had tonight," I replied. "Are you an officer of the club?"

"No, I'm Joe Gorman. I'm just a member—in good standing, though!" We shook hands.

"Then on principle, I have to refuse to let you buy me a drink," I said.

"Principle, I don't get it," he said.

"I have a rule," I explained. "When I go to speak to a club like this, I don't let anyone but an officer of the club buy me a drink."

Joe laughed and looked around the room. "You know, I don't see an officer here," he said. "That's funny, not an officer here, not even the secretary."

He got me a bourbon on the rocks and I had just taken the first sip when a tall fellow with a mustache asked, "You're Mr. Hegarty, aren't you?"

I admitted I was and shook hands.

"I'm Jesse Token," he said. "I'm supposed to introduce you tonight. When you are free, I'd like to sit with you a few minutes and get some data on what you want me to say. I meant to bring the notice, but I forgot that. I figured I'd pick one up here, but none of the other fellows seems to have brought one either. You don't by any chance have a copy, do you?"

"No, I never saw one. Don't you have the data I sent to your secretary?"

"No, I didn't know he had anything. He went to Chicago last night, and he called me from the airport asking me to take over."

"I'll give you a copy of what I sent him," I said. He followed me over to the head table. I got the copy out of my brief case. "I'll study this and give it back to you," he offered.

"You don't need to," I replied. "I carry a number of them for occasions like this."

"This has happened before?"

Has it? So often that I have had the material mimeographed. If the introducer does nothing but read it, it will be a good introduction. It gives the name of my company, my title, a plug for my books, my education, and my business experience step by step. Experience taught me to carry those copies for I have found that the material seldom reaches the man who is called on to introduce me. I was explaining this to Mr. Token when Gorman came up with the second bourbon on the rocks. "I assumed you wanted this," he said.

I did. I suspected that Gorman had found that the two drinks would loosen up a speaker. "When you finish that, we'll be ready to sit down, Mr. Hegarty," Token said, "unless you want another."

I was shaking hands with a number of members now. Each acknowledged the introduction and moved away. No member wants to be connected with a guest speaker he hasn't heard. Since I have listened to thousands of guest speakers, I can't blame them.

As we were about to sit down, the president of the club arrived, breathless and still hurrying. "Well, well, Ed, I'm glad you could make it. I have four meetings to attend tonight and I'll have to run before you speak. Sorry I won't get to hear you, but I sure appreciate your coming."

I wondered if he had dictated the letter he sent telling me about how much good I could do the club. He probably meant the club, not him. But he was off to take care of some other job.

"He's a pistol," Token said.

I wanted to ask, "Water or what?" But it struck me that the thought wasn't funny, and perhaps was pointless.

The president thanked me again before he left. I was introduced, the man read the printed piece, he told one funny story about me that didn't make me too mad, I made the speech. It was good. I had done it many times before, so that all the material was tested. How could I say it was good? I watched the faces. They tell a speaker much better than the laughs.

The chairman now introduced a presenter. This man's job was to make a short talk and present me with a gift, a

The guest speaker has just started.

practice of many clubs. "The club likes to give the speaker a small token of our esteem, a sort a memento of the occasion," the man said. He handed me a small box, gift-wrapped. I opened it with misgivings. I was right—it was a cigarette lighter with my initials engraved in gold. I have a collection of them, all with my initials. I don't smoke.

Next morning as I checked out of the hotel, I told the cashier that the room was to be charged to the club. "There's no note of it here," she said. "I'll have to check the manager on that and he is down in the coffee shop."

I signed the bill and left. I was almost certain that in a few days the bill would follow me in the mail.

You may say, "What you beefing about, Ed? You got paid for the speech, didn't you?"

Not that one. That talk was on my company. My expenses to get to the place were about one hundred dollars. And after that club scheduled me, no one seemed to worry about the speech but the speaker.

Is such treatment unusual? It isn't, I can tell you from experience. Unless the guest speaker needs practice in speaking, you wonder why he keeps it up.

Of course all clubs are not like that. Some go all out the other way. They treat the speaker as if he were somebody. Here's one experience I had. It has been over ten years since it happened, but it still sticks out as something different.

The club was the Birmingham, Alabama, Sales Executives Club. My train arrived in town at 7:45 A.M. When I stepped off the train six members of the club were there to greet me. Now that is a bit early for so many men to be out, but there they were. They took me to the hotel where a suite had been reserved. We had breakfast in the room. At breakfast, one man told me he was in charge of the meeting room; later he showed me the room and we made arrangements to handle my charts. The chairman asked about my plans for the day. I wanted to work over the notes of my speech in the afternoon, and so we arranged to see the town in the morning. One of the members was assigned as my guide. The man knew the town and he gave me the deluxe tour. At lunch time the committee met again at the estate of one of the members, and later we went on to the country club for lunch. After the lunch I was taken back to the hotel. At dinner time the group came back to the suite. The chairman had asked me ahead of time if I had any friends I would like to invite. I gave him some names and these friends came in for a drink before dinner. After my talk that night, the group took me to the train.

That club was treating a speaker as if he were a guest. I have had many clubs approach that reception, and I am sure that in every case my speech was better because the club showed that it appreciated my coming as its guest speaker.

WHAT A CLUB CAN DO TO HELP ITS GUEST SPEAKERS

Here are a number of suggestions for clubs to use when a speaker has agreed to speak at your club.

GET THIS INFORMATION FROM HIM

1. His name.
2. His business title.
3. His education.
4. His business experience. This should furnish reasons why he can talk on the subject.
5. The title of his talk.
6. The length of his talk.
7. When he will arrive in your town and how—train, plane, car.
8. Whether he will be alone or have his wife with him.
9. Any arrangements you can make for him—hotel, motel, pick-up at the station or airport.

TELL HIM THIS

1. Place of meeting and how to find it.
2. Time of meeting—noon, evening, etc.
3. Who'll be there—the name of the club may not be too descriptive of the membership. Also tell him if the ladies will be there.

4. If this is a special occasion.

5. How much time he has.

6. Adjournment time, if you have one set. Once, right in the middle of my speech, the chairman arose and told me, "Ed, we have a special adjournment time, one-fifteen, and it's about that. Can you bring this to a close?" I agreed I could and sat down without finishing. Nobody had told me about the special adjournment time, and much of my time had been taken up with a rhubarb about a golf outing.

HANDLE CONTACT WITH THE GUEST SPEAKER YOURSELF

Many times a member of the club will offer to get a guest speaker for you. This may be a man from his company, a fellow he went to college with, an acquaintance. You want this kind of help. But you will get along better with the guest speakers if you handle contact with them yourself. Let the member make the initial arrangements, but then take over. Recently a friend of mine in Cleveland asked me to speak before a club. I agreed and made the note on my calendar. I sent the friend my publicity material and heard no more about the date. About two weeks before the date of the appearance I telephoned my friend. I asked if the date was still on. "As far as I know, Ed," he said. "You know I haven't heard from those guys at all." He telephoned the right man and confirmed the date. But let's say that as soon as the club had my acceptance, one of the officers had written me, giving me the data mentioned above. I would have felt surer of that engagement, wouldn't I?

I believe that most speakers would prefer to deal direct with the club. A friend asks me to speak before his club and he doesn't give me the information I should have. If it is a service club, I know the type of audience I will have;

but if it is another type of club, I may be confused. My friend will say, "Gee, Ed, I thought I told you that." But if he doesn't tell me, my speech may be completely off the beam. Don't depend on what you tell the speaker on the telephone. Confirm it all in writing.

Let the friend make the original contact, then you take over and handle the arrangements from then on. You can tell the friend of the speaker, "Look Sam, there's a lot of details to be taken care of. You don't want to be handling them. We want you to introduce him, though." Nine times out of ten, Sam will be glad to bow out.

If you run the meeting, you handle the details and you will be sure of what the status is at any time.

WORKING WITH GUEST SPEAKERS

Here are a number of ideas that clubs use with a guest speaker:

1. *Give Him Full Information.* The more detail you can give him the better. I've had clubs sign me for a date and not tell me whether the meeting is at noon or in the evening.

2. *Tell Him Who Is on the Program.* Tell him about the other speakers and when he talks, before or after the other speakers.

3. *Keep in Touch.* At times I have had to telephone clubs long distance to confirm dates that had been made months ahead. There are a number of ways to keep the speaker posted. Recently a club sent me a copy of the notice for correction. The secretary said in his note, "Note that I have given a list of the points you will cover." I checked his points against what I planned to cover to make sure that I would make good on my advance publicity. I'm sure that

by listing those points in the notice he felt that he was obligating me to cover the points.

It pays to let the speaker know he is expected. You may have to make a date with your speaker months ahead to get on his schedule, but don't forget him in the meanwhile. Just last week I had to write a club to ask if my speech was still scheduled. It was, the club had put out an elaborate story on me in their monthly magazine, but nobody had sent me a copy. A friend in the town wrote me that he heard I was going to speak in the town. That told me that some sort of notice had gone out. When I met the club president I suggested that the club should write speakers and send copies of the publicity. He said, "That is the job of the program chairman." But the program chairman wasn't handling it. Perhaps what that club needed was a Chairman to Keep in Touch with the Speaker. In that same month I appeared before a sales managers' conference sponsored by a Sales Executives Club. The club surely knew how to keep in touch. They sent me copies of the letter to the hotel about my room, copies of the letter assigning a committee to meet me at the train, a list of the other speakers, and information on when I appeared on the program. The more information the speaker has, the better job he will do for you.

4. *Mail Him the Notice.* Send him two or three copies of the notice that you send out. He may want to build some character at home by showing these to the wife or kids. He might like to send one to the boss. Many times when I show up to speak at a club, I say, "I'd like to see one of the notices you sent out to your members."

5. *If He Ships Aids.* If he is shipping any visual aids, delegate someone to check on them. Let him know that if

he wants to ship any aids, you will arrange to take care of them.

6. *Ask If He Needs Help with His Visual Aids.* He may need an operator for a projector or porters to help him set up. Offer to get him any help that he needs.

7. *Know the Meeting Place.* Know the personnel of the hotel or public building in which the meeting is to be held. Know what is available so that if the speaker wants some special help or a special type of visual aid, you know what you have to do to get it.

8. *Ask If He Has Friends He Would Like to Invite.* The speaker appreciates this and the friends do, too. Seat the friends at the head table, or at least introduce them.

9. *Offer to Meet Him.* This always reassures the speaker that he is speaking to a live club. He may not need any help, but you get credit for offering. Recently I appeared at a sales conference put on by a club, and the club secretary sent me a mimeographed schedule showing when all of the speakers were to arrive. The sheet was made up to guide the reception committee. By sending the sheet to me he showed me the club was on the job, that I was expected.

10. *Register Him at the Hotel.* Even if he is not to stay overnight, register him at the hotel. Get him a nice room or a suite, the best the hotel has. It costs only a few bucks more, but it makes an impression. If the man is to arrive on an early morning train and the hotel is full, register him on the day before so that he has a room available when he arrives. It is not easy to get ready to make a speech in a hotel lobby.

11. *Leave a Note at the Hotel.* If he says that he doesn't want to be met at the train or airport, leave a note for him at the hotel asking him to telephone you when he arrives.

12. *Ask What He Wants.* He may want to be alone. But ask. He may want to do some sightseeing, or need transportation to some of his customers or friends.

13. *Assign a Member to Take Care of Him.* I have had these men assigned to me, and they have been of great help in explaining the membership, showing me the town, and otherwise making my stay pleasant.

14. *Pick Him Up, Escort Him to the Meeting.* Offer to pick him up at the hotel and take him to the meeting hall. If the meeting is in the hotel, offer to bring him down or meet him.

15. *Ask What He Wants the Introducer to Say.* He may have sent you a complete written introduction. Still, it is well to ask him again. Perhaps he became a grandfather this week.

The guest speaker has just told his first joke.

16. *Ask Him Again about Time.* He told you that he wanted forty-five minutes, but that was perhaps months ago. Ask again. The other day I heard a chairman ask that question of a speaker. The speaker said, "Twenty minutes at the most." I had noted that the man had been assigned a full hour on the program. Don't cut his time, either, because something has come up. Give him the time you agreed on.

17. *Help Him Set Up.* The man may need some help in setting up his speaking aids. If he does, get hotel porters or whatever he needs.

18. *Show the Speaker the Meeting Room.* Most speakers will want no change in the way you set up the room for your meetings. They will speak from a head table, a platform, or any other arrangement you have. Some, though, may have exhibits that might go better with a different arrangement. I use charts in many of my speeches and a high lectern on the table can hide the charts from a portion of the audience. Usually I arrange for a man in the audience to lift the lectern out of the way as I start to speak. The chairman may want it for his notes and other speakers may want it but I want it out, not because I could not use it, but because, if it stays, the audience will be straining to see what is printed on the charts.

At a meeting recently I had to have a platform set up at a different part of the room because the head table set up was so impossible. All the time the porters were moving in the platform, the secretary was stating, "We've always had it like this, Mr. Hegarty." He had arranged for the set-up and he didn't like to have it changed. Once, before any of the club executives arrived, I even had the head table changed to the short side of the room. Nobody seemed to notice. It may help you have a better meeting if you talk to the speaker about the room and ask if what you have is O.K. for him.

19. *Tell the Speaker about the Acoustics.* If the hall in which you hold your meetings has any peculiarities, tell the speaker about them. The size of the room and the size of the audience may fool the speaker. If he is going to be heard in all parts of the hall, he has to speak in a voice that fills the hall, rather than one that carries to the audience. I run a number of meetings in a large auditorium. The groups in the meetings may vary from twenty to two or three hundred. A speaker who gets up to talk to twenty

persons is not inclined to sound off in a loud voice. If the room were filled, he would try to speak loud enough to be heard by all. But when he sees that twenty, he speaks loud enough to be heard by twenty. In working with speakers in that room, I advise, "Speak louder than you feel you need to." I also agree to sit in the back and signal when they cannot be heard. There may be some points about this hall you use that the speaker should know. Not long ago a chairman told me, "The railroad runs along this side of the hotel. When a train comes, you might just as well stop." The trains came, I stopped, and the room and the speaker got along O.K.

20. *Ask about His Meal.* The speaker may prefer a fruit salad or some light bit instead of that leathery veal chop you are serving the club. Ask him about this. You may save a meal entirely.

21. *Warn Him.* If you have any taboos on stories or other material, let him know. If you expect that certain of his material might start a rhubarb, warn him in advance. He may want to stick his neck out, and then again he may want to play safe.

22. *Make Changes Gracefully.* If you have to change your meeting procedure to accommodate the speaker, don't keep reminding him of it. One club had to change its meeting routine to allow me the time I needed. They allotted thirty minutes to the speaker. I needed forty, and so they had to handle some announcements and other window dressing during dessert. But that was a break in club routine, and at least four of the officers reminded me of the great favor they were doing me. I had traveled hundreds of miles at my own expense to make that speech. The club didn't even pick up my hotel bill, yet they were doing me a favor. The audience didn't worry about that ten minutes; they could

have taken much more. So accept any changes gracefully. Particularly if you get the speaker for "free."

23. *Help Him Pack Up.* He may not want any help. But if he has some properties to pack, offer to help him get them packed. You might offer to take care of shipping them home to him.

24. *Pick Up His Hotel Check.* This won't break you and it is an appreciated gesture. You arranged for a nice room, one that may be better than his expense account will stand. So arrange with the hotel to pay it.

25. *That Gift.* If your club makes a practice of presenting a gift as a token of thanks, try to give something that the speaker can use. I've had clubs telephone my secretary and ask her what she thought. At least find out if he smokes. I don't, and as I have said, I have a fine collection of cigarette lighters with my name engraved on them. I can imagine some chairman saying, "We gave that guy the best cigarette lighter we could buy, and his speech wasn't so hot either." If you are going to put the man's name on the gift, be sure to have it spelled right. Check it carefully before you make the presentation. If it is not spelled correctly, just pass up the gift altogether and send it to him. He will never know that you were intending to hand him a gift.

TREAT SPEAKERS LIKE CUSTOMERS

You can sum up all of these suggestions with the advice, "Be a good host." A former president of our local Sales Executives Club once said, "We treat them like customers." That is a salesman's way of describing how a guest speaker should be treated.

IF YOU'RE PAYING THE GUEST SPEAKER

Here are some suggestions to follow if you are paying the guest speaker for his talk.

26. *He's a Guest.* Treat him as a guest just the same as a speaker you got for free. If he is worth paying, he is important. Other groups treat him well. Do you want him to feel that your group is not so hot?

27. *Give Him Full Information.* Tell him what you can about your group. Since he is being paid he wants to give the group a talk that will be helpful. If he knows who you are, he will slant his talk at the problems of your group. Recently, I made a talk to a group of manufacturers' agents. The secretary of the group sent me a booklet with the name of every member, and a list of the lines that member represented. Don't you think that my talk to that group was better because I had that information?

28. *Register Him into the Hotel.* If this is a convention-type session, your group will no doubt have filled up the hotel. Handle his registration for him. Tell the hotel that you will take care of his expenses. You are paying them anyway, aren't you?

29. *Badges, Tickets.* If it is a convention-type session, have his badges and tickets ready for him. He may not want to use the meal tickets, but if he does, you have taken care of them. I have come up to registration desks at meetings where I have been a guest speaker and have been told by the help that I had to pay the registration fee before I could get into the meeting. I have had that happen a number of times, even when the group was paying me to speak to them. At most such meetings, when I tell them who I am the girls dig out an envelope for me and in that envelope

are all my tickets and a badge. They show me I'm expected
and welcome.

30. *Tell Him Where You'll Meet Him.* If you do not
meet the speaker at the airport or station, tell him where
you will meet him. If he comes into the hotel, have a note
waiting for him.

31. *Send Him Notices.* Send him copies of any publicity
you get out, notices, circulars, and other promotion. The
more he knows about your meeting, the better job he will
do for you.

32. *Explain the Time.* Let him know the time he will
be on the program. If there are other speakers he should
know about, mention them and explain when they will
be on, before or after him.

33. *Thank Him.* Write him a thank-you note, just as if
you did not pay him. Tell him how you liked the talk and
what the members thought of it. He may want to use the
testimonial in his publicity.

34. *Have His Check Ready.* Arrange to write him a
check when he is finished speaking. If you are paying him
a fee and expenses, have a check for the fee ready, and
have him send you a note on his expenses. The man may
need the money to get back home.

HANDLING SPEAKERS IN THE OFFICE MEETING

So far the suggestions given on handling guest speakers
apply to the club or association meeting. But speakers have
to be lined up and handled in office meetings, too.

One man in charge. That is the secret of successful office
meetings. This may be the boss himself, but if the boss
does not have the time, one man should be the meeting
manager, chairman, or director. The boss should let those
taking part know this man is the stage manager, and that

the others are to work with him. In over-all company meetings this job usually falls to the advertising or sales-promotion manager. But let's say this is a department meeting —the accounting department. O.K., let the chief accountant put one man in charge of getting the meeting together and putting it on. Let's assume the boss has just given you the job of putting on a meeting. Here are some suggestions:

35. *Lay Out the Program.* This can be a list of subjects on a sheet. Opposite each subject write the name of the suggested speaker to cover that subject. If the subjects and speakers need approval of the boss, get that.

36. *Call the Interested Parties Together.* Explain the plan to the group and get agreement that Joe will cover this, Pete that, and Bill this. Have the boss in the meeting long enough to explain its importance. Get the speaker's acceptance of the subjects assigned, or make any changes the group feels advisable. Explain that you will make a more detailed suggestion for the coverage of each subject.

37. *Work with Each Speaker.* Make an outline of what each man is to cover. Explain that you are not trying to tell them what to cover, you are trying to make sure that there is no duplication. Offer to work with each on his talk.

38. *Have Each Use Visuals.* Visuals may not be easy to sell to some speakers. Too many dopes in this world feel they can do just as well by talking, but it will pay you to sell the idea of visuals. You know that a speaker with a set of charts (even handmade) or some glass slides, a blackboard, or an easel pad, does much better than a speaker who tries to get by on speech alone. Some reasons why a speaker should use visuals are given on page 108. Use these to help you sell the idea.

39. *Rehearse.* Have each speaker go over his presentation. Set up the room just as you would for the meeting.

Have the man's speaking aids there. If the company owns a tape recorder, have the man record his speech. Play it back for him, and he will realize how important this rehearsal is. After he has heard himself, he will know that he can do better. Everybody does.

40. *Use Other Departments.* Ask the advertising, promotion, or sales departments for help in laying out your meeting and in staging it. They have to use showmanship in their meetings, and they will be able to make suggestions to speakers, and to suggest meeting material that the company owns but that you might not know about. It's amazing how much help you can get if you ask for it. If your company puts on sales meetings for its distribution, sit in on them and note how the sales group sells ideas. You can liven up your meetings by using the sales approach. Usually your meetings are to persuade somebody to do something, aren't they?

41. *Don't Dodge Showmanship.* If a skit or some role playing is called for to put over a point in your meeting, try either device. You have a full quota of ham actors in your office and it's easy to get together a skit that shows the right and wrong way. Such skits get away from the constant speaking. TV or radio program ideas can be used to make good presentations. You might suggest to a man who is not a good speaker that he pattern his presentation around one of the currently popular radio or TV programs.

The guest speaker has just said, "In conclusion—"

The audience will know the program and will like the novelty of a presentation built around it.

42. *Help All You Can.* Work closely with the man on his presentation. Sit down with him. Go over his outline. Discuss in detail what he will say on each point. By working with him you help him think through his presentation. This means work for you, but it pays off in better performance.

IT'S YOUR MEETING

From these suggestions you may get the idea that you are doing most of the work. And that's right, you are. But if you are the person in charge of the meeting and you want it to be good, you have to do that work. The other day a meeting manager said, "I beat my brains out getting these meetings on the road, and sometimes I wonder if it is worth all the work."

Just then an executive said, "Good meeting, Joe."

Joe thanked him as they shook hands. I looked at Joe's face, and I knew that he was getting that thrill that comes only when a man has done a good job. He knew that the meeting was a success. And he knew that it was his work that made it so, his work and his planning.

IF YOU WANT TO BE A GUEST SPEAKER

Nobody really wants to, you say. But they do. It's strange, but they do. O.K., if you are one of the ones who would consent to make yourself available to speak to groups for a modest fee or for free, here is some advice.

1. *Write Out a Biography.* Write out a complete story on who you are and why you should be speaking to this club on this subject. Have this mimeographed and send the club a number of copies. Give complete details of your schooling,

your business experience, the organizations you belong to, the offices you have held in these organizations. Don't be too modest in this. The poor fellow writing the notice of the meeting or the newspaper release will appreciate complete information. Not long ago Mrs. Hegarty looked over a printed program of a meeting at which I had spoken. The club had printed a complete story on each speaker. "They have more in here on you than on any of these other men," she said. They had, but it was because I had given the committee more information than the others.

2. *Get a Good Photograph.* They'll ask for a photograph, so get a good one. Don't send that confirmation picture. Send a recent one, one with a suggestion of a smile on your face. The picture helps sell the members on coming out to hear you. Send as many copies as the group asks for, but ask that they send them back when they have used them. The prints cost money. Type your name, address, and title on the back of the photograph so the brothers will know who it is.

3. *Write the Newspaper Notice.* If there is anything in your speech to interest the general public, write out a story for the newspapers and send the club copies. Leave blanks for the names of the club, the date, place, and time. Suggest that the club secretary have this typed with the data filled in and send it to the newspapers.

4. *Write Out Your Introduction, Carry an Extra Copy.* Write out what you want the chairman to say when he introduces you. Have this mimeographed and carry copies with you. The ones you send to the chairman will always be lost. With extra copies, you'll be prepared when the man says, "I'm supposed to introduce you, Mr. Speaker. What do you want me to say about you?" Just open your brief case and give him the sheet.

5. *Copies of Your Speech.* Some associations want these for printing in the proceedings. If you want to release copies, have these mimeographed and ready. There is no need to have copies if you don't feel they can help you any. Some speakers make copies available, others don't.

6. *Ask for Samples.* Ask the secretary to send you copies of the notices sent out, the stories that have appeared in the newspapers, and other publicity. You may want to keep a scrap book, and what one club does might give you ideas for future publicity.

7. *Make a Note of Names.* If you are speaking for pay, keep a list of the names of the men who run clubs. Save the letters that thank you for your appearance and tell you how good you are. These can be used as testimonials.

8. *Build a Mailing List.* A list of the clubs that hire speakers with the names of the men who run those clubs can be used for an annual mailing. Usually when a club has heard you once they are finished with you for a period of four or five years. But if you're good, they may get stuck and need you. The reminder that you're still making speeches can help get jobs for you.

These are a few suggestions that will help make your life as a guest speaker easier, but let's get back to the job of running meetings. With the speaker lined up and handled, what can you do about helping him with his visuals?

7 / Helping the Guest Speaker with His Visual Aids

The other evening a chairman asked me if I could use an hour with his group instead of the forty minutes that we had agreed on. I told him that if he got me a blackboard I would explain a procedure to the group that had gone over well with similar audiences. The meeting was in a hotel in Buffalo, and as we enjoyed the social hour in the hotel, the blackboard was brought in. It was a beat-up job with a hole in the writing surface as if some previous user had tried to move a chair or bureau through it. The chairman said, "They must have a better board than that."

He went to the banquet manager and was told, "That was the blackboard the hotel used." But the chairman didn't stop there. He telephoned the manager and asked that worthy to come and look at the blackboard. The result —a new blackboard, one of the most modern ones. I don't know whether or not the hotel sent out and bought a new one, rented one, or what. All I know is that meeting manager was on his job. He was thinking of the job this speaker was doing for the club, and he wanted to give the speaker the best tools available.

Many times when I have asked for a simple speaking aid such as a blackboard or easel, the chairman of the meeting has acted as if I were imposing on him. One such told me, "No speaker has asked for one before." Another said, "I don't know whether we can get one." Most of them are willing to do anything, but some don't seem to want to co-operate.

When a speaker asks for some aid, you may know that he has a plan for using it. If he has a plan, you may be sure that his speech will be better. You know too that he is doing the club a favor for he is showing them as well as telling them. And, because he is showing, he is more likely to hold their attention. Most clubs ask you beforehand what you want them to get for you. Some clubs have one man appointed to get the speaker what he wants. Your speaker appreciates help like that. Here are some ideas that good meeting planners used to help the speaker with his speaking aids.

1. *Help Him Get What He Wants.* He may want anything, a blackboard, easel, pad screen, movie projector, a talking parrot. If he tells you what he wants, get it for him. I once had a speaker ask me to get him a dozen quart milk bottles. I didn't ask why, I got them. I've seen speakers ask a chairman, "Did you get me that list of things I asked for?" The chairman had turned the list over to somebody and that somebody was not present to give a report. No matter what the speaker asks for, try to get it for him.

2. *Let Him See What You Got.* If he has asked for a blackboard, show him the one that you have and ask him if it is all right. Tell him that you will get him any kind he wants. The one you have will usually be usable, but

show him you want to please. It is your club and you want the speaker to put on the best show possible.

3. *Offer to Help Him Set Up.* Note that the suggestion is "offer." Don't move in and try to set up an exhibit that you have never seen before. I usually travel with a set of charts. They are of the throw-over type, and I carry an easel to hang them on. The whole—easel and charts—rolls into an easily carried canvas kit. Managers ask, "Need any help in setting up?" My answer is, "No, I have all I need here." Yet even when I have declined help, I have had managers take the kit from me, start to set up the easel, and then ask, "How does this thing work, anyway?" If the speaker says that he does not need help, take him at his word. He knows what he has and how he wants it set up. You may be in his way if you move in and try to help.

4. *Check on Visibility.* When you select a place for this speaker's blackboard, check to make sure that it can be seen from all parts of the room. In a hotel ballroom the other evening the managers set up a blackboard under a crystal chandelier and the glare from the light made the figures on the board invisible. Recently I saw a speaker and the meeting chairman making marks on a blackboard and checking to see if the marks could be seen. The chairman explained, "We want to see how large he has to write and how heavy to be seen in that back row." It is the same with an aid like those milk bottles. Will they need more light? If the audience can't see the aids, the aids will not help the speaker. I did a talk in a hotel room that is famous as one of the night clubs of the country. We had to bring in some spotlights to make my charts visible.

5. *Help Him Pack Up.* Offer anyway. So often, when the speaker finishes, the club members run for the check room or the bar. The club managers get into a discussion of club

business and unless the speaker has a brother-in-law in the town who came to hear him, nobody pays any attention to him. Perhaps he doesn't want any help. His visual aid may pack in a certain way and you may not be able to help. But offer to give it to him.

6. *Get Outside Help.* If the speaker wants to show a film, offer to get the equipment and a projectionist for him. If he has visuals that are heavy, get enough porters from the hotel to help him. Last year I appeared on a program with a speaker who had one ton of visual aids. "I had to hire my own men to set this up," he told me. Most speakers will not have any such mass of visual aids, but any speaker might want some chairs or tables moved. If your speaker does, get him the help he needs.

7. *Know the Facilities.* If your club meets in its own hall, know what you have available in the way of visual aids. Know too where you can borrow or rent certain types of aids that the speaker might ask for. If your club meets in a hotel regularly, you should know what is available. Many times the hotel manager can help you in renting or borrowing such aids as projectors or recorders. When the speaker asks for an aid, he is reassured when you say, "Yes, we can get that for you."

8. *Have Him Check the Room.* Not long ago I arrived in town for a speech and the chairman telephoned me at the hotel, "I'd like to have you check the room, Mr. Hegarty." I always try to do that whether I'm asked or not. I have had clubs move me away from the head table and set me on a platform at the end of the room. I felt that I had better audience contact from the new position. When you ask the speaker his opinion of the set-up, you give the impression that you are trying to help him. That gives him a good impression of your club, and makes him want to

do better for you. This, though, is not the reason for having him check. Perhaps your set-up may be such that he cannot do a good job. It may be that a slight change will make all the difference to him.

9. *Don't Talk about His Props.* If you are the chairman who introduces the speaker and he is using a set of charts, you don't have to explain to the group that he is making a chart talk. He will show them that he is. If he has brought a ton of equipment, don't regale the group with the trouble you had setting it up. The less you say about his equipment, the better.

10. *Don't Try to Help Unless Asked.* You have seen the chairman who tries to help the speaker use a chart, or get a chart out of the way, or do some other task that he thinks helps the speaker. Never works well, does it? Recently a chairman turned my chart easel at an angle. I stopped speaking and looked at him. "So they can see over there," he explained. I don't think he helped the visibility any. He just couldn't keep out of the act. I have seen chairmen, with wholly good intentions, get a speaker's visuals so balled up that the speaker never did get them straightened out. I have had that happen to me, and how I have loved those chairmen!

11. *If He Asks You to Help in the Presentation.* Find out exactly what he wants you to do. Not long ago I wanted a chairman to hold up certain cards for me one at a time. He said, "Supposing we go back into the next room and rehearse what you want me to do." I agreed and we went through the routine. When we did it in front of the audience, it went well. That rehearsal was a good idea. You may say, "Why, any dummy can hold up cards!" You're right, but chairmen must not be dummies. Think of the times you have heard speakers ask a chairman to do some-

thing, and then say, "No, not like that, like this." If the chairman had been like the one who wanted to rehearse, he would have done the task right the first time. So, when you are asked to help, find out exactly what you are to do, and practice doing it.

12. *Get Set Up Beforehand.* Where you have the one speaker in your meeting, you usually will get what he needs set up beforehand. When you have two or three, there may be complications. If the aids of the first speaker have to be moved to make room for the aids of the second, call a recess while you make the change. A speaker and a porter

"This is how it will look."

trying to move a chart easel into place can get laughs from almost any audience. If the first speaker has left his aids all over the place, they may cramp the style of the second speaker. A meeting should be an orderly procedure and anything the chairman can do to make it orderly will help.

WHY VISUALS HELP THE CLUB

I heard a meeting chairman complaining about the amount of help one of his speakers wanted in setting up his visuals. "You'd think those gadgets he uses are the most important—" There was more of it, and I felt like moving in and explaining just what those visuals did. They helped the speaker, yes, but they helped the audience more. And the audience was the concern of that chairman, even though he could see no reason why he should be concerned with the speaker's visual aids.

Let's examine why a visual helps that audience. Here is a fact. We remember:

Most of what we see.

Less of what we read.

Least of what we hear.

The speaker who uses talk alone delivers the least effective message. The one who uses showing as he talks is making it easier for the audience to understand. That's why the audience likes the speaker who shows something —he is making it easier for them to understand his message. You have the responsibility for setting up this meeting. You want it to be a good meeting. O.K., if the speaker has gone to the trouble of preparing some visual aids, he has shown that he wants to get his ideas across. You, the meeting planner, and that speaker are working toward the same idea, so give him all the help you can.

WHEN YOU HAVE TO SELL AN IDEA TO THE CLUB

Perhaps you are the type of speaker that can get up and talk the group into doing anything. That's great if you are. But most of us are not in that class. My suggestion, when you have an idea to sell, is to make up a set of charts to help you in the presentation. Here are some suggestions.

Get some sheets of paper from a printer. If 22 inches by 28 inches is large enough, he will probably have that in stock. If you want the charts larger, he can cut or get the size you want for you.

Next, get a marking crayon and letter on the charts what you want to cover. If you are no good at this, have a sign painter letter the charts for you. He'll do them in crayon or in ink, however you want them. Make a deal with him before he starts on what he will charge you.

Laying Out the Chart Presentation. My plan is to take a large sheet of paper, draw a number of squares on it, and letter in the squares what I want on my charts. This gives me the opportunity to look at all of the charts at once and to rearrange them, if they need shuffling. In planning the lettering on a chart, follow these don'ts:

Not Too Much. Don't put too much on one chart. If you have a lot of data to go on one chart, make two or three charts out of it.

Large Lettering. Make the lettering large enough so that it can be seen from any part of the room in which you will use the charts. I use three-inch block letters. These can be seen in almost any size room.

One Idea Only. Cover only one idea in each chart. If you can describe the idea in one word, do that. Use short words that are sure to be seen and understood.

WHAT THE CHARTS DO FOR YOU

The set of charts can help you in many ways. Here are a few:

They Serve as Notes. The set of charts can serve as the notes for your presentation. You have seen the speaker fumble through his notes looking for that point he wants to make. With the charts, you don't have to do that. You turn a page, and there is your reminder of what you want to cover next.

They Keep You on the Track. In any presentation a speaker is inclined to get off on a tangent. With a set of charts, he keeps on his orderly way.

They Hold Attention. When you turn a chart, the group

looks to see what is on it. If attention has strayed, your turning of that next chart says, "Here, look at this." The listeners look, and you again have the chance to sell the group.

They Help Explain. When you make a point with speech only, I may not get it. I may not hear exactly what you said, or I may not understand. The lettering you have on the chart helps me to understand.

They Appeal to a Second Sense. You hear me talk about the idea, you see it explained in the lettering on the chart. We all know that we can sell better if we can appeal to more senses.

They Clarify Figures. The chart is especially helpful in explaining figures. You mention a figure of cost and I may not understand. You show me the figure and you give me a second chance to understand it.

They Indicate You Have Prepared. This is important. Too many speakers come before a group to ask for help with a plea that shows no indications of preparation. The listener feels, "If he didn't think any more of it than this, why should I get steamed up about it?" But if you have gone to the trouble of organizing your story and making a set of charts, they feel that you are serious about this plan, and that is important to you and perhaps to the club.

They Make It Easier on Everybody. I believe that the success of most chart presentations is due to the fact that it is easier to understand the plan that is presented with charts. You don't ask your audience to study the details. I talk to you about an idea and you have to concentrate fully on what I am saying. If I picture what this idea is, you do not have to concentrate so much. Thus I make it easier for you. With the charts, I lay out my presentation,

I talk only about what I want to cover, and I cover my points, all of them, in order.

SIMPLE PLANS FOR CHART PRESENTATION

You can make up this chart presentation in a number of ways. Here are some ideas:

The "Answer the Questions" Plan. I saw one of these recently. The man making the presentation made a list of the questions that the group might have about the plan; he listed these questions, one to a chart. He turned the chart and answered the question covered, then asked if there were other questions on that point. If a question did not refer to the point under discussion, he asked the questioner to hold it until later when that subject came up. This is a good plan of organization. It can be improved by making the first chart a list of the questions that you plan to cover. It will help too if there is a last chart that sums up what you want the group to do.

The "What You Do" Plan. When you are after the group to do something, lay out the plan on a set of charts. Let's say you want each individual to call on ten persons. You want them to:

First, call on the person.

Second, show them a circular.

Third, ask for some kind of action, a pledge, a check, a promise of some effort, something.

Your first chart might then cover the three things you want the listener to do, your second would cover the first step. In speaking of that step, you would discuss the persons to be seen, and would explain how the worker gets the names. Your third chart would cover step two. If there is a special way you want this circular used, you would explain that. The next chart would cover step three, and in talking while using that chart, you would explain exactly what you wanted the worker to do, and how he should go about it. Now you might wind up with a chart that covers the three things as a summation.

In making up your charts, follow the three suggestions I have given earlier.

(*a*) *Don't crowd.* The other day I saw a speaker try to explain an idea with one chart. But he had too much on the one piece of paper. After the session I suggested that he make what he had on the one chart into three charts. He did that and after the next presentation he admitted, "It was much better; they seemed to understand quicker." You are using the charts to help the listener understand, aren't you? So don't try to crowd too many ideas on one page.

(*b*) *Use large lettering.* You have heard the speaker say, "I don't know whether or not you can see this." Don't have any doubt. Use letters at least 3 inches high if you have an audience of thirty. You may say, "I can't get it all on the chart if I do that." O.K., then try to cut down what you put on the chart or put some of it on a second chart. Remember that you are not making charts, you are trying to explain to a group.

"*This page explains—*"

(*c*) *One idea to a chart.* The human mind can take in so much at one flash. Don't try to make over the minds of your group. Give them one idea per chart and they will understand better. You have seen the speaker who has too many ideas on his chart. As he tries to explain, you try to follow. Then you find it too much effort and you lose interest. This group of yours is no different. Don't try to put everything on one chart. Give them one idea at a time and they will understand.

THE SPEAKER APPRECIATES HELP

I travel about with a roll of charts that are easy to carry and easy to set up. I need no help with those charts, yet committee members carry them for me, they want to know if I need any help in setting them up, they want to help take them down, they offer to ship them back to me. I need no help, but they show a willingness that makes up for the groups that do none of these things, that seem to think, "He wants to speak to us, let him get himself ready to speak." The suggestions I offer here are not only to help make a good impression on that speaker; they help you get a better effort out of him. If he needs help, give it; if he doesn't need help, offer it. Show him that you know he is a guest. That goes even if you are paying him. The speaker who is treated well will usually do a better job for you.

Now that we have that guest speaker handled, let's discuss the room in which you hold your meetings.

8 / Setting Up the Room

The room can help your meeting.

Of course, it would be grand to have the ideal room every time, but that's not possible. Still, I have seen meeting managers use a room in a way that did not help the speakers or the audience. Recently I was billed to appear at a sales congress, a full-day meeting. I got in the night before and the committee invited me up to the hospitality room to talk over what I needed. After our session, they asked if I would like to see the room. I said I would, and so they took me to it. It was a long room, rather narrow, but the speaker's table was set up across the short side of the room, and while the ideal room might have been a bit wider, the arrangement would work well.

"This will be the set-up for the morning meeting," the chairman said. "But at noon we are going to set a head table up on this side of the room, and then we'll run the afternoon meeting with that arrangement."

I asked, "Do you have to do it that way?"

"That's what we planned," the chairman said.

That set-up would have been bad. The audience would have been about ten persons deep and sixty or seventy wide. An audience spread like that is difficult for the speaker and, if the speaker uses exhibits, he is almost certain to get in front of them and hide them from some of the audience.

I pointed this out to the group and they were able to change. I'm sure that the meeting was much better because of the room arrangement.

One of my friends is active in the League of Women Voters. I gave her a copy of my meeting book, she read it, and at the next meeting of her group, the chairs were arranged so that the speakers faced the windows and the audience sat with its back toward the light. One of the big shots in the club asked, "Why did you do that? Congresswoman Ajax is to be the speaker, and she might not like to speak while facing that light."

"It's the audience that should be comfortable," my friend said, and she brought out my book to prove it.

After the meeting my friend got a number of compliments on the room arrangement. "That light in my eyes always gave me a headache," one member said. "Why didn't somebody think of this before?"

Nobody thought of it, because nobody understood how the room can help the meeting.

The other day I met two of the younger members of one of the local service clubs in the hotel. "How was the speaker today?" I asked.

"Not so hot," they agreed.

"Well, the food made up for it," I offered.

"No, it wasn't good either," one said.

"How many good speakers do you get in a year?" I asked.

"Maybe five or ten," one answered.

"But that isn't what bothers me," the other said. "I can't figure why I come down here every week and sit and look at those windows. My eyes hurt all the rest of the day."

Now I know that hotel room. It is a better meeting room with the head table set up at one end against a paneled wall. But it is easier for the hotel to set up with the head table in front of the windows. And the men who run those meetings feel it makes no difference.

Once I made a speech on "How to Run a Meeting" in a hotel. The room was arranged poorly and I explained to the group how that room should be set up. A month later I was back in that hotel for another speech and the banquet manager was waiting for me. "What do you mean telling these clubs that our room is not set up right?" he started. There was more of the same. The man was nettled because I felt he did not know how to set up a room. He had been in the business twenty years, he knew how, and he let me have it.

I let him run on. Then I asked, "All you're interested in is selling meals, isn't it?"

He admitted that was right.

"O.K., then," I went on. "How many of the club members don't show for meetings because they have to sit looking at those windows?"

Of course, I never got anywhere. He was thinking of his interest, the time it took to set up the other way. I was thinking of the audience.

And since you are running the meeting, you should think of the comfort of that audience.

Let's review some of the things a man running a meeting should know about the room.

WHAT THE MEETING MANAGER SHOULD KNOW ABOUT THE MEETING ROOM

1. *The Shape.* In a speech I do, called "How to Run a Meeting," I use a playing card to illustrate the ideal shape

for a meeting room. I suggest that the speaker be placed at the narrow end. In such a room the speaker has most of the audience in front of him. He does not have to turn too much to the left or right to watch every face.

2. *Entrance at Rear.* The entrance of the room should be behind the audience. If the entrance is behind the speaker, every late arrival will steal attention from the speaker. Anyone who passes the door will attract the eyes of the group. When you arrange the room it may be easier to set up with the speaker's table near the entrance, but the extra work is worth the trouble in the effect on the meeting.

3. *Backs to Windows.* That has been mentioned before. Seat the audience so that they do not have to look out of the windows. The light from the windows makes it difficult for them to see the speaker or his aids. Let the speaker face the windows. Perhaps the boss won't like it, but you should try to please the audience first.

4. *Use a Stage.* Put your speakers up above the audience. In hotels they always set the head table above the floor. Any elevation helps the speaker; it lets the audience see him. If you hold your meeting in a room with a stage, fix it so that a speaker has to use the stage. There are a lot of speakers who will try to speak from the floor in front of the stage. They say they like that intimate feeling that comes from being on the same level with the audience. But they will do better if they are up on that platform. You might move the front row up closer to the stage. You don't need a wide aisle there anyway, do you?

5. *Background behind Speakers.* Stand the speakers before a blank wall so that there is no movement behind them. Get all of the audience in front of the speakers. Set up a screen behind the speaker so that any movement be-

hind him cannot steal attention from him. If he works from a stage, close the curtain.

6. *Seat the Chairman in the Audience.* A chairman sitting behind or at the side of the speaker can do nothing but sabotage your attraction. Get the chairman, the secretary, the preceding and following speakers, and anyone else off the platform. Give the speaker the spotlight alone.

7. *Size of Room.* Try to select a room that fits the audience. A small group in a large room seems lost, and the speaker is inclined to speak to the small group and not to the room. Note the next time you have a meeting in a crowded room. The speakers seem better and the audience

"At this time I'm asking you gentlemen at the head table to take your chairs and sit down in the audience."

seems to like the meeting better. If you have to use a large room for the small group, you might enclose the group with screens or set the chairs in one corner of the room. If you have a room with fifty seats and you have forty-nine in the audience, you have an ideal arrangement.

8. *Ventilation.* "Yes, we don't have any." That could be said of many meetings for in most rooms there is no way to freshen up the air. The hotel manager will tell you that the room is air-conditioned. He means that it can be cooled, but there is no way to pump enough air into meeting rooms to keep the air fresh and clean. And as the group breathes

that stale air over and over, they tire and begin to sag. For a short luncheon meeting, you can get by without ventilation, but if your meeting is to run for longer than one hour, try to figure out how you can freshen up the air from time to time. I have seen all of the windows thrown open at recesses. I have seen ventilating fans turned on for short periods. All such efforts to give the listeners fresh air will pay off in the attention you get from the group.

9. *Fans Will Help.* Electric fans will help give the air a lively feeling. But if you want to run fans, put them behind the speaker. Aim the air stream so that it will blow along the walls and not at the audience. I suggest putting the fans behind the speaker for this reason. If he hears the fan he will talk louder. Put the fan in the rear of the room and some busy-body in the audience will hear it and turn it off. The whir of the fan makes it more difficult for him to hear the speaker so the busybody decides to help you run your meeting, and turns off the fan.

10. *Get Rid of Smoke.* As soon as your club member sits down in your meeting, he takes out a cigarette or pipe and starts to pollute the air. I have seen rooms in which the speaker could not be seen from the back of the room because of the smoke. I have tried all sorts of plans to cut down on that smoke. "No Smoking" signs in the room can help. The idea of the smoking break can help. The plan of opening all of the windows at recesses or running a big ventilating fan helps. Remember that you can't keep windows open because the listeners sitting by the windows will close them. That goes for even a hot day; if it isn't a draft from the window, it is the street noise. If the meeting room is difficult to ventilate, you might agree with the group on no smoking or on smoking recesses.

11. *Lectern High Enough.* Have the speaker's stand high enough so that the tall speaker is not reclining when he leans on it. The short speaker will stand up to it, but anything you can do to encourage your speakers to stand up straight when they speak will help. No speaker can put a lot of enthusiasm into what he says when he is leaning.

12. *Light.* The lighting in most meeting rooms can be improved with spotlights. That's true if the speaker intends to use some exhibits that he wants the audience to see. If you can, have the spotlights mounted overhead. If your group is one that likes to take notes, give it lighting at the seats so that it can see to write. You don't want them calling, "Give me a little light, I want to write that down."

13. *Visual Aids.* Check your speakers beforehand and try to help if they use visual aids. Find out what they will need and try to help get it for them. Don't assume that the hotel has anything before you check it. I have had chairmen tell me, "I was sure they would have a blackboard in this hotel." I had written weeks ahead and asked that the chairman get me a blackboard and chalk. The chairman assured me the matter had been handled, but nothing had been done. A speaker who uses visual aids will usually do a better job for you. If he is using such aids, explain the kind of room in which the meeting will be held. Tell him, "You'll speak from the stage in a high school auditorium." The speaker will understand that kind of set-up. When I told a chairman recently that I used a set of charts, he wrote to ask, "Will you need an easel for them, and will you want any special lighting?" That chairman knew his job.

14. *Acoustics.* Usually you can do little about the acoustics of your room, but it will be well to check to see what problems you have. In many buildings there are beams in

the ceiling that seem to trap the sound and make it difficult for persons in the rear of the room to hear. Recently I heard a speaker ask, "If I stand here, can you hear me better?" He moved out in front of a ceiling beam and the group said they could hear him better. I once ran a series of meetings in a room that had been treated with acoustical material. In that room a speaker had to speak louder to be heard. If the room you use has any acoustical faults, tell your speakers about them.

15. *Signs on the Wall.* If there are any signs on the wall that might not be in keeping with the purpose of your meeting, see what you can do to get them taken down. In a hotel room not long ago I attended a church fund-raising meeting and there was a large banner on the wall advertising a well-known beer. The beer people had had a meeting there earlier and had not taken down the advertisement. The sign did no harm, it was good for a laugh— but it might have offended some of the good people at the meeting. Look over the walls of the meeting room you use.

16. *Posts or Pillars.* If there are post supports in the meeting room, try to set up the audience so that the posts interfere as little as possible. I have seen groups seated in rooms with such obstructions in a way that made it most uncomfortable for both the speaker and the listeners. In many cases the chairs could have been arranged so that the posts would not interfere.

WHEN RENTING A ROOM IN A HOTEL

At times you have to rent a room in a hotel or other public place for your meeting. Here are some suggestions.

17. *Look at It.* Look at the room that the management assigns to your meeting, and if the one offered is not what

you think it should be, ask to see others. I have arrived at hotels to put on a meeting and found that the room was not at all suitable for the session. The local man who had arranged for the room had telephoned the hotel and said, "We need a room for a meeting of fifty on the 19th." The management put the date in the book and assigned a room that would seat 50 but was not suitable for what we wanted. If you have to rent a meeting room, look at it. Make sure that it is what you want. Those hotel people are not mind readers. I have a friend who puts on a lot of meetings in hotel rooms. His local representatives engage the rooms for him, but he gives the local men complete specifications for the room. He claims that he usually gets what he wants. So often when you arrive the day of the meeting, and find the room is not suitable, all of the other rooms are taken.

18. *Shape of Room.* My friend's specifications on the room he wants specify the shape, too. He wants a room that is about the shape of a playing card. He would like a room that can be set up so that the audience does not have to face the windows or the doors. He specifies a room with no posts.

19. *Electric Supply.* You may have to run a projector; so check to see that the electric supply is right for the machine. If there is any doubt, the hotel electrician can tell you what you can do. If you have any special lighting for your visuals, you might check to see if the place is adequately wired to take the load.

20. *Where Is the Elevator?* If your room is on one of the upper floors, how far are the elevators from the meeting room? Your speakers may have some exhibits that will be difficult to get to the room.

21. *Checking Facilities.* What is the audience to do with hats and coats? There should be a checking facility handy.

The hotel usually has a check room, but how far is it from the meeting room? You don't want guests coming to the meeting room and then going back to the lobby to check their wraps. They might have to pass a bar on the way.

22. *Quiet.* A room on a noisy street will not help your meeting. If the street traffic is right outside the windows, try for a different room. In the summer time you will have to open the windows.

23. *Hotel Help.* It is important that you have hotel help to provide you with the little things you need to keep the meeting moving. If you use a public address system, know how to get the engineer quickly in case something goes wrong. You have seen the confusion a meeting is thrown into when some hotel help is needed and is not to be found. You may want to move some chairs or set up a projector and screen, or the head table is not fixed the way the speaker would like it. Who is going to do it?

At a meeting recently I was arranging for a lapel mike for a part of my talk. A committee member brought the engineer to talk to me. I explained what I wanted, and he told me where the lapel mike would be when I wanted it. "I'll be here, too," he said. "I'll be right there in that booth. I'll regulate the sound for you. I've been doing it all morning." The public address system had worked well all through the morning meeting. I told him he had done a fine job, and he thanked me. But the committee had done that fine job, or the hotel management. Whoever was responsible for that man being there had done the job. That sound system was important to that meeting and the meeting manager knew it.

I have attended such meetings when one of the members of the committee was responsible for the public address system only, and that fellow didn't take any chances. He was there checking before the meeting started.

24. *Look at Other Rooms.* If the hotel has more than one room to offer, ask to look at what they have. They may offer you a room that is easier for them. It may be on a noisy street when there are similar rooms at the back of the house that are quiet. I once was told by a club chairman that I would have to talk to the club in the main dining room while the regular guests were having dinner. True, the club was set off on one side of the room, but there was a microphone on the head table, and my speech would carry to all parts of the room. Since it was a business speech I doubt that many of the paying guests, who were not members of the club, would appreciate it. I suggested to the chairman that we might eat in the dining room, then move to another room where we wouldn't bother the other guests. The chairman said there was no other room. The banquet manager came by during the meal to ask how the food was. While he was speaking to the chairman, I broke in and asked about another room. "We have a number of meeting rooms you could use," he said. After the group was fed we moved to one of the finest meeting rooms I have ever used. It pays to check. The next day the banquet manager told me, "They never asked for a meeting room. They told me they wanted to eat in the main dining room. We can't serve food in those meeting rooms, they're just too far from the kitchen."

Most hotels have facilities for anything you want to do. If you will ask for what you want and get them to show you what they have, you'll get the best set-up possible.

SETTING UP THE ROOM

After you have your room, what can you do to make it a better meeting room? You have to seat your audience in it, and you have to make a set-up for your speakers. The way you arrange that room can have a lot to do with the success of your meeting. Here are some suggestions:

25. *Close Together but Don't Crowd.* Work out a seating arrangement that puts the listeners close together but does not crowd them. You ask a hotel to set up a room for one hundred guests and they will put chairs with twelve-inch seats about two inches apart. You crowd men with an arrangement like that. Just recently I took two chairs out of each row in a meeting room and moved the other chairs to take up the extra room. The chair seats were not wide enough for the men who came to the meeting, but the few inches between chairs gave them room to be comfortable. Men sitting close together feel that they belong. And with the group close together the speaker has an easier time. He doesn't feel that he is speaking to empty chairs or to large areas of floor. He gets a response from the listeners, nothing but discouragement from the empty chairs or the floor.

26. *Close to the Speaker.* The set-up where you leave about twenty feet between the speaker's rostrum and the first row of listeners is not too good. Get that front row close to the speaker. You have seen speakers move up almost into the empty seats in the front of the audience. They are trying to get closer to those listeners for they know that it is easier to get a response from an audience that is close to them. The speaker has an easier job when all of the seats are filled, front and back.

27. *Keep the Audience Together.* I have spoken to groups that about half-filled the seats in the room. That would be O.K. if those listeners were all in the front seats,

but they weren't; they were scattered all over the room. Just last week I spoke in a school auditorium from a stage. There were about three hundred in the hall, but the first four rows of seats were practically empty. Fortunately, there was a recess before my speech, and I went out among the group and got a number of them to take front seats after recess. The committee said that the speaker ahead of me had not done a good job, that he showed no enthusiasm for his subject. The man wasn't an experienced speaker but I am sure that those empty front rows did not help him one bit.

You have a similar problem to this in the large dining room that your group doesn't fill. The hotel manager is inclined to leave more space between the tables. Recently I was in a room that had a wide aisle right in front of the speaker's lectern. This meant that the speaker would have no listeners in front of him, just that ballroom carpet. I moved men from the nearby tables into that open space and I had more response than I would get from that carpet. In setting up the dining room put a row of tables directly in front of the speaker. He will do better if you do.

28. *Comfortable Chairs.* I have spoken of the hotel chairs with seats not wide enough for the average man. You probably cannot do much about the chairs you use in the rooms in which you hold your meeting. They're there and you take them and like them. But if you have any opportunity to equip a meeting room in your church or clubhouse, try to get chairs that are comfortable but not too comfortable. In a meeting I ran not long ago, there were some large upholstered chairs in the back of the room. The meal was served at tables in another part of the room, and I watched some of the club members hurry up

the pie and ice cream and run for those chairs. I bet myself that at least one of those men would be dozing during my speech. Two of them were. I like to feel that it wasn't my speech, that it was due to those comfortable chairs. While you should get chairs with seats wide enough to accommodate the fat brothers, watch that you don't get them too comfortable.

29. **Theater Arrangement.** You can't beat the theater arrangement when you set up a meeting room. Note how a theater follows the suggestions given here. All the chairs face the same way. The audience faces the stage and sees nothing but actors and scenery. All attention is focused on what the playwright wants you to see. When you set up your meeting room, think of this theater arrangement and ask yourself, "How close can I come to the theater arrangement?" Your room arrangement can help your meeting a lot. Try to give your production the best setting you can.

HOW TO FILL UP THE FRONT SEATS

The people who attend meetings are a contrary lot. For some reason they won't sit in the front seats. Usually when I run a sales meeting the first arrivals take the rear seats. When I ask them to move, they say, "Let the late comers take those front seats." That is fine for them, but the tardy member taking a seat 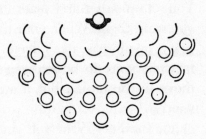 down front disturbs the speaker and the audience. You know how it is in the theater—you took the trouble to get there on time, you're seated and the show is started, and now come the ones that stopped at the cocktail party. Their seats, of course, are right in front of you. In the theater you can do nothing. But in your meeting you can show you are smarter than those back-seat drivers. Here are some suggestions:

30. *Use Ushers.* The ushers may not be able to get the first arrivals to take the front row, but they will get them down front. The later arrivals will then be easier to guide down front.

31. *Rope Off Back Seats.* I once ran a lot of meetings in an auditorium that had about twice as many seats as needed. I roped off the last twelve rows. When anyone said, "I'd like to sit back here," he was told, "Those seats are reserved for the factory people." It worked. You could use the choir, the glee club, the high school students as the group for which those seats are reserved. The rope will work on most listeners. I was asking the custodian of a building to rope off some back seats not long ago. He agreed and produced some rope of the right length. "You've done this before," I said.

"Yeah, and we also use these." He produced two signs that read "wet varnish."

32. *Set Up Only Front Seats.* Let's say you expect fifty. You set up only thirty seats and these are down front where you want them. When your thirty seats are about filled, you bring in more seats. I have seen this worked where the listeners were to be seated at tables. It is more trouble to move in the tables, but it seats your audience where you want it.

33. *Use Seat Tickets.* If you are in a room with numbered seats, you can pass out only the tickets for the front seats. Somehow people look at those numbers and feel that the other seats must be taken.

34. *Use Badges of Different Colors.* The blue badges take the front row, the yellow badges take the second, the

green the third, and so on. I've seen this used with ribbons of the colors on the seats in the row.

35. *Put Best Chairs in Front.* I've run a number of meetings in an auditorium that seats four hundred. There are two kinds of seats: one, small metal fold-away chairs that are not too comfortable; two, a larger metal chair with a lot of spring in the seat. We set up the room with the best chairs in front. Nobody takes one of the hard chairs until all of the easy ones are taken.

36. *Get Easy Chairs Out of Room.* If there are a number of easy chairs at the back of the room, or along the sides, get them out of the way so that they won't help scatter your group. Remember, if there is an easy chair within miles, some of the brothers will spot it. I've seen easy chairs dragged in from another room.

37. *Tie in with Door Prizes.* Announce, "Every third door prize today will go only to those seated in the front four rows. You may have the number drawn but if you are not in those first four rows, you can't win." I saw that stunt pulled just as the numbers were about to be drawn and those empty first four rows filled up fast. Try it sometime.

38. *Reserve Front Seats for the Bell Cow.* Hold a seat up front for the boss. The "yes" men will want to sit near him. In a political club they always save a seat up in the second row for the Judge. The workers vied for the seats next to their hero. You can, of course, save them for the officers.

39. *Appeal to Your Friends.* If the front seats are not taken by the committee members or some special group, you might get enough friends to take them. I once ran a club and stood outside the auditorium as the members arrived. As I greeted a friend, I asked, "Joe, will you sit in the second row tonight?"

MOVING A GROUP ONCE IT IS SEATED

This is a tough job. You have no doubt heard a chairman ask, "Will you people please move down into the front seats?" He pauses for ten seconds while nobody moves, not even his relatives. Then he goes on with the introduction of the speaker. And there is the speaker starting his talk with those front seats empty. I have had this happen to me when I was a guest speaker, but I found a way to get most of those front seats filled. Here is my plan:

First, I figure out which listeners I want to move and which seats I want them to take.

Second, I ask those listeners to stand. For some reason, the same listeners that won't move will stand up when they are asked to stand up. When they are on their feet,

Third, I ask them to march down to the seats I want them to take. I lead the rest of the group in counting off— one, two, three, four; one, two, three, four, while the others march.

If you try this, explain why you moved the group. Tell them it is difficult to talk to empty seats. Explain how you get no response from empty chairs. But with human beings in those chairs, you get a response that helps you make a better speech. And they want to hear a good speech, don't they? O.K. now, you as their speaker are set up right to give it to them.

Under this plan there is confusion while the movers get seated, but they are laughing about how they were moved, and the speaker starts with a good-natured audience. If my chairman doesn't move my audience for me and I have to do it, I get started right with them. This speaker is different, because they have never seen the stunt done before.

WHEN YOU USE TABLES

40. *The "U"-shaped Table.* Many meeting managers like this set-up. It may be good for a discussion, but it is not

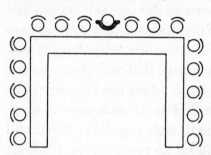

so good for the speaker if he speaks from the position shown. All he has in front of him is bare floor. A narrower "U" with men on the inside of the table would help. Then the men on the inside could move enough so that the speaker would have listeners in front of him. I have run meetings with a table set up as shown, but have asked the men on the outside of the "U" to move inside before the speaking starts.

41. *The Long Tables.* This arrangement adds distance between the speaker and his listeners. It is quite difficult if the committee does not see that the front tables are filled. The tables help the audience to take notes, and give the listeners something to lean on.

In an afternoon or a day-long meeting, they usually need that prop. The listeners have little trouble seeing, but they are further away than necessary. If you don't have a public address system, you'll have to caution your

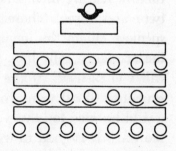

speakers to speak louder. The tables can be set at right angles to the way they are shown in the illustration. This is probably better for the speaker, for he feels that the listeners are closer to him. It means that to write, they have to turn one shoulder to him, and I feel that the extra effort to take a note will cut down on the note-taking.

42. *The Round Table.* For the dinner or luncheon meeting I like the round table. Note how the audience seems

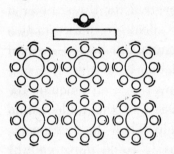

closer to the speaker in the illustration showing round tables than in the one using the long tables. But watch that the caterer doesn't put the tables too far apart. Recently I spoke in a hotel room to about eighty guests. The hotel had set up ten tables and had set them up so that the tables filled the room. The room was large enough for about twenty tables and the audience was much further away from the speaker than it should have been. When you use round tables, get the caterer to put them close together.

43. *Fill Up the Close Tables.* You have the same problem here that you have in the auditorium. You help the speaker if you get those near tables filled. One club handles this by seating members who bring guests at tables one, two, and three. These are the tables right under the speaker. When the member buys the ticket for his guest, the secretary tells him, "Sit at table one, two, or three, will you please?" If the member asks why, the secretary explains, "We'll want you to introduce your guest and it would be nice to have you up front where everybody can see you." It is good to work out some plan for filling these near tables. Your members will not take them unless you figure out some way to make them do it.

44. *The Head Table.* Usually you are stuck with a head table in your meetings, but those big shots sitting at the head table are of little use to the speaker. In fact, all they

can do is sabotage him. While he speaks on they light cigars, talk to one another, draw pictures on the table cloth, go to sleep, look bored. If you use a speaker in your meetings, work out some plan to get everybody out from behind the speaker before he starts. Not long ago a chairman told me, "Ed, we ask our head table to move before the chairman introduces the speaker. When the chairman is finished with his introduction, he gets out, too." That's a fine arrangement. If you have more than one speaker, ask number two and number three to sit in the audience while number one speaks. Then ask number one to do likewise while the others perform. The next speaker does not add much sitting in full view of the audience worrying or checking his notes.

You may say, "Those details don't help too much." You may be right, but they help some, and they are worth the trouble you are put to to handle them. Many times a chairman has told me, "Ed, I know we shouldn't do this, but we have to."

I agree, but I always wonder why the man will not take the trouble to do things right.

45. *When You Have Dancing Plus the Speaker.* Twice recently I have attended dinners where they had a speaker and dancing. In one case they had the orchestra on the stage behind the head table, an open dance floor in front of the speaker, and the audience seated at tables along the sides of the dance floor. In the other case they had the head table on one side of the dance floor, the orchestra on the other side, and the audience at tables on the other ends of the floor. The speakers were supposed to speak to the group scattered like that. In front of him that expanse of bare floor, and his nearest listener thirty feet away from him. Both set-ups were almost impossible. In one case the

speaker was a humorist and all through his speech he kept fighting to get the laughs that he knew he should get. In the other case I was the speaker and I arranged beforehand with members of the audience to move into the space in front of me. Now this meant that both men and women had to move their chairs to get where I wanted them, but they moved on the signal I had suggested. I had perhaps one hundred in front of me when I spoke. I was the guest speaker at this affair and perhaps you would say that I presumed a lot to move another meeting manager's audience, but I'm sure that I gave a better performance and the group liked the meeting better because of that move.

If you run a meeting-dance like this and want to dance during the dinner hour, try to work out some plan so that the speaker does not have to speak to that waxed floor. He gets no response from that floor, and no matter how hard he works, he will have trouble doing his usual fine job for you.

THE THREE BIG FUNDAMENTALS

You may say, "I let them sit where they want. It's enough trouble to get them here. Why herd them where you want them?" You can work that way. Get out the audience and let it seat itself. But you are reading this book to learn how to put on better meetings. And if you get your room set up right, it will help you have a better meeting.

The three big fundamentals of this setting-up the audience are:

1. *Close Together.* Don't let the listeners scatter about the room. Seat them close together, not too close, but close enough so that they know they are attending the same meeting.

2. *Close to the Speaker.* Don't give him an expanse of

floor, carpet, or linoleum to speak to. Let him speak to people. If he has the feeling that the listeners are sitting in his lap, he'll do a better speech for you. You have seen the speaker move closer to the group as he starts to speak. He is trying to get better contact with his listeners. Try to set up so that he has that contact.

3. *Think of the Theater Arrangement.* Nobody has come up with a better idea than the theater arrangement for a meeting. Try for that when you put on a meeting. It will help the audience, and it will help your speakers.

Now for some ideas on the types of meetings you can put on.

9 / Not Just More of the Same

Not long ago I met a European businessman and during the conversation I asked him, "What are some of your impressions of this country?"

"One thing," he said, "businessmen over here seem to be going to or coming from meetings."

Ain't that so?

We're going or coming, and sometimes we don't know which. But most clubs live or die on the quality of their meetings. Just last week a man told me, "I'm going to resign from that club. I'm not getting what I thought I would out of it." When I told the treasurer of one club that I meant to resign, he said, "Why, you are one of the charter members." I was that, but I decided that I would rather stay home that one night per month than go to the meetings of this club. Why? I wasn't getting anything out of the meetings.

So, if you are the person in charge of the meetings, you can do a lot for that club. Perhaps your type of club determines the kind of meetings you will have. Let's say that you have just been made chairman of the programs of your local Service, Inc. The club meets at the hotel every Tuesday for lunch, you have a guest speaker each meeting. O.K., then your problem is to get the guest speakers, or to get the members of the club to help you get them. You can't do much more than have a guest speaker at a luncheon meeting for the brothers want to get back to the office.

If you are running a church club, you have a different problem. Your club meets in the evening and there are a number of different types of meetings that you might have. One night you may have a guest speaker; another, a discussion session; a third night, a movie. Because you are meeting in the evening and have perhaps two hours for your meeting, you can have a variety that the luncheon club cannot have.

If you are the program chairman of a business club of advertising or sales executives, purchasing agents, or credit men, you again have that chance at variety. Your subjects have to be related to your business, but you can have a wide variety of programs within that limitation.

If you are running a business meeting in the office, you can have the time that your subject should be given. But you still can vary the meetings so that all of them are not built over the same pattern.

And that variety in types of meetings can help you hold interest in your club. There are about eleven different types of meetings that can be run. And when you list them, you find that some of them do not vary too much. The types I refer to, and the ones that will be covered by the suggestions I give in later chapters, are:

1. *The Guest Speaker.* Much of the space in a book like this must be given over to the meeting that depends on the guest speaker. That's because most of the meetings that you and I attend are of that type. But there are others.

2. *The Guest Speaker Plus.* This plus can be a discus-

sion, a quiz session, or something that gets the listeners into the act. The speaker presents his story, and then the meeting is opened for discussion or for questions. Such sessions can be given the fancy names of Clinics, Seminars, Conferences, Forums. They draw well and are popular because the name gives the listener the impression that the meeting will not be one-sided. The listener himself can take part.

3. *The Panels.* In this type of meeting a group of experts is assigned to present a subject, to answer questions from the group, or handle some similar task. The panelists may each take a few minutes to present a phase of a subject, one covering point one, the second point two, and so on. The panel meeting may or may not be opened for discussion or questions. Again, the name suggests that the meeting will not be one man yak-yakking at the group for the entire time of the meeting. The panel is popular; I've sat on them as an expert and have listened to them as a part of the audience.

4. *The Discussions.* This is one of the most popular types of meetings. We all like to get into the act and this type of meeting allows us to do that. There can be many fancy names for the discussion. Some of the popular ones are the round table, the shirt-sleeve session, the work shop. How to stage the discussion session is explained fully in Chapter 16.

5. *The Quiz Session.* This type of meeting can be built almost wholly on answering the questions asked. It can be dolled up with the trappings of the radio and the TV quiz shows. Chapter 15 gives a number of suggestions as to how this type of session can be put on.

6. *The Joint Meetings.* I have read of two or three of the service clubs in my town getting together for a prominent

speaker. Our Sales Executives Club and the Purchasing Agents get together for a joint meeting each year. The Men's Clubs of different churches do it. Members of both groups like the idea, and the guest speaker gets a larger crowd to hear his message. The joint meeting can be a discussion. For instance, recently at a joint meeting of the purchasing agents and the sales executives a panel from each group told what it did not like about the other. This made for a lively meeting, much better than if either had staged its own meeting with two guest speakers.

7. *The Committee Meeting.* All groups must have them. In business the meetings might not be called committee meetings but they run much the same. Chapter 16 gives suggestions that can be used in the committee meeting.

8. *The Social Meeting.* Most clubs have them, and the business too has its social gatherings. There are so many angles this type can take that this book will not discuss the subject at all. But it's great to belong to a group that devotes at least one meeting each year to having fun.

9. *The Entertainment.* There comes a time when the club must hire the orchestra for the dance, or the accordion player and singer to go about the tables during the annual dinner. Business must do the same.

10. *The Fund-raising Meeting.* Every town has them; the church groups, the civic groups, and most of the meetings held are not as effective as they might be. Chapter 18 gives some ideas as to how this type of meeting can better accomplish its purpose.

11. *The Training Meeting.* There are times when the meeting is supposed to train a worker to do some task. The club member may be asked to solicit memberships. You can send him out to talk to people or you can train him to speak to those people effectively. The training meet-

ing calls for a few more elements than the ordinary lecture and Chapter 18 tells how to run the training meeting.

THERE ARE OTHER TYPES

There are other types of meetings, of course. Perhaps the one that you are running next week does not fall into any of the classifications listed here. But the ones listed

"I think a dance would be more fun."

are the ones that are constantly before the man or woman who runs a luncheon club, a discussion group, a business group, a church group, and the special types such as garden clubs.

There is nothing about parliamentary procedure or rules of order in this book. I have been running the types of clubs listed above for years and I have always been allergic to such formality. Still, with some clubs, you need that order and there's an excellent book on the subject called *Standard Code of Parliamentary Procedure* by Alice F. Sturgis. The main objective of my suggestions in this book is to give you ideas to make your meetings more interesting. The business meeting is discussed, too, not the sales meeting. For sales executives I'd suggest my book *Making Your Sales Meeting Sell*.

LUNCHEON OR DINNER MEETINGS

Not long ago a man who ran the meetings of his sales executives club told me that they had changed from luncheon to dinner meetings. I asked why, and he said that they liked the extra time that the dinner meeting gave them. What are some of the advantages and disadvantages of the two?

THE LUNCHEON MEETING ADVANTAGES

Most club managers agree that it is easier to get the brothers out to a luncheon meeting. The member says, "You gotta eat anyway." If the luncheon is held at a centrally located place, the member figures that every Tuesday or every other Tuesday he'll eat with the club. Just recently a friend said, "You meet the gang and eat too."

The luncheon meeting is short, it doesn't steal time from anything. As a guest speaker I've noted how practically all the members run when I finish my talk. Many don't wait until the chairman thanks me for the effort.

The members know the speech will be short and even if the speaker is not too good, they can take a short poor speech if it is short enough.

The member may not be too much interested in the subject. He may feel that a short talk will give him all he wants to know about the subject.

The time is convenient. The member has set the time aside for eating. Most members have to go outside the office to eat. Why not go to the place the club has selected?

THE LUNCHEON MEETING DISADVANTAGES

With the luncheon meeting the club is limited to the one type of program, the guest speaker. Of course, one of the other types of program could be used, but there is little time for even questions after a guest speaks. The time available usually is not enough for the guest speaker to develop his subject. I've had clubs ask me to speak for twenty minutes when my publicity material on the speech said that the time was forty-five minutes.

The members worry about the time. The committee announcements and the wise cracks of the president and chairman have them fidgety. At a luncheon club the other day I asked one of these fellows who kept looking at his watch, "What you worrying about?"

"We're going to be late," he said.

"So what?" I asked.

"I gotta get back to the office."

"So you can put your feet up on the desk?" I asked.

He laughed and relaxed. "That's about it," he said.

But the member feels he has to hurry back even if he has no more important work than getting his feet back up on that desk. And so the program is rushed to get him back. An audience worrying about the time is not an easy audience for the speaker.

The tight time schedule gives the member the impression that the meeting is in a rush to get finished. The chairman and the committee chairmen who report say, "I'll make this fast." That's agreeable to the listener, but if they are in such a rush, why shouldn't he be too?

The business of the club can't get the time it should in meetings, or the discussion from the members that it should have.

Variety in the club programs is limited since new types cannot be introduced because of time.

THE DINNER MEETING—ADVANTAGES

The speakers have adequate time. Last month I spoke at two club meetings in one day, one a luncheon and the other a dinner meeting. At the luncheon meeting there was quite a rhubarb because I wanted forty minutes for my talk. At the dinner meeting the chairman told me, "We'll put you on at about eight o'clock and you can go to nine-thirty, if you want to." I didn't, but I didn't feel bound to rush either. I was speaking on the same subject but the extra time allowed me to use a blackboard for a ten-minute demonstration. The demonstration was helpful to the audience, I'm sure.

Program variety is one of the advantages of that extra time. You can run a discussion, a workshop, or any of the other types of meetings you might want.

THE DINNER MEETING—DISADVANTAGES

You have more trouble building attendance at the dinner meeting. In the smaller towns the member quits his work and goes home at five o'clock or thereabouts and you have to sell him on coming back. If he stays downtown for the meeting, he has some time to kill. One club I know has attacked this by having the social hour at five-thirty, the dinner at six, and the adjournment at eight. "We get the member on his way home," the president told me. "You have to offer a good program to get that member away from his TV after he is once home," another program chairman told me. One club I know changed its meeting night so that the members would not have to come out on the night of a popular TV program. The trouble with that scheme is that the program that is a "must" this year may not be on the air next.

The dinner meeting competes with other attractions in the town. I've mentioned the TV, but there is bridge with the neighbors, the community theater, the church activities.

Some of your members may travel and they like to spend their time with the family when they are home. The business clubs feel this, a sales executives club, for instance. A sales manager who spends a large portion of his time on the road is not too keen about evening meetings when he is home.

The dinner meeting costs more. The meal is higher in price and there is the expense of the social hour.

THE AFTER-DINNER MEETING

This type has the advantage that it lets the member eat at home with the family and then go off to his meeting. Because it starts later, it usually ends later. With a long-winded session it can run far into the night. Otherwise, it has the advantages and disadvantages of the dinner meeting, but usually it costs the member nothing.

SOME THOUGHTS ON THE TYPES OF MEETINGS YOU MIGHT PUT ON

THE GUEST SPEAKER

It Is Easy. All you have to do is to get Joe to agree to speak and you have your program. One man only is forced to work, the patsy selected as the guest speaker, and he may have a speech that he has done many times.

It's Expected. If your club has always had guest speakers at its meetings, the members expect a guest speaker and whether they know it or not, they resist any change. It's been good enough for us in the past; why not in the future? A club member told me recently, "Ed, we tried having some of these shirt-sleeve sessions, but they didn't work. We had

to go back to the guest speaker." This type fits best with
most clubs.

THE DISCUSSION

It Gives Novelty, Variety. There are so many forms the
discussion can take. How many times have you heard a
club member say, "The talk the man gave was not so hot,
but when he started to answer questions, he was good"?
One of the reasons the member felt that the speaker was
good was that the member got a chance to ask one or more
of those questions. Let's say your club has been having a
series of guest speakers; now tonight you stage a discussion
session. This is new, different, and the members' interest
is increased.

We Like to Get into the Act. The member may not admit
that he likes to get into the act, but he does. I do many
stunts in my talks in which the audience is asked to take
part, and they love it. I have watched audiences do simple
tasks like holding up their right hands to show approval of
a proposal, and I've seen them walk around their tables at
the request of a speaker. Because he had asked them to take
part, I'm sure that they liked his presentation more.

Gives Novelty to the Publicity. The name of the event
can be a help in getting out the group. You can call the
session a round table or a clinic, the shirt-sleeve session, a
work shop, a grass-roots session. The member may not be
too sure what the name promises but it does indicate that
this meeting is going to be different. And so he plans to
come. If the session is to cover a number of points, you can
list the points and ask the members to come prepared to
ask questions or to offer ideas on the points. If it is to discuss business problems, you can ask the members to bring
their problems and throw them at the leader. The publicity

can tell the man that this is his session and promise him that he can get something out of it if he comes.

Gives Work to Members. You can't run a discussion session without a number of your members getting together and preparing for the session. This gives work to those members. It makes them feel that they are contributing to the club. In most clubs the average member feels out of the management of the club. In this type of session you bring him in, put him to work.

"Hold up your right hands, like this."

Rhubarbs Hold Interest. Most members find any discussion interesting. No matter what the subject, there are sure to be opinions that do not agree. I present my ideas, another member presents his. Perhaps what we say shows that we are opposed on certain points. O.K., some member jumps up and asks why we don't agree. Now we have a friendly discussion on our views. The audience likes nothing better than to see the two experts arguing.

Introduces Your Members. After one of your members appears before your club, the group feels it knows him. The discussion session shows the kind of members you have. You know how you feel about a man you have heard state his views. If he has made his points clearly, you're inclined to feel that he is a man of ability. Thus the member-participation program helps build up your members.

Builds Enthusiasm for the Club. I once took over as chairman of an anemic church club. There were a handful in attendance at the meetings at the time, and the question was, "What can we do to build attendance?" I organized and staged a number of discussions on subjects that were in the news at the time. I picked teams, one man to present one side, another to present the opposite. While the sessions were not debates, the members thought of them as such. The men made their presentations, then we opened for discussion. The meetings were publicized as well as they could be with a small budget, but we got out over two hundred men at the first meeting, and from two to three hundred at later meetings. Within six months we had a most enthusiastic membership.

Can Be Staged. When clubs plan discussion sessions there is always the fear that certain points will not be brought up, and the committee feels, just to be sure, that someone should be assigned to bring up these points. Now it is all right to assign the member to bring up the point, but it is seldom necessary. If the point is one that should come up, it will be brought up. Assign the member if you feel that it is better to be safe, but tell him to hold off until late. Your discussion will usually go over without too much such managing.

DISADVANTAGES OF THE DISCUSSION

You Need a Leader. Discussion leaders are not too easy to find. If you check through Chapter 16 you'll see why. It is not easy to lead a discussion. Too many leaders want to make a speech stint out of the job. Others want to do most of the talking. Others make a great number of the mistakes that are listed. If your club is planning to run a number of discussion sessions it might be a good idea to train your discussion leaders. You might use Chapter 18 as the text for the training.

It Requires Planning. Many times I have been told, "Ed, we're not asking you to do a lot of work. All we want you to do is to lead the discussion on this subject." Such a statement shows that the man making it doesn't know much about leading a discussion. The leader needs a plan. Now some of your members will go all out to do that planning. Others will be like that man who makes the statement. They won't know that they have to plan.

Difficult with Large Audience. If your club turns out over fifty members, the discussion may not give everybody the chance to sound off. This can be handled by appointing a team of discussers. The others can write out questions or points that they would like to see brought up. These are passed on to the discussers. But the ones who do not get to talk have a feeling of being left out. They all want to get in, and with the large club it is difficult. The "buzz" session idea can be used to get everybody in, even if the club is large. I've seen groups of over one hundred broken up into groups of eight or ten. The small groups discuss a point, and the leaders of the small group report back to the large group. This gets everybody in. The "buzz" session idea is discussed in Chapter 16.

THE PANEL

It's Different. Perhaps that is one of the reasons for its popularity. Recently I saw a group of four men do a panel presentation for a service club. Each man took six minutes, and the club seemed to enjoy the novelty of listening to four speakers instead of one. At another meeting I saw a panel of five experts answer questions put by the audience. Both meetings were called panels.

It Has Appeal. Your club member watches a number of these panel shows on TV and he likes them, apparently, for the shows seem to run on year after year. Thus the panel before your club should help draw attendance.

It Puts Members to Work. The alert meeting manager makes up his panel with members of his club. This gives a number of members an opportunity to take part in a club meeting. Members are made to feel important when they are put on programs. They are more inclined to feel that the club is doing a lot for its members. A club member told me recently, "Ed, we got members in this club that can speak much better than the imported talent that we bring in, but do we ever use them? No." Perhaps there are members in the club who can contribute. The panel gives them their chance.

DISADVANTAGES OF THE PANEL

Difficult to Control. The panel needs a good moderator or leader. One club I know uses the same man for all such jobs. When asked why, the president explained, "He's good, he knows how to do it." You do need that moderator. If the moderator isn't a strong character the panelists may get off the reservation.

It Should Be Rehearsed. You can put on a panel without a rehearsal. I have sat in on some that were unrehearsed and others that were rehearsed. The latter go over better with the group. At an unrehearsed panel I sat on, two of the four panelists got into an argument that got quite hot, and the meeting wound up on that note. The moderator did not know what to do about it. He tried ineffectually to break it up and then gave up. The audience loved it, but I'm sure that the listeners didn't get as much out of the meeting as they should have.

More Prima Donnas. Not long ago a club manager explained why the club had given up on panel programs.

"We had four prima donnas to deal with instead of one, Ed," he said. "So we went back to the guest speaker." He was telling me that the guest speaker type of meeting is easier to put on. It is, but if the club wants some variety, any of these other types of meeting should be tried.

Names Can Help. In this chapter I have mentioned many names commonly used for meetings but you have so many to choose from that you can easily find a new one. I asked a meeting man, "What is this seminar you're putting on?" "It's just a discussion, Ed," he explained. "We keep changing the names to help build attendance." But think of the names you might use—convention, work conference, shirt sleeve, seminar, clinic, institute, symposium, panel, forum —there are more if you search for them. But the name can help tell the club member or the man you want to attend that your meeting is to be different.

THERE'S LITTLE EXCUSE FOR DULL MEETINGS

Variety in your meetings can help keep your club alive and your club attendance up. If you are losing attendance, if the members are not coming out as they once did, try to figure out why. Ask a number of the ones that have not been out lately. I did that recently for a club and the main answer was, "Well, we don't get anything out of the meetings." O.K., if I were running that club, I'd try to do something about the meetings. In later chapters there are many suggestions as to what you can do to change the routine of your meetings. These chapters are in the main "how to." From them you might get an idea or two for making your meetings the kind that the members don't want to miss.

10 / Starting the Meeting

Perhaps your club has a standard way of starting the meeting. It might be with a prayer, a song fest, a ringing of the big gong, a pledge. If so, you may not be able to do much about it. You have a starting procedure; it works. Why try to change it? In the business meeting you can use any variety of starting devices. If you have taken over the meetings of your club and feel that it might be well to do something about the starting procedure, there follow some ideas that may help you plan an opening that might be a trademark of your club. When you have such a standard, organized, starting procedure, you give the impression that the club knows what it is doing.

One point to watch is the group that might resist any change. The brothers may not want the new procedure. Joe's been playing a few piano selections for maybe seventeen years now, and what's the matter with that? And who said these meeting openings needed pepping up anyway? A club member told me not long ago, "These meetings start like a funeral, Ed, and so often they continue in the same tone." You may feel that way about the manner in which the meetings of your club start. And perhaps you are right in wanting to do something about it.

Just think of your meetings in the light of the impression they make on the guest speaker. Let's say you start on the low beat. The speaker sits there watching. He may wonder, "How did I get stuck with this date anyway?" If you start with an unusual bang, he may think, "I've got to put some life into this talk, these brothers are hot." I've been the speaker at meetings in which everything up to my speech was fumbled. I've been at others in which everything that happened up to the time I went on needled me to be better.

I've heard meeting men say that there are three parts to the meeting: the opening, the in-between, and the closing. Quiz those men, and they'll tell you that the opening and the closing are most important, the in-between is not so important. I express that idea in my speech-writing theory when I advise, "Write the end first." If you have a good ending and you build the rest of the speech up to that ending, you'll usually do all right. Other speech-writing experts advise, "Get the listeners with you in those first few words." As a luncheon speaker I have stood up after my introduction and smiled at a group whose looks said, "I

"Who cares about the minutes of the last meeting? Is that your question?"

dare you to interest me." And it is a challenge. They're
full of food, many of them feel that they ate too much,
they're breathing smoke-filled, second-hand air. The fat
fellow over there on the left ate some green peppers in that
salad and green peppers don't agree with him. But I have
to interest all of them, not only my fat friend, but all. Many
times as I looked over a group like that I would have loved
to say, "Gentlemen, there's a hole in the seat of your pants."
That would qualify as the startling line the speech experts
advise. Some of the brothers might even rise up from their
chairs and start investigating.

It would be great if we could open our meetings like
that, wouldn't it? I've seen speakers, introduced to a tired
audience, ask the group to stand and stretch. The speaker
is trying; he wants what the club manager wants in his
start of the meeting. But then there isn't too much difference in the problems of the club manager and the speaker.
Let's analyze what a speaker is advised to do. He should:

Start with a smile.

Compliment the group on something.

Speak their language.

Show why they should be interested.

Look over those bits of advice and you can see that you
would like to follow all of them in starting your meeting.

THE CLUB BUSINESS

You may say, "We always have a lot of club business
that we have to handle and if we wait until the guest
speaker is finished, too many of the members leave." If
you are running that kind of club, and are stuck with these
petty things, it is better, I believe, to run them off and then
bring on the speaker. But don't show that any of these affairs are petty. If Joe Blow is in charge of one of them, Joe
doesn't think his project is petty. Not long ago I had the

problem of discussing a club project at a meeting. The project was large enough to deserve a full meeting, but the zealous program chairman had scheduled a guest speaker. Now we had two meetings, for the committee on the project felt that at least two and perhaps three of the committee members should speak on the project. We settled by having the discussion first and fortunately it did not develop into a rhubarb that ran far into the night. The guest speaker got on at a reasonable time. At meetings where a meal is served I've seen this routine business handled while the brothers were eating. Then the meeting proper got under way with the introduction of the speaker.

In running a club you have this routine business to handle. I'd suggest you bring into the meetings only what you must. Handle as much by correspondence as you can. Recently, while a Joe Blow was discussing a change in the by-laws of a club, the member next to me said, "These guys don't care about by-laws, they come here to be entertained." If that's the attitude of your club, that routine business may not be nearly as important as you think. But we're talking about starting the meeting—here are some ideas for starting meetings, ones I have picked up from traveling the knife-and-fork circuit.

1. *Start Positively.* Let there be nothing chicken about your start. If you pound the gavel, bang it. If you ring the big bell, ring it loud. Let the group know that you are ready to start.

2. *Start on Time.* If you said that the meeting was to start at eight o'clock, get going at eight. You may expect more members, but if they see that you start on time, they'll try to be on time at the next meeting. One club I know that meets in the local hotel sends a committee into the bar to rout out those that are in the hotel but not in the

meeting room. Starting on time shows that you are running a good club.

3. *Start with Prayer.* In some parts of the country every meeting starts with a prayer. It would be better if the other sections took up this procedure. If it has not been the practice in your club, you might try it. If you have a cleric as a member, he might be asked. If not, ask one of the brothers, a different one each time.

4. *The Group Singing.* This one is popular with the luncheon clubs. We all like to sing. Most members will tell you that they can't sing for sour apples but they'll join in lustily when they are part of a group. Not long ago a club member told me, "Ed, I've never been asked to do anything for this club but join in that group singing." You may have members like that. For this brother sang, a bit sour and off key, but loud.

5. *The Meal.* If your meeting starts with a meal, you are set for an opening. A little singing before, then the grace before you start to eat, and you have the thing handled.

6. *The Weekly Quartet.* One club I know has the idea of starting the festivities with a weekly quartet. Instead of the entire group singing, a quartet is picked from the group and it is asked to sing "Sweet Adeline" or some other favorite. The assignment comes as a surprise to the men selected; they know about the quartet, but they don't know they're it. The stunt makes a big hit with the club. The day I saw it done, two of the men selected had guests with them and the guests were pressed into service, so this day there was a sextet. It made for a lot of fun.

7. *The Business Talk.* Some clubs open the meeting with a business talk by a member. A limit of five minutes is put on the talk. The member speaks for his five minutes on his

business. He gets a great kick out of the opportunity, and the group gets better acquainted with him.

8. *The New Member Presentation.* One club I know gives five minutes to a new member to tell about himself. This introduces the new member to the group quickly and gives him the opportunity to show himself to all. The club gives the member a mimeographed outline of what he is to cover and he takes over from there. This idea works with the club that takes in only a few members each year.

9. *The Big Bell.* One club I know has a big bell. The chairman starts the meeting and asks for attention by banging on this bell. A club can get a lot of mileage out of such a bell. Recently I heard a chairman ask one of the members to come up to the head table and bang the big bell three times. When the member asked what it was all about, the chairman announced that the brother had just become a grandfather again.

10. *Announcements.* When I have appeared at clubs and asked for forty minutes for my talk, the chairman has told me, "Well, we have a few announcements, but we can handle them during the eating." After watching a few of these sessions, I'm inclined to believe that it's a good idea

"Just one short announcement—"

to do this whether or not you are pressed for time. It gives the meeting the impression that this is a live club, that you have much business, and are doing a lot for the members. There are always lulls in the serving of the food, during which the member sits wondering what he can say to the fellow next to him. Committee reports and announcements can well fill in this time.

11. *Name the Announcements.* One club I know names the announcements. There's the appetizer announcement, the entree, the salad, the dessert, the coffee. You can take it from there. The chairman says, "Our soup announcement today will be from Joe Whosis, Chairman of the Entertainment Committee."

12. *The Exercise.* You have probably seen this done. The chairman asks the group to stand, to march around their chairs, to hold up their hands. Last week I saw a chairman put the audience through an applause test. He was about to introduce a group of guests and he wanted one clap for each. He drilled the group in that one-clap routine. Such exercises get the audience into the act and tend to get the meeting started on a high note. The member of the group tells himself, "This is going to be different." He likes the novelty.

13. *Close the Bar.* At meetings where there is a social hour, the closing of the bar can be the signal for all to get seated. The chairman signals for the bar to close, and he asks everyone to take seats. A good bartender is an expert at closing that bar fast. The chairman announces that you are to take your seats, you turn to the bartender, and there is not a bit of hard stuff in sight. I've heard the chairman announce as he went through the crowd, "Get a drink if you want it for we are going to close the bar." An experienced chairman knows when to close that bar. The

group gets just so loud, and it is time to start the meeting. I've seen the closing of the bar done with a ceremony that gets the group seated when the chairman decides he is ready to go; then I have been at meetings where the bar was never closed. All through the dinner the lushier members kept going back for more. This is not good. If you have a bar, close it when you start the meal.

AUDIENCE "TALK-BACK"

14. *Routines.* I have started many meetings with a greeting. I say, "Good morning, everybody." The group responds, "Good morning, Ed Hegarty." This can be anything, a pledge of allegiance, the club slogan. You get started right when you get the audience into the act right at the start.

15. *The Stunt.* You have seen the chairman who stands before you with a piece of rope, his hands playing with the rope. You've seen the one who puts on a funny hat, or the one who stands there shuffling a deck of cards. Your attention is caught. You wonder what he is up to. You can get the audience to take part in such stunts—let's say you have each of them wave his handkerchief at you. Sounds silly, but it is effective. If you attend many meetings you will see such stunts tried. When you find one that might be used with your club, make a note of it and try it at the next meeting. Most clubs need something to liven up the proceedings.

16. *The Smile.* Please, when you act as chairman and stand up to start this meeting, put on your best smile. I've seen chairmen who look so worried and harassed when they start that they must transfer some of that worry to the audience. Even if your speaker hasn't arrived, and the audience is slim, and you have found that the amount

you are charging will not cover the meal—smile. Those worries are yours. Don't inflict them on the group.

17. *The Opening Talk.* Most meetings have to have an opening talk. And most of those talks are too long. The chairman stands and yak-yaks and the group does not pay too much attention. If you need a lengthy explanation of why the meeting is called, try to divide the job among a number of speakers. The listener likes action, and this splitting up gives it to him. Too many chairmen start off with a few ill-prepared remarks. The listener has come to expect this and so he feels that there is no percentage in listening now—later, perhaps, but not now. If you have to start with a statement of the purpose of the meeting, get the statement in as few words as possible. Prepare what you are to say, outline the points you want to cover on a card, and stick to the outline. You can't possibly help the meeting by speaking on and on when a well-prepared statement would get you off to a fast start.

Not long ago I heard a chairman say, "Now if everybody will read the statement on the sheet in front of you, you will understand why this meeting is called." He waited while the group read the statement. Then he asked, "Any questions?" That was getting started fast but right.

18. *Your Introduction.* If the group doesn't know you and you have to start the meeting, you might start by qualifying yourself. Give your name, your connection with the project, tell why you are opening the meeting. In such a start try to make yourself appear a good Joe, a fellow the group would like to work with. Avoid describing yourself as a big shot. You are just a country boy trying to get along like the rest of them. Infer that they could do this job better than you can.

19. *The Anecdote.* This is the standard start of most

speaking efforts. You start, "Before I left the house tonight, my ever-loving wife advised me—" You'll get attention with that type of start. A story of how the project came into being might serve well. But there is no appeal like the anecdote. Everybody listens when you say, "Once upon a time—"

20. *Introduce the Guests.* Most clubs feel they have to do this. Joe has bought an extra meal, and he wants the brothers to know that he has a friend he thinks enough of to buy him a meal. A number of suggestions of how this may be done are given in Chapter 12.

SOME STARTING DON'TS

Don't Wait to Start. Some of the members will take the trouble to read the notice and to get there on time. Others will come in late. It's a shame, but that's how members are. I have seen chairmen hold up the start of a meeting for thirty minutes hoping that the tardy ones will show up. Now think of this fellow who came on time. He probably figured that he would be out at a certain time, and here you are postponing that time for him. If you have most of your audience there, I'd say start your meeting and let those others come in late. If you feel you have too few to start, work out some plan that will give these early birds something to do. Don't let them sit there watching you fidget. Introduce them to one another. Get them to take the front seats, and start a quiz session or a discussion on some point in which they will be interested. If you are waiting for the speaker, explain that. If you have a good reason for waiting for a larger crowd, explain the reason. But get them active in some way. At a meeting recently I saw a group put to work on a list of questions to ask the guest speaker. One man was appointed secretary and he wrote the questions down as the others suggested them. The chairman started about twenty minutes late, but because he had put the group to work, they did not resent the wait.

Don't Start with an Apology. When you start the meeting, be positive. Don't apologize for the poor attendance, for the competing attractions in the town that night, for the weather, for anything. Recently I heard a chairman I knew was disappointed by the poor attendance say, "Well, we're lucky to have this small crowd tonight for this subject lends itself to discussion, and the group is about the right size." Too many chairmen are inclined to worry the group about the chairman's troubles. I heard another chairman tell the guest speaker, "We have about half our club here tonight, but what we lack in numbers we make up in quality." Perhaps there are many things wrong about the attendance tonight, but don't worry the group with the problem. They are there, and they want to get what they can out of the meeting. So run the meeting just as if the crowd is what you expected.

GET THE SHOW ON THE ROAD—FAVORABLY

Years ago I went to see a radio program in a studio in New York. It was a comedy show and before the show went on the air, the comedian and his cast came out and did a few routines until the studio audience was laughing and applauding. The radio people called that a warm-up. In that warm-up, the announcer and the star of the show were not trying to warm up themselves, although that helped; they were trying to warm up the audience so that when the show went on the air, you and I sitting in our living rooms would be hearing the applause of that warmed-up group. You might say they were rehearsing the audience.

Your problem when you start this meeting is similar. You want to get the show started. Just the other night, the president of a club at which I was to be the guest speaker said, "O.K., let's get the show on the road." As the meeting manager you want to do that, but you want one more thing: you want to get it on the road favorably. You want acceptance for this meeting at the start. If you get off to a good start, you have a better chance of continuing that way.

O.K., so much for starting. You need a good start—you also need a good ending. Here are some thoughts on that—.

11 | Ending the Meeting

Get it over.

That's what the group is waiting for.

Strange, but the eagerness of the American public to come to a meeting is exceeded only by its urge to get out of it.

You have heard of the fellow making a speech who had so many good places to finish, but didn't. He would zoom into an ideal place to end, take another deep breath, and fly on.

Many meetings are like that. You hear Lowell Thomas say, "So long until tomorrow." You don't expect him back, do you? Not until tomorrow. Or Ed Murrow, when he gives that thought for today. You know he is finished. Those are finishes, wind-ups. If you are going to be the chairman of the meetings of this club for a period, why not work up such an ending? Perhaps the fellow who takes on after you will carry on the tradition, he may even go you one better. The other night I was the guest speaker at a meeting. After my speech, the chairman said, "Thank you for a good message, Mr. Hegarty. Meeting's adjourned." He banged the table with his gavel, and that was that. The abruptness jarred me. Afterwards I asked the friend, who invited me to make the speech, about it. "He always ends that way," the friend said.

You have to admit the man had a plan. Perhaps he should have said a few more words of thanks to the speaker, but we are not considering courtesy here. We're speaking about ending the meeting. And this man's plan had one advantage, it finished the meeting. There was no doubt in anyone's mind. When I watch chairmen fumble around trying to get a meeting finished, I am not too sure that my abrupt friend did not have an idea.

There are, of course, many ways to plan the ending of your meeting.

O.K., let's discuss a number of them.

1. *Organize the Ending First.* In my book *How to Write a Speech,* I suggest you write the end of the speech first. The idea is good for meetings too. Plan the end first. Why? Well, the ending gives the group the impression it takes home, doesn't it? And you want them to take home a good impression. In planning a fund-raising meeting recently, we concentrated on the ending. We did all the planning on the instructions we wanted the workers to take home. First we wrote out a plan of what they were to do. Then we concentrated on explaining how they would do it. We planned to get all of the courtesy speeches out of the way, then concentrate on getting the workers to understand what they were to do and how they were to do it. That ending was built over a formula. First, the worker did this; second, he did this; third, he did this.

This first, second, third plan will work well for the ending of a speech or the ending of a meeting. Let's say you are called upon to give your opinion on a subject to which you have not given much thought. You can stand up and talk all around the subject and prove to the group that you know almost nothing about it. But let's say that you stand up and talk around the subject for a few minutes, then say, "Well, gentlemen, here's my suggestion as to what we should do about this subject: first, this; second, this; and third, this." Now you sit down. You agree, don't you, that the latter plan will make a better impression on the audience?

In some meetings all you want the group to do is to come back next week. O.K., plan your ending to remind them of what will be on the program next week. That blurb about the next week's speaker might be a good ending. After you have just heard a speaker, the blurb about the next speaker may sound too much like, "We're going to have a better one next week." But you know who the speaker is and you can plan an ending around how good he is. Of course, if you have a few disappointments in a row, the members may discount those blurbs.

I stress planning the ending because the ending of the meeting is so often overlooked. You plan to open with Charlie, and he will say this; then you will introduce Jack, and he will cover this phase; then—. You leave the ending last in your planning and the audience knows it when you come to the end. You are much like Porky Pig in the cartoon movie; he says, "That's all, folks!" With some meetings this does not make much difference, but every meeting can stand some work on the ending. Plan it first and the listeners will take home a better impression.

2. *The Planned Summation.* One club I know winds up its meeting with a summation of the session. If the attraction was a guest speaker, the chairman sums up what the speaker has given them. I have attended meetings in which one of the members of the club was asked to do this sum-

mation. Not long ago a member of a club wrote me about a month ahead of my scheduled appearance and asked me for a copy of my speech. He said he had to sum up after my talk and he wanted to be prepared. I was fairly certain that that meeting would end on a high note. It did. I asked the chairman about the idea and he said, "Ed, it works great. It gets a member of the club into the proceedings, but the members like it, and you can see how it buttons up the meeting."

"What if the speaker does not have a copy of his remarks?"

"That happens, but the club member assigned talks with him before the speech and gets enough."

A variation of this is a sort of brainstorming session in which a number of the men in the audience are asked to name ideas they got from the speech. Each man is asked to name one idea. The chairman tips off the men ahead of time so that each can be looking for his idea. I've listened to this type of session after I spoke and I have been amazed at the ideas men got from my speech. I'm sure I did not express some of those ideas, but what I said sparked them, proving that you never know where an idea is coming from —a thought I have expressed in many speeches.

Any plan that reviews what the meeting covered is certain to make the meeting seem more important to the listener. In working out this review stunt, plan it so that it fits your club. The review by the chairman is likely to give the impression that he is the wise father trying to tell the dumb group what they could have learned from the session. When one of the listeners does it, you get away from this feeling. When the group does it, the summation may not be as well done but it will be more popular with the group. One danger with this type of free-for-all is that it gives certain individuals an opportunity to sound off on a favorite subject. But an alert chairman can keep on top of that. In such a session the chairman should call on Joe by name and say, "Joe, give me one idea." One idea per man makes for a good session. There is no sense letting Joe demonstrate his fabulous memory by repeating all of the points the speaker made. Joe would like that, but the audience wouldn't. It's best, too, in any such session to have Joe state the idea he got and then have him tell what it means to him. He doesn't repeat what the speaker said. He tells what the idea meant to him, how he can use the idea,

"Our next speaker has exactly two minutes."

or he elaborates on what the idea can mean to the group.

I once ran a session with a group of salesmen. The speaker had been allotted forty minutes. He came with a fifteen-minute speech. With twenty-five minutes to kill, we started a summation session. Each man in the group was asked to tell one idea he got from the speech, and to explain how he could use that idea. As you might expect, the discussion had to be cut off. After the session one of the group said, "That's the way all meetings should be run." There is little doubt that this type of summation made a good ending.

But good as they are, they should be planned. A chairman with some imagination can work out many ways to use the summation or review to give his meetings a better ending.

3. **End in High.** So many meetings seem to fall apart at

the end. You know it is ended by the fact that there seems nothing left. In a demonstration I do on how to end a meeting, I purposely let the session die. Then I ask the listeners to look around the room. I call attention to "the fatigue that shows on every face, the perspiration on all the bald heads"; I point out how low the interest is at this moment. Then I get the group to go into some routine to bring them back to life. I get them to stand, to hold their hands above their heads, to wiggle their fingers ten times with me. Then I ask them to sit down, to look at the group now. I explain that they are now all alive and alert, and while they are in that condition, I say, "Mr. Chairman, I am giving them back to you." That ending makes a hit with the group. It is the kind of ending we should try for in every meeting we put on.

You may say that you can't bring yourself to that kind of monkey business and perhaps you are right. But I'm using the example to show what is needed in that ending. You are asking them to come back another day. Why not send them home wanting to come back again?

One of my friends says, "I try to stop while interest is high." He has an idea there. If you stop while the listeners are interested, they will want to come back. Recently I saw a chairman cut off a discussion, I thought rather abruptly. There still seemed to be life in it, but he cut it off. I asked why and he said, "I want to stop while the interest is high."

Chairmen make the mistake of holding a number of routine announcements until after the inspirational speaker is finished. Not long ago the chairman of a fund drive said, "Ed, we got this breakfast and after this inspirational speaker, we'll put you on to tell them how to do it." I suggested that he let me tell them how, then have the inspirational man come on to inspire them to do it now. The latter plan was more in line with ending in high.

4. *Make It Definite, Certain.* Let the group know that the meeting is ended. Too many meetings end on the note, "Well, if there is nothing else—" If you are running the meeting, you decide that it is time to end and this is it. Think of the ending of the school session. I was speaking to a class in one of our colleges. I had finished my talk and was answering questions when the bell rang. That was an ending. The boys and girls started to leave immediately. "They have to go to the next class room," the teacher who had invited me explained. But they had to go and go they did. I imagine that most club members would like that bell idea in their meetings. Brrrr--ing, and that is it.

But since you don't have the bell, as chairman keep control of the meeting. You decide when you are finished. Don't ask the group if they would like to go on. Stop or go on because you feel that you should. The fellow who thanked me in ten words and then shouted, "Meeting's adjourned," had the idea. He let them know that the meeting was finished. The suddenness was a shock to me, but the club had come to expect it from him, and he let them have what they were expecting. So pound the gavel, ring the bell; they made you chairman to run the meetings. So run them. If it has been a good meeting up to now, keep it good by the right kind of ending. If it has been a poor meeting up to now, get out from under by a definite ending. Leave no doubt in anyone's mind that you are ended.

5. *Work Out an Ending Routine.* If your club has none, now is a good time to start. It might be a prayer, a song, a pledge they recite. If your club is a church group, a prayer is in order, but don't be afraid of a prayer ending for any club. Too few of your members give much thought

to prayer. All of them feel it is a good idea, but somehow too few of them ever get around to it. This routine can be made a trademark of the club. I knew a sales force that always marched out of the meeting room and down the hall singing a silly song about the merits of the product. Do you think that those men felt silly? They did not; the senseless song helped tie them together as a group. The routine does not have to be elaborate. Some simple bit, done over and over at each meeting, will help make your regime as club chairman remembered.

6. *The Thanks to the Speaker.* If you have a guest speaker, you can make a good ending out of this duty of thanking the speaker. Why not let one man do it this week, another next, and so on? Give the thanker a time limit, say two minutes. After a time each will try to outdo the others and you will have a feature that the members look forward to. I know one club that uses this plan but gives the thanker an outline of the points he must cover. A committee of judges rates the man on his effort and if he passes a certain grade, he gets his lunch free the next session. If your club gives a gift to the speaker, you might try to work out some plan to make more of this. Most times the speaker is handed a beautifully wrapped package and he doesn't know whether or not to open it. Most times he doesn't. He thanks the club for the thoughtful gift, and that's perhaps well, because he may already have a dozen of these celluloid ash trays at home now. I know one club that has a foghorn-voiced member who, when the speaker accepts the gift, calls "Open it." The member is assigned that task, and so the speaker opens the gift and learns the worst. If he is an actor he still smiles. A chairman who helps his thankers plan these short talks can aid in getting the high point he wants at this time in the meeting.

7. *The Good Speaker Last.* If you have more than one speaker on your program, try to wind up with the best one you have. I've sat through all-day meetings where the program committee did not seem to understand that it is best to wind up with a speaker that the group will like. Not long ago, when I suggested a change in a program when I knew that the last speaker would wind up on a low note, the chairman said, "We promised him that he could be on last and we don't want to hurt his feelings." The program stayed as planned, the last speaker was a bust, and the group went home from the meeting with a poorer impression than if the meeting had wound up with one of the better speakers that had gone before. Recently I suggested that I be put on last on a program. "I'll send them home happy," I promised. The man had told me the names of the speakers he had, and I knew that I would do better in the last spot. They gave me the closing speech, and the meeting did end on a high note. Don't think that I am egotistical when I say this. I am egotistical, but I know how to end that meeting in high, and even if the audience is half asleep at four in the afternoon when I come on, experience has proven that I can wake them up. If you have more than one speaker, try to get a good one last. A poor speaker might destroy all the good work that has gone before.

8. *Relax Them Before.* When you want to assign a job at the ending, it's sometimes a good idea to let the group

"Is this the time to ask questions?"

relax before you assign the task. Let's say the group has listened to a number of speakers on the fund drive. You had to introduce all of them, and let each say his piece. But you knew that you had too much. Now you come to the important part, the time when you assign the job. Most meeting planners would say, "We've run the meeting too long now, we better hurry and get them out of here." But the wise planner might say, "They're tired now, in no condition to listen to what we want them to do, let alone understand it." So he will plan a recess at this time. Give the group a break, let them take ten minutes to stretch. Then when they are relaxed, he would give them the plan and tell them what they are to do about it. If you have a job of this type to do, try this idea. You'll get more of your listeners to understand what they are to do. You may say, "But they don't want a recess, they want to get the meeting over." Surely they want to get the meeting over. But you want them to take home your plan. If you let them take a breather before you assign that job, you'll find that your meeting will have much better results.

9. *The Quiz or Discussion.* You can wind up your meeting with any of these devices, but so often a discussion just dies out, the talkers keep on talking, and the member who came to learn something is disappointed. If the meeting must end with this kind of device, try to organize the quiz or the discussion so that it helps serve the purpose of the meeting.

Not long ago I sat in a meeting that ended with a quiz. After the second question was asked, I knew that the questions had been planted by the chairman. I didn't realize until about ten questions were asked that the questions had been numbered so that they were asked in a certain order. That's what I mean by managing the quiz. Let's say the meeting is to wind up with the answers to a question like, "What do you think about it, Joe?" You want some favorable testimony of the plan or some pledges stating what the members are going to do about it. O.K., work up what you want Joe to say, then call on Pete for his bit. But talk the thing over with Joe and Pete before and make sure that they will say the right things. If some member is likely to get up and sound off against the plan, make sure that you have enough members for it to overshadow what he says. Perhaps you do run a democratic group, but a managed democracy works better to get the right kind of ending for your meeting.

You have been in meetings where the discussion at the end gets out of hand and all of the work that has gone before is wasted. Recently a chairman complained to me after such a fiasco. "Might as well not had the meeting. The members that are for it clam up and the loud-mouths against it do all the yapping. Why is it all the guys against things are loud-mouths?" The chairman did have cause to complain, for the againsters had a field day, but I felt that he should have organized that ending so that while the group knew there was a difference of opinion, it wouldn't have felt that it was so one-sided.

As the meeting planner, plan the meeting all the way. No matter how you end, you keep control. Chapters 15 and 16 give you many ideas for keeping on top of quizzes and discussions.

10. *What to Do Now.* You have run a fund-raising meeting, or you are starting a membership drive. The purpose of this meeting is to get the group to do something. Why not wind up with a plan to tell them what to do now? I came out of a meeting the other day and the man walking with me asked, "What do they want us to do now? Oh, I

know that they want us to get new members, but they didn't tell us how."

That "how" offers a great possibility as a meeting ending. So often in the meetings, when the group is asked to do something, the people running the meeting give the impression that they don't know how the member is to do the task requested. Let's say that you want the member to:

Make a list of ten prospects.

Go see those prospects.

Get a pledge card signed by each.

Return the cards to John Whosis, your secretary.

That seems like a simple task, doesn't it? But you have been in meetings where a task just as simple was made to appear so complicated that you wondered how anybody would get it done.

Of course, with such a canvass, you would need a story for the member to tell. Perhaps you should have that written out for him to learn. Let's say you have the story written and you are trying to get the members to follow this plan. Why not work up this type of ending, have two members get up before the group and demonstrate how it should be done? Have one be the solicitor, the other the prospect. You might want to write out a skit and have the men memorize what they say. (This type of skit is described in Chapter 18.)

I prefer to use a plan outline. I write the four steps the solicitor follows on a blackboard. Then I explain to the group that the solicitor is not using a memorized speech, he is simply following the four steps on the board. The group watches the play acting, they learn from it, and the meeting has an interesting ending. If you have called this meeting to get the listeners to do something, don't let them go away asking, "What do I do now?"

11. *Different Man, Different Group.* This is an idea I have seen used by luncheon clubs. The ending today is assigned to one man or to a group of two or three men. They are to stage a two-minute ending. The only restriction is the time. The man might recite a poem. The group might stage a rhubarb—one start to speak and the others interrupt. The possibilities of such a device are endless. But in time the members will come to look forward to these ending stunts. They will be thinking what they will do when they get their chance.

A member of a luncheon club, stuck with this ending assignment, asked me, "Ed, can you tell me something to do?" I suggested that he do something with the morning newspaper he was carrying. Here's what he worked out. He cut a few pages of the newspaper into pieces about the size of a sheet of letter paper. He passed these out during the luncheon and asked each member to hold on to the piece until he told him what to do with it. Then when he was introduced to end the meeting, he explained. "Here's what I want you to do with these pieces of newspaper. They have been well shuffled and I want you to match them up so that you have the pages back together again. Will every man who has a piece of newspaper stand up?" He paused while the men stood. "Now, I don't think you'll find any matching pieces at your table, but they are in the room and if you talk to enough people, you will find them. You'll also speak to a lot of members and get better acquainted. Now, please, start looking for the pieces that match yours. The idea is to put these pages back together again. Gentlemen, I realize it might take most of the afternoon. Unfortunately, I can't wait until you get this task done. I'm due back in the office. If any of the rest of you are, you can go, too. Meeting's adjourned." You may say,

"What's that got?" Not much, maybe, but it did wind up the meeting on a different note and it made a hit with the group.

12. *Make It Businesslike.* Don't get too much horseplay into such an ending. Use stunts, yes, but fit the stunts to the type of meeting and to the group. The stunt with the newspaper just described was used by a luncheon-club member, and the man who staged the stunt knew all of the men involved. The same stunt might not go at all with a group of strangers. The stunt that asks a member to do too much clowning may not be right at all for your group. It will get the laughs, but it might not set too well with the members. So try to keep the ending stunt in character.

SOME DON'TS ON THE MEETING ENDING

13. *Don't Let It Die Out.* You have heard the speaker say, "Well, that's about all I can think of on this subject. Thank you." He sits down and you wonder whether or not to applaud. So many meetings die out like that. The ending should be a high point. Try in your meetings to make it different, interesting, on the up beat.

"Now all together—hip, hip—"

14. *Don't Follow a Good Speaker with Routine.* Let's say that you have had a good speaker, he has done a grand job. Now you follow him with a number of routine announcements such as the one about the policeman's ball, etc., etc. The speaker has left the group on a high plane. Now you bring them back to earth. Try to plan your meeting so the meeting adjourns on that high note.

15. *Don't Try to Salvage.* If the meeting has been a flop, let it lie. Figure that it is lost. You have seen the chairman try to make the speech for the guest speaker who never got off the ground. It didn't work, did it, no matter how good the chairman was? That story you heard in Chicago won't help a bit. Be like the baseball manager, figure that this one is gone, and send in some of the subs to give them a chance to play. But don't figure you can blast a home run and save it all.

16. *Don't Tear Down.* No matter what the speaker has said, don't try to explain that his are not the views of the management and that he has to take full responsibility for them. You have heard the chairman try to relieve the club of any responsibility for what the speaker has said. It doesn't do much good. Perhaps the group did not get the impression that the speaker meant what you thought he meant. Once a chairman thought I said that I did not believe a salesman should go to college. After I finished, he went on to explain why he felt a college education would be helpful to a salesman. There was nothing in my speech that implied a salesman should not go to college. I asked a number of men in the group if they had heard me make that statement. None had. If the speaker makes a slip, let it go. Usually the audience will not be as conscious of what he says as you will.

17. *Don't Try to Explain.* You have heard the chairman

try to explain what the speaker has told the group. Why tell them that they, dumb as they are, did not understand, but that you with your superior intelligence did understand? The device of summing up can make a good meeting ending, as explained earlier in this chapter, but it should be prepared. Beware of the summation off-the-cuff by the chairman.

18. *Don't Drag It Out.* Chop it off quick. Many of the suggestions in this chapter repeat this thought—get it ended. You have heard speeches that you thought were about to end, then the speaker seemed to draw on some inner resources and started off on a new track. There are meetings like that, too. The chairman just can't seem to make up his mind to go home. Perhaps you do have a lot of detail to cover, but try to work out some way to get it handled before you wind up. Make your ending interesting. Details and announcements won't do that. You have heard the chairman shout as the group is crowding out the door, "Don't forget next Thursday." I've always wondered how much such an announcement helps. Or how much attention and action those endless announcements at the end get. Get the meeting adjourned, quickly, easily, painlessly. Get it ended.

Now let's analyze that chairman's job and see what we can do to make it better.

12 / How to Be a Good Chairman

Recently a club president complained to me, "Look at the mess of things I have to do." He shoved a number of small sheets of different sizes at me. On each of them there was a note of something he had to do. It was a luncheon meeting and, with time pressing, I felt that he had too much. Another chairman I sat beside that same week had his notes neatly typed on pages in a three-ring binder. He had organized his job. "Let me see that, will you?" I asked. He passed over the book. He had made his notes, one to a sheet. As he completed one task, he turned a page and there were the notes on the next job. While the one man fumbled reading those small pieces of paper, the second seemed to handle the job with no effort at all.

What makes one man a good chairman and another a fumbler? Well, here are a few suggestions.

1. *Know What Is Going to Happen.* You would think that a chairman would. But how many times have you heard the chairman ask the secretary a question about the program? The look on the secretary's face tells you that the secretary has told the chairman once, but you know from what has been said the chairman isn't sure. You have

also heard the secretary break in to correct an announcement of the chairman. There is no need for that. The chairman should know. A good chairman finds out what is to
happen beforehand, and he makes notes so that he can run
the meeting without help.

2. *Speak Louder.* It helps if the chairman speaks louder
than he feels he needs to, even if there is a microphone
and a public address system. When the speaker starts, he
is likely to start in a voice that matches the chairman in
volume. Most speakers are better when they speak louder.
They put more energy into their voice and so appear to have
more conviction. The listeners like that energy too. Recently, after a speech, a listener said, "Boy, you put a lot of
pep into that speech." I couldn't figure whether he liked the
speech or the energy I put out, but I know that the energy
helped. If you, as the chairman, whisper when you introduce the speaker, why should he start shouting? So speak
a bit louder than you feel you need to. It helps the other
fellow start off right.

3. *Prepare.* I am not suggesting that you look up a number of choice wisecracks so that the group feels that you
are witty. I am speaking of the kind of preparation the
chairman with the three-ring binder did. Let's say you
have three announcements. When are you going to make
them—all at once, or one here and one there? You may
say, they are only announcements—what difference does it
make? Maybe none. But perhaps one is more important
than another. Don't stand in front of a group with a number of tasks to do without planning what you will do about
each.

4. *Hold to Schedule.* Keep the meeting moving but don't
worry the group about time. Chapter 13 gives many suggestions for handling time.

5. *Keep Order.* If you open the meeting for questions and some brother starts an argument with the guest speaker, move in and bail the guest out. If a discussion about the picnic seems to be taking too much time, stop it. If two members get into a squabble, postpone it. A meeting should be an orderly gathering and a good chairman keeps it so.

6. *Check on Comfort.* If there are guests standing in the rear with plenty of seats down front, stop the proceedings until you get everybody seated. If some of the group are sitting holding their wraps, see that a place is provided for the wraps. If the chairs are too close together, have the janitor move them so that each guest has enough room. You'll have a better audience if it is comfortable.

HOW TO INTRODUCE THE HEAD TABLE

If you have a head table at your meeting, you will have to introduce the people who are sitting there. Here are some suggestions for doing that:

7. *All the Same.* If you have five or six people at the head table, try not to give any one of them more prominence than another. Perhaps Joe who sits down at the end

"I didn't expect to be called on."

is your pal and went to college with you, but don't say, "I have to tell a story on this fellow." Give him about the same prominence you give the other people. Some clubs announce only the name of the man and his title.

8. *One Paragraph on Each.* You might have a paragraph written on each man giving whatever data you want to give on him. Make these paragraphs about the same length so that the men will get the same prominence. When you go overboard on one man and then introduce the next man as Joe Whosis, you embarrass both of them. It is safer to read these paragraphs, not to try to do them from memory.

9. *Vary What You Say.* Try for as much variety in what you say about each one as you can. You have to use the same vital statistics on each. But you might put them in a different order or handle them in a way that makes them seem a little different.

10. *Punch the Last Name.* Listen to the MC's on the TV and the radio. They introduce the singer and, unless it is a big star, you have trouble catching that last name. If the man's name is John Townsend Yumph make that Yumph prominent. I've heard chairmen spell out names that are hard to understand.

11. *A Card on Each.* You might have the data you want to use on each on cards, but don't shuffle the cards. Check before you start the introductions to make sure that the cards are in proper order and that you have names and men in the right order.

12. *The List in Position.* It's good to work from a sheet that lists the men in position. Good meeting managers usually give their chairmen such a list and see that the men are seated according to the list; thus the chairman has little chance to make a mistake.

13. *Keep the Listeners Awake.* If you are running a long

meeting, watch the faces and see how they are standing it. If they show signs of fatigue, use some device to relieve fatigue—a recess, a stretch. You can give them something to do—an exercise, a note to write, or something that demands attention. Don't introduce a new speaker to a tired audience. I have had chairmen introduce me to an audience that was half asleep. That's not fair to the speaker. In such cases, I ask the audience to stretch, to do an exercise. In a way this is a break for me, because the group realizes immediately that this is not an ordinary speaker. But it is not the job of the speaker to keep the audience on its toes. The chairman should keep the listeners awake. Some suggestions for recesses are given later in this chapter.

14. *Adjourn While They Still Want More.* The chairman who cut off the discussion did that. Perhaps this is not possible in your meetings, but don't drag out the ending. The chairman had this idea when he thanked the guest speaker in twenty words and then shouted, "Meeting's adjourned." There is no sense in dragging out the ending. The group has had it, and they are ready to go home or back to the office. So don't try to hold that spotlight longer. Quit while you are ahead.

HOW TO INTRODUCE SPEAKERS

"Without further ado, I give you Jonathan Ajax."

That's the line with which most chairmen wind up the introduction. I don't know the history of the expression, but it must be in a book of instructions somewhere. The chairman runs out of words, then the life saver—without further ado. I say, don't use that line, if for no other reason than to be different. But there is a lot more than an ending to a proper introduction. Listening to thousands of chairmen introduce speakers has given me these ideas.

15. *Get the Right Attitude.* Not long ago I was talked into being a Master of Ceremonies at a Chamber of Commerce dinner. They had hired a guest speaker and they wanted to give him a good introduction. The speaker turned out to be a small, pompous gentleman, the president of a university I had never heard of, but nevertheless a gentleman swelled up with his own importance. I sat next to him through the dinner and he regaled me with his prowess as a speaker. When I stood up to introduce that man, I couldn't tell the listeners that the speaker tonight was a pompous little so and so, but I had been suckered into the job and with good nature I used the publicity guff that had been given me. He made his speech. It wasn't too good and, after he was finished, he chided me for leaving out some important facts in his introduction. Afterwards one of my friends said, "The way you talked about him, Ed, I thought he was going to be good." Well, I was cleared on the point of attitude. As the chairman you have to display the attitude that the speaker is to be good, that his subject will be interesting, and that the group will get some information, some amusement, or some ideas from it. After you have displayed that attitude, many speakers will let you down. But it is your job to build up.

16. *Don't Make a Speech.* I was at a meeting not long ago in which the chairman followed each speaker with a summation of what the man said. I asked one of the members of the group if this was a part of the plan. "No, when that guy gets up there he thinks he is the speaker." I imagine that during that day the chairman did get as much time as any one of the speakers. And the meeting ran overtime by just the amount he took. I've heard chairmen sound off on their personal political and economic and social views when they got a shot at an audience. I've heard

others tell long stories that were speeches in themselves. Then you hear that refreshing chairman who sticks to his job. He gets the speakers on and off, and you wonder why more can't be like that. If you want to be popular as a chairman, handle the introduction in a businesslike way. Stick to your objective.

17. *Use a Formula.* A good formula for the introduction of a speaker is:

(*a*) Why this subject?

(*b*) Why this speaker on this subject?

(*c*) Why this speaker on this subject at this time?

Formerly, when I went out to speak before clubs, I sent them a long biographical sketch. I found that most chairmen did a fine job on this sketch but they slighted my subject. I rewrote the material and worked it into a piece with the title, "Suggested Remarks to Use in Introducing Ed Hegarty." The remarks followed the above formula. The chairman was given a script that read, "Today our speaker is Ed Hegarty, and his subject is 'How to Run a Meeting.'" Now there were some two paragraphs building up the subject of meetings. Then the part that told how Ed Hegarty was Mr. Meetings himself, and why he was competent to speak on this subject. The biographical material went in here. Next the script told why meetings were more important today, and the humorous thought that we've been trying to get this fellow Hegarty for three years and this was the only day we could get him.

With this new script I felt that the introduction was handled better. The chairman gave a little build-up to my subject and that helped.

You can follow this formula with any speaker. Let's say you have the local banker in to tell your luncheon club about the economic outlook for the next year. Why the subject? Well, they are all businessmen, aren't they? And the economic outlook for the next year is of interest to all of them. Why the speaker on the subject? Well, who in the town should know more about it, who attends the meetings at which the future economic problems are discussed? It's old Frosty the banker, isn't it? Why the time? Well, it is the first of the year, isn't it?

That shows how the plan works with most speakers. When the speaker uses one of these vague titles, such as "Let's Get Personal," you may not be able to use one step of the formula without giving away too much of his speech. But the idea of a formula is good.

18. *Don't Go Overboard.* In introducing a speaker, don't use so much of the old oil that the audience doesn't believe you. You can get in to your neck. "It's my privilege, my pleasure, and I'm telling you fellows that I'm getting a tremendous kick out of standing up here and introducing this—" Maybe you do feel that way about your boss, but I don't believe the average group will believe it. Think of how your speaker would introduce himself, and add a little varnish to what he would say. I've seen speakers embarrassed by what the chairman said about them. Even if the man is the Senator and you're trying to get him to help you get a job for your no-account brother-in-law, remain calm. I've heard chairmen go all out on the speaker, and handle the job in such a way that the listeners thought they meant it. That's the pay-off. Do you sound as though you believe? If you have more than one speaker to introduce on the same program, don't say, "This one is particularly important." That's about as bad as the chairman in the cartoon in *The Saturday Evening Post* who said, "You have heard from a distinguished guest, a learned orator, a brilliant wit. Now for a change of pace." If you have a

number of speakers on the same program, give them all the same treatment.

19. *Contribute.* Try to help the speaker in what you say about him. Don't tear down by making his speech. I've had chairmen who promised so much in describing the speech that I was about to make, that I'm sure the audience must have been disappointed. You have to remember that your job is to put the speaker on, that's all. In trying to build him up, you may tend to tear him down. One chairman said, "You should listen to Mr. Hegarty; he has come a long way to speak to you." That is not much reason for listening to a speaker. But he thought that he was doing me a favor. You might tell the group why they should listen, "It's not often we get a chance to hear an expert like this." That statement has some appeal. You tell a group that about a speaker and it may have some effect on him.

20. *Biographical Material.* If you don't have a chance to study the biographical material that the speaker gives you, you might read it, particularly the pertinent points. I've had chairmen introduce me as an executive of my company's chief competitor. Now there is no excuse for that. The man was just careless. Yet he was following a printed piece that had all the data under his nose. But he was one of these gents that had to ad lib, and he did. When I have been chairman, I have used the printed material that the speaker furnished so that I would not make one of these mistakes. I've had chairmen ignore the carefully prepared piece that I sent them. Chairmen ask me, "What do you want me to say about you?" One asked me recently, "Do you want me to read this?" "It would be fine if you would," I replied. It is usually better when you read what the man has provided. It would help, of course, if you had read it

over two or three times before you got up to read it. Recently I heard a chairman put his personality into the reading of a biographical sketch. After reporting each fact, he would make a comment like, "I wonder how he ever got into that business." The audience and the speaker enjoyed the fun, but the audience got the facts.

21. *Your Notes.* Keep the notes you use in an orderly manner. I've seen chairmen fumble through a number of small pieces of paper to get the data to tell the story about the speaker. I once saw that done as a gag. The chairman took small pieces of paper out of his many pockets, one by one. On each he had a note about the speaker. Oh yes, he gagged it up. He read one and said, "I better not use that"; on another he said, "This is on another speaker." One chairman I met planned to read what was said about me in the souvenir program. But when he came to introduce me he could not find the program.

Another chairman asked what I wanted him to say about me. He scribbled a number of notes and when he needed them, he could not read his scribbling. The speaker does not get a good impression of your organization when you fumble with your notes. Further, the club isn't proud of the chairman that fumbles either. I advise typing all of the data you have on the man on the one sheet needed. Then use just that one sheet when you are making the introduction.

You may not like that plan, but have some plan. Work it out and stick to it.

22. *Your Friend, Your Old Pal.* This type of introduction is fine if you know the man and went to school with him or had a business connection with him. I have had men tell what a great guy Uncle Ed was, and I had met the fellow just a few minutes before. I admit to being the man

he described, but how would he know? I had one fellow take my biographical material and talk himself into it throughout my entire career. I had never met the man before, and I doubt that he knew very much about me. But here we were, old buddy-buddies. I have always wondered how this goes over with the audience. From the biographical material, the listener learns that the speaker was born and brought up in Colorado. He knows that the chairman is a local boy. The speaker was in the Marines, the chairman was in the Army Engineers. How did the two get to be such friends? All of it may be true but if the audience will not believe, you might better leave it unsaid. Recently I heard a man introduce his boss as "our great leader." Perhaps the man felt that way, but with a number of the listeners feeling that the boss had holes in his head, I don't believe that the introducer could make them believe that he was sincere. And can you name one man who got to be a vice-president because he went overboard every time he introduced the boss? Stick to the truth, the audience will come closer to believing.

23. *To Introduce or Present.* Choose your words when you have to introduce a man that the group knows. Let's say that it is the leading banker of the town. He's Joe Whosis, and every one of your members should know him. Well, you don't take pleasure in introducing Joe; you present him.

"My script says, 'Tell a joke at this point.'"

24. *Your Stories.* Let's skip that story you heard another chairman tell with the speaker as a hero. At a meeting recently, where a chairman used one of these stories on me, I asked the group, "Does he use that story about the farmer's daughter in introducing every speaker you have?" The query got a laugh. I happened to know this chairman for I had worked with him a number of years. I could hit back at him like that for the story did not show me in a complimentary light. But I imagine many speakers would like to have some fast comeback to get even with the chairman who tells such stories. I've had chairmen make me the hero of a vulgar story in introducing me. The audience laughed, of course; they were supposed to. But how do you think the speaker felt? And how could a chairman prove that he rated low in social intelligence any quicker? So use the material that you have on the speaker and forget your funny stories. You're there to get him on his feet speaking, not to show that you can tell funny stories.

25. *Let the Speakers Do It.* Where you have a number of speakers, you might let each introduce the speaker that follows. This may not work so well for the club meeting, but for the business group where each of the speakers is known to the others, it saves the chairman from bobbing up and down between the speakers. Give each speaker a note on what you want him to tell the audience about the next subject and speaker. Then you can sit back and watch the show.

AFTER THE INTRODUCTION

26. *Get Out from behind Him.* After you have introduced the speaker, get off the platform, let him have the spotlight alone. When I speak, I move the head table out from behind me. The head table group can only sabotage

the speaker. You know, because you have watched them. But the chairman is the most effective saboteur of all. He lights cigarette after cigarette, he looks at his watch, he studies his papers, he signals to the men in the group, he walks over to check the secretary on the schedule. Now when you are behind the speaker, the audience sees all of that. They make book on whether or not the chairman will have a stroke before the speaker finishes. But if you take a seat in the audience, they won't see you worry. So get out from behind that speaker, let him be the whole show.

27. *Stay in the Meeting.* You have seen the chairman who introduces the speaker and then, as he walks down from the platform, signals to a couple of the officers to meet him in the back of the room. Why do that? You have just told this group that they can learn a lot from this speaker, and now you are showing that what you said applied to them and not to you. When you introduce the speaker, stay in the meeting. If he is as good as you said he was, you will want to hear him too.

28. *Listen to the Speaker.* Perhaps that will be difficult, but do your best. The Nervous Nelson type of chairman bouncing around, fumbling through his notes, steals attention that the speaker should have. Recently a chairman introduced me with this futile line, "I want you to pay strict attention—" Then he demonstrated that he was not going to listen to a word I said, for he started calling men out of the room for talks with him. "I had to give them some new prices," he explained later. Another chairman introduced me and then, during my talk, he kept moving about the room, speaking with certain of the members. Later I asked, "What made you so nervous?"

"I was checking with the various members of the picnic committee. Good thing I did, too." Why he couldn't have called that committee together after my speech, I don't know. But if he did not listen, why should the group?

29. ***Don't Help with the Props.*** If the speaker is using visual aids, don't try to help him use them, unless he asks for the help. You have seen the chairman get so tangled in the speaker's aids that he has to call for help. The aids belong to the speaker, he understands them, and if he needs any help he will ask for it. The other day in a meeting the speaker was showing some large cards. The chairman, figuring that he could help, said, "Here, I'll hold that up." He took the card from the speaker and held it higher than the speaker had, "So they all can see," he explained to the speaker. "He's bound to get into the act," the man next to me grumbled. In this case the speaker had rehearsed his presentation with those cards, he knew what he was doing, and what the chairman did was of no help. There will be times when you feel that you can help by moving in like this chairman did, but hold back. Of course, if things get in such a mess that you know help is needed, move in. But if the speaker is having no trouble, let him be the whole show.

30. ***Help Out with the Quiz.*** The biggest help you can be in the quiz is to repeat any questions that the audience asks. Your repetition gives the questioner a chance to agree that you have stated the question correctly. It gives the speaker a few seconds to think of the answer. If the speaker wants questions, you might have him give you four or five that he would like to have asked. Write these on cards and give them to club members who will ask them at the proper time. Tell the men you select to memorize the question and not to read it. This plan will assure enough questions to start. Others will come once you get the flow started. In any quiz session there may be questions that are unfair to

the speaker. If you feel that the question asked is not proper, move in and state, "I don't think that question is on this subject, Joe. Do you have another that is closer to what we are discussing?" In the quiz you also have to watch the member who wants to start an argument with the speaker. Move in on these brothers. Try to protect your speaker at all times. If you open the session for questions and no one volunteers to ask the first one, ask one yourself. Next, ask one of the members, "Surely you have one, Joe, I saw you making some notes." Don't ever quit, if the speaker is willing. The weakest ending you can have is, "Well, Mr. Speaker, you must have covered the subject well, for there are no questions." Chapter 15 gives you many other suggestions for the chairman of the quiz session.

31. *Don't Argue with the Speaker.* The speaker may express some thoughts with which you do not agree, but don't start an argument over that. He's your guest, remember. If one of the audience tries to start an argument with the speaker, step in and stop it. I have seen speakers get pushed around by groups while the chairman sat back and enjoyed the show. I have seen other chairmen move in and stop any such display. A chairman is supposed to run the meeting. He should protect his speaker, no matter how he feels toward him.

32. *Thank the Speaker.* Recently, after I had finished my speech, the chairman thanked me, not in the usual, "It's nice of you to take time out of your busy day to come here, etc., etc." He said, "Mr. Hegarty, I liked your speech, and here's why." He then went on to quote some of the ideas I had presented. As I spoke he listened, made some notes, and his thanks were for me personally. He wasn't using the standard words; these thanks were addressed to me and to

me only. It is not too difficult to do that, if you follow a plan. Here is one that will help:

> *First,* tell why you liked the speech.
>
> *Second,* mention something the speaker said with which all can agree.
>
> *Third,* tell why the club members were helped by what he said. Don't gush overboard on these thanks. Say just enough to let him know that you are speaking to him.

Cover any one of those three points and you have a better thank-you speech than most. So often the thank-you speeches could apply to the speaker last week, just as much as to the one today. The speaker has put himself out to talk for your club. Show that you appreciate what he has done by making the thanks personal.

WHEN YOU MANAGE THE CHAIRMAN

As the meeting manager you may have to sit in the background while the president or the chairman carries on the meeting. Here are some suggestions on how to handle that job.

33. *Know What You Want.* Get a clear picture of the job you want the chairman to do. In most cases you will have to give it to him fast. I've had chairmen who would sit down with me and go over each point taking enough time to thoroughly understand the job. But those are few and far between. I sat next to a meeting manager not long ago while we watched his chairman butcher his carefully planned meeting. "Next time I'll have to make him sit down and go over it step by step," he said. But before my friend can do that he has to know exactly what he wants the chairman to do. Don't ask him what he thinks. He hasn't many ideas, and if he has one or two he will suggest adding them to your prepared plan.

34. *Give Him an Outline.* I like to use an outline similar to that shown on page 211. The chairman who follows this will stay on the beam. Let's say, when you show him an outline like this, he asks, "Where are you having the program committee report?" If you have left off the report purposely you can tell him why, if you forgot you can write it in. When the chairman is at the head table with such an outline, all he has to do is to look at it to determine who comes next.

35. *Outline Any Speeches.* If the chairman has to make any speeches during the meeting, outline what he might say. Offer these in the form of suggestions. You are not telling him what to say, but he is a busy man and this is a suggestion to help him. You'll be surprised at the number of times the chairman will follow the outline. It's good sense for him to do it, for you have given some thought to the subject and quite likely he hasn't thought of it at all. If he has to make a longer speech, you might give him a script to follow. He will come close to following that, too.

36. *Work Out Signals.* There will be times when you want your chairman to do something. There will be times when:

> The audience can't hear the speaker.
> The chairman doesn't seem conscious of time.
> He should break in and stop the discussion.
> He should protect the speaker.

At such times you will want to signal him. Work out some signal, a signal that the audience can't see. He needs someone in the hall watching these things for him.

37. *Don't Break In.* If your chairman makes an announcement that is not correct, don't break in unless it is absolutely necessary. You can reach him later and have him change the announcement. By breaking in you cause confusion, and you may give the impression that your chair-

man does not know the score. Remember that the group feels your chairman is running the meeting, and you want to build him up, not tear him down.

38. *Data for Introductions.* One plan is to write this out, give it to him, and suggest that he follow it. Some chairmen will take the time to study the material on the guest speaker and write out their own introduction. Most will not. They will, however, take the material handed to them and read it. You're more certain to get the facts right when the chairman reads the introduction. I've had some chairmen rewrite my material and come up with a grand introduction. I've had others use my material and a joke book and come up mighty sour. But I can't recall a chairman who read my material and did not do an adequate job.

39. *The Head Table.* Give the chairman a list of the men at the head table. List these in the order they are sitting at the table. Under each name give whatever data you want the chairman to use, his business, his company connection, etc. If the chairman is acquainted with the men he may not need the list but it is better to give it to him anyway. I've seen names and short descriptions of each man given on cards, a card for each man. If you want to use a paragraph on each man, the use of cards is good. But I have seen a chairman shuffle these cards and, when he looks to the left for Joe Ajax to arise, Joe isn't there. Instead, a sheepish-looking Joe stands up on the chairman's right. This gets a laugh, but it doesn't seem like good managing. Use the cards or list, whichever suits you best, but give the chairman some help. The use of either is advised. Don't depend on the chairman to do the job well without some kind of guide. The list or cards give an order and importance to the job.

40. *Get Together Beforehand.* If possible, get together

with your chairman beforehand and plan what he is to do about each meeting. On weekly meetings this may be difficult, but if the group meets once each month, why not have lunch with him and plan his work in detail? Always have something down on paper for these meetings. I've found that a suggested program helps guide such a discussion. The chairman reads it over, he makes suggestions, we discuss them, and the final meeting outline is ours, not mine. Whenever you want to get an individual or a group to agree on a plan, get your outline on paper and work from that. You'll find that you can put over your ideas much easier when you have them written out.

41. *Make the Instructions Complete.* I have spoken of outlines, and lists of men at the head table, and data for introductions. All help you have a better meeting. The more complete your instructions are, the better your meeting. You may want to call them suggestions, but make them complete. The chairman is up there before the audience, he may have a marvelous memory, but if he has that piece of paper that tells him what comes next and what he is to do about it, he's more likely to do what he is supposed to do.

42. *Make the Instructions Usable.* Think of the chairman when he has to use this information that you give him. I watched ex-President Truman do a speech on TV recently and he had his script in a three-ring binder. That's what I mean by usable. The three-ring binder organized his material so much better than loose sheets of paper. A speaker couldn't shuffle those pages; they came up one by one in order. In giving your chairman his instructions, you might use this binder idea. Have the club buy a binder; then on page one cover what the chairman does first, page two second, and so on. Use the large typewriter on this, too. You have seen a chairman working from pieces of

paper, fumbling, and trying to make out the handwriting. Not very orderly, is it? Try to make your chairman seem orderly. You can help that if you give him his instructions in usable form. The other night a chairman and his meeting manager were kidding about the relationship. "I resent your telling me everything I have to do when I am up there," the chairman said.

"You feel the meeting runs better when you have those suggestions?" the manager asked.

"Yeah, but I'm just a puppet and you're pulling the strings," the chairman went on.

"Who gets the credit?" the manager retorted.

The chairman, of course. Lucky is the chairman who has a good meeting manager to help him run his meetings.

KEEPING THE MEETING MOVING

One of the chairman's most important jobs is to keep the meeting moving. Here are some thoughts on that.

"Now comes the best part."

43. **Stick to the Order.** You have your plan for the meeting. At the start you figured that this would be your order. Well, stick to the order you agreed on. Arrange your events in what you feel is the best order and stick to it.

44. **Organize Discussions.** If you plan any discussion,

organize it. Explain to the men who will take part what you want them to do, and when they are to do it. If your whole meeting is a discussion, it may be well to have a rehearsal.

45. *Streamline the Details.* Try to streamline such details as minutes and reports of committees. If you have to bring them into the meeting, see what you can do to make them go as fast as possible.

46. *No Waiting.* Never let a meeting wait. If the speaker is delayed on the way from the bus station, call a recess, and let it run a little overtime. Call the group to order again when the speaker is ready. If you have to fill in, don't explain that you are filling in. Give the impression that you planned it that way.

47. *Make Sure of Questions.* If you open the meeting for questions, make sure that you will have some. Start by asking one yourself. Better still, pass out a few that you want the members to ask. The chairman seems to be fumbling when stony silence greets his query, "Are there any questions?" Everybody is embarrassed at such an impasse. I've always figured that it is the chairman's fault. One told me last week, "Ed, I didn't want any questions, we were running behind in time." O.K., then why didn't he skip the request for questions? If you ask for questions, make sure that you will get them. It's easy; there are always members who want to get into the act. Some suggestions for keeping the quiz moving are given in Chapter 15.

48. *Plenty of Recesses.* When you are running a meeting, it seems there never is time enough for recesses. But don't kid yourself. No matter how interesting the material, the group needs those breaks. Here are some suggestions:

(a) Never skip one, run it as scheduled, even if you are behind time.

(b) Schedule one at least every hour in a long meeting.

(*c*) Try to give the impression that you are not too anxious to get started quickly. The leisurely mood pays off.

(*d*) Don't try to run a recess in five minutes; it is not enough time.

(*e*) Don't ask the group whether or not they'd like to skip a recess so they can finish earlier. You decide.

(*f*) Try a coffee or coke break. Bring in the beverage.

(*g*) Space your recesses according to the difficulty of the subject matter. If the meeting is covering a technical subject, call breaks oftener.

ORGANIZING THE HEAD TABLE

At a luncheon or dinner meeting the head table is more or less a place of honor. Your club may use it as such. Some clubs put the officers at the head table every time. Others feel that the officers should sit in the audience with the members. One meeting manager said, "Our officers had a habit of always sitting at the same table. You'd look around and four of them would be at the same table. Now they're assigned to tables, one to a table."

Here are some suggestions on head tables.

49. *Fill It Up.* The head table looks lost when you don't fill up all the places. If you have room for five chairs at the head table, get five people up there. If you don't have five people that you want to sit at the head table, cut the size of the table to the number of people. Don't let the hotel set up for more.

50. *Make Up a List before the Meeting.* Make up a list of people who will sit at the head table before you come to the meeting. It might be well to telephone the men to tell them that you want them at the head table. If you telephone a member ahead of time, and ask him to sit at the

head table, he'll usually agree. If he can't attend that day, you can ask another.

51. *Vary the Group.* Some clubs work on the plan of not having the same people sit at the head table every meeting. Others vary the group. One club I know will put the doctors at the head table today, the lawyers up next week. Any such tie-in with a man's business or profession helps.

52. *Assemble and March In.* The other day at a meeting, the meeting manager took the men who were to be seated at the head table into one corner of the room. Then he lined them in the order in which he wanted them to sit at the head table. Next he marched them to the head table. He got the men in order without confusion or without any studying or hunting for place cards. This march is an orderly way to get the head table in place.

53. *Work Out a Rotation.* One club I know appoints a new member each meeting to fill up the head table. The man may fill it up with his friends or his associates, but the head table is filled and there is a reason why the people scheduled are there. Another club reserves the head table for the committee chairmen who have to make reports. Since these men aren't always the same throughout the year, there is quite a variation of men at the head table.

54. *Settle It Beforehand.* Don't go about the room looking for people to sit at the head table. It doesn't sound good to the other members when you are trying to induce the member to leave a table where he is seated. He says he would rather sit with his buddies, and most men would, but you want to do honor to the speaker too.

55. *The Speaker's Friends.* When you have a banker speaking at your club, you might have the local bankers sitting at the head table. You can work this kind of arrange-

ment with any business. Clubs write me, "Do you have friends in town you would like us to invite?" The friends I name usually sit at the head table. The speaker is glad to know that other members of his profession are willing to come out and honor him by sitting at the head table.

56. *Remember the Workers.* There are certain men who are the spark plugs of your club. They bring in the new members, they put on the affairs. Remember these men at the head table. It is well to recognize the work they do. A spot at the head table now and then is mighty small recognition for the hard work they do.

INTRODUCING GUESTS OR NEW MEMBERS

There are a number of ways to introduce guests or new members at your meetings. Some clubs handle it in a way that makes it seem important, others act as if it is something to get out of the way. Here are some plans:

57. *The Chairman Does It.* Since the chairman is up in front of the meeting he will probably talk loud enough for all to hear. It does give him the problem of finding out how the man pronounces his name. One club I know has the man who brought the guest write out the details on a card. These cards are collected and given to the chairman and the chairman handles the introductions. If there is anything different about the pronunciation of the man's name, the host tries to give this to the chairman. It takes some work to gather the material for such introductions, but it does make the guest feel more important, and so more welcome.

58. *Let the Host Do It.* The trouble with this is that the host mumbles what he says, so very few people in the club understand the name and get any idea of who the guest is. He gets to his feet, says he has two guests tonight, Mr.

Wahoo of Umhoo, and Mr. Hoowah of Honum. The others in the room applaud, but they don't have the slightest idea whom the man brought. All they know is that he brought two guests. I heard a fellow next to me at an SEC meeting say, "Sounds like he picked them up in a bar someplace." We laughed, but it did. Recently I heard a chairman say, "Say that name again, will you, Joe—louder." Joe did and we heard the name. I have seen a club give the host who brings these people a card, and they suggest that he follow the outline on the card. This card gives the name of the man, the town he comes from, the business he is in, and some other data. As the host reads this the visitor feels a bit more important.

59. *Let the Guest Do It.* This never seems to work well. The guest is probably a better mumbler than the host. He is scared too. He gets up, says he is Mr. Also, sits down. The club members applaud but they haven't the least idea of what he said. The chairman can help in this. I've seen chairmen ask a man who had introduced himself if he would please say his name again. Then he asked, "What's your first name?" In this way he made the man's name seem important to the group. I've mentioned before the rude MC on the radio or TV who introduces a guest with a big fanfare. Then when he comes to the man's name, he mumbles. You heard the fanfare but you did not get the man's name. A good chairman goes after that man's name and gets it presented so that everybody hears. I have heard chairmen ask, "How do you spell that?" A fellow trying to introduce himself is anxious to get it over with quick. He isn't too concerned with making everybody understand what his name is. Thus he is inclined to mumble.

60. *Let the Neighbor Do It.* This is a plan that I have seen worked in a number of meetings. Each man in the

room fills out a card giving data on himself. He writes his name, where he came from, what his business is, and any other information that might be needed. The man then passes his card to the person next to him, and this person introduces him. This is an excellent idea when the group is made up of strangers. The first man starts out and does little more than read what is on the card. The next man elaborates a bit on what is written, others add more, and by the time the introductions are finished the device has made the group fairly well acquainted. A sample of the card that might be used is shown below. This same idea might be used on out-of-town members. Usually when the out-of-town member of your organization comes to a luncheon, he gets up and tells who he is. Why not ask him to fill out one of these cards, and have a local brother assigned to introduce him with the card? This would give the guest much more prominence and he would feel much more welcome.

LET'S GET ACQUAINTED!

1. Name _____
          (FIRST)   (MIDDLE)   (LAST)
    Nickname _____

2. Birthplace _____Birthdate _____
        (CITY)   (STATE)   MO. DAY YR.

3. Your Business _____

4. Married _____ Children ___ How Many ___ Boys ___ Girls___
    Grandchildren _____ How Many ___ Boys ___ Girls ___

5. What sports are you interested in _____
_____
_____

This, in reduced size, is an acquaintance card used by one club. A member can make a good introduction with this data.

At one two-day meeting I attended, after the introductions the cards were collected and the data given on the cards was put on a separate sheet, reproduced, and returned to the members of the group. Thus, each man had quite a bit of data on each of the others.

61. *The One-minute Boasting Talk.* You might give the guest one minute to tell who he is and to boast somewhat about his business or his accomplishments. This works for new members too. Most of the new members will handle this in a light vein and will make an impression on the group. If a new member knows that he is going to have one minute to get up before the group and tell who he is, he can prepare and without doubt will do very very well by himself.

62. *"Your Name, Please."* You have been at the meetings where each man who asks a question is asked to tell who he is, and where he comes from. This is a good idea, but usually the man mumbles some of the information, and people in the group do not understand who he is. In many gatherings where this device is used, I have never seen why the name was important. If it is important, it will be well to have the chairman ask the man to repeat, to give his name a little louder, or do whatever is needed to clarify his interest in the question.

63. *The List of Names.* If the meeting is to run through a full day, it might be well to produce a list of names and business connections and towns, and pass this out to the men attending the session. This helps clarify names. The list is valuable when the man returns home from the meeting with a record of the name and address of the man to whom he promised to send something or who promised to send him certain information.

64. *The Biography.* I have attended meetings where a

short biography of every speaker was given to the listeners. This biography is a help to the listener. Perhaps the man does get a good introduction from the chairman but if the men who attend the meeting have the biographical sketch on the speaker in printed form, they can file it with the notes on what the man said. In schools I have used this device to cut the lengthy introductions that seem necessary when an important person comes before the group. By giving the class members a copy of the biography, there is

"I hope you folks are not expecting a formal speech."

little need to go into details when you introduce the speaker. Of course, I explain the idea to the speaker.

65. *Name Badges.* Name badges for the guests help, and when the time comes for the introductions, use the data on the name badges. Either have the man read what is on his badge, or have his host read it.

66. *Have a Formula.* You might set up a pattern that each member uses when he introduces a guest. Let's say he has to tell the man's name, where he comes from, the business he is in, and his position in that business. O.K., you make that a standard routine. Then you set up a fine of a quarter for the member who misses any of the points in introducing his guest. Let the secretary print a number of cards with this formula on it. The cards are available to the member who brings the guest, but if the member

fouls up on the pattern, you sock it to him while the other members cheer.

67. *First Names.* Where the group is made up of strangers, you can liven up the proceedings by having all the Joes stand, then all the Bobs, and so on. When they are standing, ask each to state his last name. If your meeting is the kind where you want that first name familiarity, you might have the men's first names in large letters on the badges.

68. *Make the Guest Feel Important.* The proper kind of introduction makes the guest feel important. It makes him feel that he is welcome. At a club meeting not long ago I heard the chairman ask the president, "Shall we skip the introductions tonight? Over half of these people are guests." He felt that he did not want the guest speaker to know that half were guests. That club had a membership problem and many of the guests were there as prospects for membership. For that reason the introductions were important. The club should have wanted to make these prospects for membership feel at home. The other night I heard a chairman tell the guests, "You are welcome to ask questions. Remember that now." I heard one chairman say, "Let's have this question from a guest."

WHEN YOU'RE THE CHAIRMAN BE YOURSELF

If you have to be the chairman of a meeting, don't try to put on. Be yourself. Remember that many of this group know you, they think that you are a good Joe. If you try to be funny like the fellow on TV, or the brother in the night club, you may not do too well. Be just good old you, and you will go over well with the group.

Now for one of the biggest headaches of the meeting planner—that fugiting time.

13 / That Ole Debbil Time

Time is the nemesis of a meeting planner. You never have enough. But remember this—it's your problem. Never worry the audience about it. Don't tell them, "We have but a few minutes left." Don't say, "We're running behind." When you are the chairman act as if everything is going right, as if this is the way you planned it. It may be difficult. In Columbus recently I watched a chairman die while one windy general went on and on beyond the time assigned to him. I thought as I watched him, "This is a good argument for having the chairman sit in the audience after he introduces the speaker." I'm sure that the audience was more conscious of the chairman's discomfort than of the speaker's message. I can't offer any suggestions on how to cut off speakers who go on and on over the time assigned, but I can report how I have seen some meeting managers handle this time problem. Here are a few suggestions:

1. *Write a Synopsis.* One plan used by many clubs is what I call a synopsis. It is more or less an outline of what is to happen. Here is a sample:

> The president opens the meeting—one minute.
> He asks Mr. A to lead the singing of the national anthem.

Mr. A leads the singing—three minutes.

The president thanks Mr. A and the accompanist—one minute.

After the luncheon the president opens the meeting and asks Mr. B, chairman of the picnic committee, to report.

Mr. B reports—five minutes.

The president thanks Mr. B, pats the committee on the back, asks for any action necessary—three minutes.

The president asks the chairman of the program committee to introduce the speaker—one minute.

Mr. C, chairman of the program committee, introduces the guest speaker—three minutes.

The guest speaker does his stuff—thirty minutes.

Mr. C presides over a question-and-answer period—ten minutes.

After the questions and answers, Mr. C thanks the guest speaker, presents the gift—one minute.

Mr. C turns the meeting back to the president—one minute.

The president closes the meeting—one minute.

Time—sixty-one minutes.

That might serve as a synopsis for a luncheon club meeting. With a written outline of the action and a time schedule, you can let everybody know what is expected of him. The experienced meeting planner sends copies of this outline to everybody on the schedule. How does it help? It helps most in keeping the club members in line. Recently, I heard a member complain, "But what can I say in one minute?" The chairman said, "Try and see." The complaining member did, and got his job done well. Too many clubs run on the principle that nobody knows who is going to do what and when. The synopsis should help in that. It helps with the speaker, too. Let's say that the speaker tells you that he wants forty minutes. O.K., you might cut out that question-and-answer period.

It helps to send the copy of the outline to the speaker. Many times I have had to tell meeting managers that I needed more time than they assigned to me. If the manager had not sent the copy to me I would have shown up with a forty-minute speech and he might have felt that by taking those extra ten minutes I was ruining his meeting. You might try this synopsis idea. It will convince the club officers and committee chairmen that you have done some planning.

2. *The Time Schedule.* I use this a lot in business meetings. Recently I ran a meeting for a group of professors of economics and the social sciences. They were coming into the company's factory, and we were trying to explain the economic problems of our business to them. The first step in planning the time in such a meeting was to work out a time schedule similar to the one at the right. This was sent to the speakers with an explanation of the meeting, and an outline of what the speaker was to cover under his subject. The time was set. We had so many minutes. The factory trip had to be run at the time it was scheduled because of a change in working shifts. Usually there are changes in this first attempt to schedule the time. One speaker wanted more time, another less. But the schedule told the speakers what the time problem was. Using a time schedule in the business meeting where a number of departments are involved can lead to rhubarbs. Each department manager feels that his is the most important message, and the meeting manager is wise if he gets the boss to rule

Economics Professors' Visit to Factory

July 2

Suggested Program

10:00 A.M.	Arrival of group by bus. Coffee break.	
10:15 A.M.	*Welcome*	Mr. Ajax
10:30 A.M.	*The Economic Problems of Our Industry* The growth problems of our industry and effect of shrinking profits on retailer, distributor and manufacturer.	Mr. Bjax
10:40 A.M.	Questions and Answers	
10:50 A.M.	*Market Forecasting* A description of the market forecasting plan to take care of the growing appliance market. Booklet to be given the Fellows.	Mr. Cjax
11:00 A.M.	Questions and Answers	
11:30 A.M.	LUNCH	
12:30 P.M.	*Factory Expansion to Meet the Needs* The economics of building new factory facilities. The story of the Columbus plant, why Columbus was selected.	Mr. Djax
12:55 P.M.	Questions and Answers	
1:40 P.M.	*The Laundry Equipment Line*	Mr. Ejax
2:30 P.M.	Factory Trip The factory trip will follow the H-1 Laundromat from the flat piece of steel to the finished product.	Mr. Fjax
3:30 P.M.	Return to Auditorium Questions and Answers	Entire Group
4:00 P.M.	ADJOURN	

A schedule such as this helps tell all concerned what is to happen.

on the time allotment to each department. The schedule on page 211 shows how this idea can be used.

3. *Personal Conferences.* I have followed up time schedules such as the one illustrated with personal conferences with each of the speakers. I go to the man with an outline of what he might cover. I make it clear that this outline is a suggestion and that it was made up for two reasons: first, to save him time and second, to fit his presentation in as an integral part of the program. In many cases the man says that he needs more time than I can give him. There are times when he asks, "How much time are you giving to Charlie?" The best answer to that is, "It hasn't been decided yet." If Joe finds that Charlie is getting forty minutes, he may want one hour. Speakers are like that. I have found that it is good to go to the man, explain what you want him to cover and ask, "How much time will you need?" Since he is thinking of getting together a speech, he may say twenty minutes, when you were figuring on thirty. We all know that most speakers who know the subject can do a grand job in twenty minutes, but we know too that it is more difficult to do a good job on a subject in a short time. Try this discussion beforehand. It helps.

4. *The Dry Run.* This idea is being used more and more in the business meeting. Not long ago I sat in on such a dry run. The management was trying to interest the workers in the factory in turning out a quality product. The workers were to be brought together in a meeting and told what a quality product meant to them. The works manager, the manager of engineering, the industrial relations manager, and others were on the program. The meeting was to take just forty minutes, for the workers were being taken off the job and being paid for attending the meeting. Time was extremely important here for the meeting was to be put on

four times for two thousand workers and if the workers were to be off the job for one hour, the cost of time alone would run about four thousand dollars. The speeches were prepared and the dry run was held. Each speech was timed, and the meeting ran fifty-five minutes. Suggestions were made on cuts and each speaker was asked to report to the meeting manager on the cuts he had made. The meeting with the workers ran thirty-eight minutes. The dry run had cut out almost twenty minutes and all of the speeches were better for it. When a meeting costs $100 per minute, a dry run seems important. Try it some time on an ordinary meeting.

5. *The Briefing Session.* I spoke at an all-day sales managers' conference not long ago and the committee had all of the speakers together at breakfast. The chairman reviewed the program, talked about the audience, the type of companies the sales manager represented, and they talked of the time problem. Each speaker was checked again to make sure that he had the time he wanted. I felt that this was good management. None of the speakers on that program ran over his time. In fact, a few of them were under the time that they asked for. This type of review is fine where you have a number of speakers on a program. When one speaker takes up time that is assigned to another, and then that fellow feels that there is no time problem and goes a bit over his time, you are in trouble. I was in such a meeting, not long ago, that was supposed to be over at four in the afternoon. We were still going at five-fifteen, and at this time the chairman, conscious of what was happening, was rushing everything. Had the group of speakers been briefed before the day started, I'm sure that the time would not have got so out of hand.

6. *The "Play Safe" Plan.* I spoke at a meeting, not long

ago, that had eight speakers—three in the morning, one at lunch, three in the afternoon, and one at dinner that evening. Eight speakers in one day. Every speaker was good, too. I complimented the chairman on the quality of his program and suggested that in the next such meeting they have fewer speakers. Two in the morning and two in the afternoon, for instance. One meeting manager I know calls this the "play safe" plan. "The fewer you have the less time they can take," he explains. Not long ago I was asked to help out at a fund-raising breakfast. I had developed a solicitation for the workers to use and the chairman suggested that I take a spot at the breakfast and explain this plan. "We usually have a crowded program," he said, "but even though they have heard the plan before and had it explained, it would be good to repeat it, don't you think?" As a trainer I knew that the explanation would help, but I did not feel that the idea was too good. "Ole debbil time" was crowding us too much.

7. *Cut the Details.* Most of the clubs you belong to have dispensed with the reading of the minutes. I heard a chairman say recently, "We mailed you a copy of the minutes of the last meeting. If there is no objection we will approve them as is." That gets the minutes out of the way fast and the club member likes it. When you hear minutes read today, you wonder why. A good meeting manager tries to get rid of as much of this chaff as possible. Not long ago I attended a meeting in which the chairman seemed overburdened with the details he had to handle. It was a luncheon session. I was told that I was to finish by two o'clock, yet the chairman was sweating through paper after paper trying to get his part of the program organized. Finally he said, "Look, I'm going to start these announcements now. I won't get any lunch this way, but I'll get you on at

one-fifteen." He did just that—announcements, door prizes, an award too. He didn't eat but he worked steadily. There was a full twenty-five minutes of it. I wondered if all of it was necessary. Door prizes are always good. But do they help get out attendance and do they get any publicity for the donor? I've never been convinced that they do either. Awards, fine, if you can give them time. But if you have to rush, what good are they?

If your club meetings are cluttered with all of these details, you'll do the members a favor by cutting out all you can. The minutes, reports of the treasurer, the reports of committees. Do you need them brought up in the meeting? If you can handle them in some other way, fine. Try it and see what it does to your time problem.

SOME GENERAL SUGGESTIONS ON TIME

1. *Don't Mention It.* Time is your concern, not any affair of the audience. In one of my speeches on how to run a meeting, I say, "Don't mention time." When I make that remark, seven or eight of the listeners look at their watches. I try to count the number and I tell the audience that the seven or eight looked at their watches. Those people had not thought of time until I mentioned it. Bishop Fulton Sheen in one of his broadcasts put it this way, "As long as I hold your interest, you are not conscious of the flight of time." In Chicago recently, at a meeting of the National Association of Radio and Appliance Dealers, Don Gabbert of Minneapolis was about to be chairman of what looked to be a crowded session. He asked me, "Ed, do you have any suggestions to give me?" I suggested, "Don't mention time." He said, "All right, I won't." I said, "I'll bet you do." So we bet a quarter—I said he would, he said he wouldn't. After the session, he collected the quarter. I told him as I

paid, "I didn't think anybody could be chairman of a panel with six members and not mention time once." He showed me a large brown envelope he carried. On it in large letters was the advice, "Don't mention time."

"That was right in front of me all of the time," he said.

You won't have that note as Don did when he ran that session. But try not to mention time. It is your business to run the meeting, not the job of the listeners. What good does it do to tell a group that you are running on time?

"I plan to stay within my time."

They look at their watches and hope there is not too much more meeting. There is little sense in telling the speakers about it. They are going to take the time to do their stint anyway. And it doesn't quiet your ulcers to mention it. So never mention it in any way. Here are some ways the meeting chairman mentions time:

HOW YOU MENTION TIME

THE SCHEDULE

We're right on time.
We're ten minutes ahead.
We're ten minutes behind.
We have a busy afternoon.
We have a crowded program.
Joe will take two minutes.

YOUR WORRIES

In the time at my disposal.
I'm not going to be long on this.
Here is a quick explanation.
Briefly, this is it.
I could go for a long time, but—

THE PROMISES

We'll get you out of here on time.
I'll cover that later.
The time you mention is their time—it belongs to them, remember that. So don't mention it.

2. *Don't Show You Are Pressed.* You have seen the chairman who introduces the speaker and then sits behind him worrying about the time he is taking. I told you about the chairman who died again and again while the General blithely ran overtime. In that instance the chairman kept looking at his watch. He'd look at his watch, drum his fingers on the table, and then look at his watch again. Once he stopped to wind his watch. I smiled when I saw that and I imagine that others in the room did too. The audience had no way of knowing that the General was running over if the chairman had kept his shirt on. But he fidgeted, he mopped his brow, he looked at his watch. He showed the group that his worry was time, and before the General was finished the audience was worrying about time too.

Once in New York State the chairman of the meeting went to the back of the hall when he had finished introducing me. I saw him standing there listening; then when I was about half finished, he started pointing at the big clock on the front of the balcony. After the speech was finished, I asked, "What were you waving at that clock for?" "I was afraid you were going to run overtime," he said. Fortunately I had paid no attention to him. I asked, "What are you most interested in, having me give a good speech, or getting me finished?"

Some chairmen seem most interested in the latter. Don't show you are running behind time by rushing the speakers. You have heard the chairman say, "Jack, can you tell us about this in five minutes?" How can you feel that Jack's message is important if he has only five minutes to give it? Don't rush your introductions. Try to display an even temperament. Perhaps you are running behind, but don't let it throw you. Recently I was running a class for a group of engineers, and I told the chairman, "I like to run these classes in a leisurely fashion, no rushing. Men don't learn faster just because you want them to."

A chairman who shows no worry about time worries his audience less.

3. *Keep Relaxed.* A school can do it. Why not you? You hear the chairman call a recess and ask the group to hurry back. He says, "Let's take five." A group of any size can't move out of its seats, out to the washroom, and get back in five minutes. They line up at the coke machine, put in their coins, and drink their drink. But not in five minutes. I have found that it is best to run the recesses and stretches on a leisurely basis. If I am not after the group to hurry back, they feel that they have had a greater amount of time than if I had kept after them to hurry. If you show that you have no worry about time, the group will not worry about it either.

4. *Let the Audience Help.* Last year I ran a series of meetings that finished at four-thirty in the afternoon. After the meeting we agreed to stay and answer any questions

that the group might have. Seldom did we get out before
six o'clock. But the overtime was not blamed on the
meeting manager. The audience knew that it was setting
that quitting time. The group was not asked, "Would you
rather adjourn now and skip the questions?" The presentation part of the meeting was finished and the questions
were the listeners' part. It was their time they were using
when they stayed to ask questions and listen to the answers. The meeting manager got no blame for running
overtime. In fact, the listeners felt that the lecturers were
generous with their time when they were willing to stay
and hash out any questions.

5. *Hold a Time Rehearsal.* That's what the professionals
do. They run through their meeting, timing every part.
After the speakers have finished one rehearsal, the manager knows how much he has to cut. I mentioned this dry
run earlier.

6. *Make a Time Record.* Have someone time the speakers with a stop watch. Then make up a sheet that shows the
time allotted and the time taken by each speaker. If you
have given me twenty minutes and I have taken twenty-
five, I am glad to know it and will try to cut my speech to
the correct time the next time I do it.

7. *Let the Boss Help.* If you are running a business meeting, the boss can be of real help in setting up the time
schedule. He can tell the long-winded brother that he has
ten minutes only, and that he has to keep within that limit.
I know one meeting manager who gave the boss the job of
making the check and recording the time that each speaker
took. The man that ran over was sure to hear of it.

8. *Change from Noon to Evening.* I mentioned one club
that changed its meeting time from noon to evening, from
luncheon to dinner. "We never had time in the noon meet-

ing," the chairman told me. "We were always running over. In the evening it makes little difference if the speaker takes an extra ten minutes. Nobody notices it, but at noon that ten minutes' excess was murder."

9. *Plan Some Cushion.* Recently on the program of starting times in a golf meet, I saw the notation, "starters' time." The names of the golfers in a threesome were listed. After each four threesomes, there was this notation, "starters' time." The man running the meet knew that there would be things beyond his control that would slow his progress and he provided some extra time for these emergencies. This would be a good idea to follow in planning the meeting. If you have a number of speakers, it is highly possible that one of them will run overtime. O.K., figure on that and give yourself some time for these emergencies. I've done that by scheduling a subject that I would handle. I gave myself thirty minutes. Then if time was needed when I came on, I cut to fifteen, twenty, or what was needed. If I cut one of the guest speakers he might feel hurt. But I can cut myself as much as I want. Another way to handle this starters' time is to give the chairman more time than he needs for the introductions and the announcements. This provides a cushion that may come in handy. Supposing every speaker does finish on time, there is no law against adjourning early, is there?

10. *Keep Control.* This time problem is yours and in no way should it be referred to the audience. I agree that it is their time that you are playing with, but it is your problem to run the meeting. Don't ask the audience, "What do you think?" Do the thinking and tell them what you are planning to do. Don't say, "If we skip this recess now, we can go on and finish by five-thirty." Skip it and finish, or take it and be late. You handle the decision.

11. ***Don't Print the Time on the Schedule.*** The other
day in a meeting the fellow next to me studied his schedule
and said, "We're running forty minutes late." It happened
that the chairman planned it that way. His last speaker
could not make it, and he had asked the other speakers to
fill in the time. But how could my friend with the printed
time schedule know that? So there he sat, worrying about
time, when it should have been no concern of his. When I
work up a time schedule, I put the starting time of the
session on the sheet given to the audience, and that is all.
I have a detailed time schedule for the speakers, but when
the schedule is printed for the audience the times come off.
There is no need to worry the listeners about time.

WHEN A SPEAKER TAKES TOO MUCH TIME

Don't bother the audience in anything you do to warn
the speaker that he is going over his allotted time. Every
meeting manager has had speakers he would like to kill
for butchering a well-planned time schedule. But there is
a law against murder. Besides, it would be too good for such
a speaker. There are a number of ways that you might warn
the man. Most times he has no idea that he is talking overtime. It is such a nice audience, so responsive, that he hasn't
thought about time. But when you must be tough, here are
some suggestions that might be used.

1. ***Agree on a Signal.*** This might be a man waving in the
back of the room. It can be a flashing light there. I saw one
meeting room equipped with a red and green light. As long
as the speaker was within his time, the light was green.
When he reached his limit, the light turned red. I once saw
a flasher on a lectern—presumably the blinking light could
be seen by the speaker but not by the audience. This time
the speaker had spectacles with very thick lenses, the flash-

ing light was reflected in his spectacles, and it looked as if the speaker had red eyes that were blinking at the group. The listeners started to laugh and, because there were no laughs written into his script, the speaker, a bit confused, brought his remarks to a close. The blinker stopped him, but not in the way intended. But the blinker is a good idea.

2. *Get a Time Checker.* One plan that works is to get the speaker to arrange with one of the group to check on time for him. The speaker and the checker agree on a signal, and the meeting manager is out of it. Under this plan the speaker sets up his own checker.

*"We're running a little behind time—
about one hour."*

3. *The School Bell.* This is sure-fire. I mentioned my experience when I was answering questions for a class at one of our universities. The bell rang, and the boys and girls got out of there as if they belonged to the volunteer fire department. I was a bit surprised, but I thought that this would be a good idea for the kind of school sessions I ran. I came home and bought a bell that could be set to ring automatically when the school session ended. Bells are so positive. The bell sounds off and even the speaker who plans to run on for another twenty minutes must take heed. We used the bell in one of the school rooms. We set it and told the speaker that he need not worry, the bell would warn him automatically. You might work out a plan to ring the bell on your speakers. It will stop even the most hardy.

4. *The Postponement.* The chairman must handle this. Not long ago in a meeting the chairman of the golf outing made his report. Like the group mentioned in Chapter 1, the committee had moved the outing from one club to another. This started a rhubarb and there were some heated words passing back and forth, while I waited to make my speech. Finally the chairman broke in. He said, "Let's postpone this until after our speaker has made his speech." The discussion was postponed, I was introduced, and I made my speech. An alert chairman can move into such disputes and cut them short. They kill time and seldom accomplish anything.

5. *The Abrupt Cutoff.* I had this worked on me one day. I was speaking at a luncheon meeting. I had told the chairman that my speech would take forty minutes, but there had been a lot of preliminaries and I had started late. When I had been going for about twenty minutes, the president rose and said, "Mr. Hegarty, we have an adjournment time of one-thirty." I was floored. Nobody had told me about this set time. As I looked at him, he asked, "Could you bring this to a close quickly?" I said, "Yes." I sat down.

Now the club was wondering. But that's how the meeting ended. I don't believe that ever before had I seen a chairman move in like that. I know that many chairmen have wanted to, with speakers that were running on and on. But I had spent about sixty dollars of my company's money to make the trip to give this talk, and here I was asked to stop before I was half finished. To this day I don't think much of that club—not because they stopped me, but because they didn't tell me beforehand. I have been invited back to speak before it a number of times. But I always think of that fellow breaking in in the middle of my speech to ask me to stop. There are times when this method is all that is left to the chairman. If the speaker will not recognize his responsibility for time, there is no other out. But it doesn't make friends of speakers. It gets the program ended, though, and if the speakers will not respond to signals, the chairman must break in and ask the speaker to stop.

THERE NEVER IS ENOUGH

You'll never have enough time. Perhaps Heaven for meeting managers will be a place where you still work as a meeting manager but have all of the time you want.

Recently, at a meeting I attended, the speaker didn't show. He was in an auto wreck on his way to the meeting. A discussion of the speaker's subject was organized and the rhubarb went on for two hours. The chairman had to cut it off finally. Afterward, he said, "Ed, you don't have enough time no matter what you do."

You never do.

You never will.

In a club there isn't too much you can do about that loud-mouth that goes on and on. In one club I know they had a pest that got into every discussion and he talked on and on. He was a good worker, and the club didn't want to lose him as a worker, but it did want to shut him up. The president told me how they fixed it. They made him the High Guardian of the Time Schedule. You laugh—well, it is an idea, isn't it? I asked how he worked out. "He's so conscious of time now that he's afraid to open his trap," the president said.

In business it is easier to take care of the time killer. The business meeting is more of a team operation. Joe will fight for the time he needs, but if he sees that it isn't possible, he goes along with what he gets. And the team has a manager and captain. The boss can always help out by saying, "Look, Joe, you got ten minutes and if you run over—well, your kids like to eat, don't they?" Yes, in business you have more control. The club manager's problem is to get that same kind of control into the club meeting.

But remember this—if you are managing, the meeting time is your problem.

Don't mention it.

Don't show your concern with it.

Don't fidget and fume about it.

And remember—the group came to hear the speaker, or to learn from the program, not to finish on time. Don't get so concerned about finishing that you forget the objective of your meeting.

Sure, it's important this time, but not that important.

Then if you want to have some fun at the next meeting you attend, that one you are not managing, relax and watch the chairman fidget over the time. Poor fellah! Not happy, is he?

Of course, some of the brothers and sisters come to eat, so let's talk some about food.

14 / When You Are Serving Food

If you serve food at this meeting of yours, that food is important. You learn that if you are a guest speaker at many dinners. As the guest speaker, I have sat next to members who have complained about

The sickly looking veal chop.

The watery tomato sauce sprinkled on it.

The hard potato with the pinch of ground parsley.

The piece of pie that is as small as—

Oh, yes, that food is important. The fellow is paying two bucks for it, isn't he? And even if you are buying the dinner, he can wonder why you didn't put up a half dollar more and get a real meal.

This concern about food could take the wind out of some speakers' egos. Recently a vice-president of a club sat beside me. I was taken by the gusto with which he attacked his food. When his plate was about clean, he noticed that I had not eaten much of the food on my plate. "You oughta eat that chop," he said, "it's good."

I explained that I never ate much before I spoke.

"Aren't you going to eat any more of it?" he asked.

"No, I'm finished," I assured him.

226

"Mind if I eat it?" he asked.

I said I didn't. He lifted my plate and his, put mine in front of him and his in front of me. Without noting my signal to a waiter to get the mess out from in front of me, he went to work on my plate. "Boy, this is good," he said.

The guest speaker seldom cares what is served. I have seen few of them eat as if they enjoyed the meal. I have suggested this before, but since this chapter is concerned with serving food, I'll make the suggestion again. You may do the speaker a favor by asking if he wants something special. He may like a salad or some soup and dessert. If he does, get it for him. If he prefers the regular fare, let him eat that.

Arranging for the Meal. Recently I asked a meeting manager, "How do you arrange for the food that is served at these luncheons?"

"We take the Tuesday dollar luncheon special," he said.

His club ate in a hotel every Tuesday and instead of discussing a menu each week, they had agreed to take the Tuesday special. That's an idea that can save much time in discussing menus. If you have a club that meets each week or each month at the same place, you can work out such a plan.

The Annual Banquet. If your club has a banquet once during the year, you first get the hotel or restaurant to suggest a menu, with prices. You next get this approved by the committee.

Cut the Courses. This is a good idea, especially at lunch. Usually you will have to fight with the hotel man on this. He is selling food, you are running a meeting. The hotel man feels that you are arguing against the soup because of the cost. You're arguing because of time. I spoke at a meeting recently. The meat course was on the table when we sat down. The pie was also served. All the waiters had to do was to serve the drinks. At another affair the same week, we had to wait what seemed an unusually long time for the dessert to be served. And at this second luncheon, they had a set adjournment time. Perhaps some of the hungrier club members may resent the exclusion of the soup, but it can save time.

Try a Caterer. This works well where you have a meeting in your place of business and have to go out to lunch. You waste time going to and coming from the restaurant, in ordering, and—because you have left the meeting place—you may lose some of the group. For a luncheon break you might try having a caterer bring in some sandwiches, pie, and coffee. There is more fellowship in the mixing that you get in such a meal. The group has to get its food, its drink, and the confusion caused mixes the group well. You cut expense over the meal served in the public dining place, you save time, and keep the group together.

Service in the Room. If you are meeting in a hotel room, you can have room service bring in the food. Run your meeting right up to the time the food is ready, then call the break. I've seen committee meetings go on while the group ate. You can let each of the group order, or you can say, "I'm going to order up some chicken sandwiches for lunch. Anybody that doesn't like chicken sandwiches?" Usually all will go along, and you have saved the time spent in looking over the menus. You can, of course, order from the

"The piece of pie was as small as—"

menu, but this takes time and adds confusion. As the chairman, I have learned not to suggest a drink at a noon meeting. Most men do not want it, but they all will go along if it is suggested. At a committee meeting recently, the chairman said, "I need a drink, fellows. How about you?" The group all went along, and that added more time and more confusion. You know your group and if its members are accustomed to having a drink at noon, suggest it. If not, let it ride.

GETTING THE COUNT

If you are planning to serve food, you must have a count of how many will be there, for those meals cost money and the restaurant or hotel will be after you for a number. Members are mean about telling you whether or not they will come. I can't figure why, but they are. They say, "I couldn't tell until tonight." And there they are without giving you warning. "These two friends happened to be in town tonight, and I brought them along. It's all right, isn't it?" You smile and say, "Any friend of Charlie's is a friend of mine." But you think of murder.

Some suggestions for getting a count and inducing members to tell you are given in Chapter 4.

The Law of Averages. Recently, at a service club luncheon, I asked the president how they gave the hotel a count. "We depend on the law of averages, mainly. We have one hundred members, so we guarantee eighty; and we come out O.K." This may work well where the group is known and meets every week for lunch. Unless you have had experience with similar affairs, you can't use the plan. But if it can be used it saves much work.

The Telephone Check. This takes time. In one club I know, the attendance committee is large and each has three men to telephone about meetings. The member gets a notice. The attendance committee member gets a reminder to telephone his three men. He telephones and reports back to the secretary. In this club the meetings are once each month and while this puts a lot of work on the committee member and the secretary, it does get a count.

Plus or Minus Five. Some restaurants or hotels will go for an arrangement of plus or minus five. You guarantee a number. If the brethren don't show, you pay for five less than you guaranteed. If you run over, the hotel manager may ask you to try to be more accurate in the future. I have drawn overflow crowds where the meeting managers had to send some members to other rooms or to restaurants to eat, but not before the restaurant had taken everybody it could.

The Pay Anyway. This is probably the best plan for the club that meets regularly—the members' dues include their meals. You try to get acceptances anyway, but if the postcards don't come back, you have insurance that you will not lose money on the meal. You can base your guarantee to the hotel on the average turnouts in the past and if attendance falls off, you have the money to pay for the ones who did not come and did not tell you that they wouldn't.

Sell Tickets. When you sell tickets, you have a fairly accurate count of the number that will be there. It is work to sell tickets and to get reports back from the ticket sellers, but usually you have fewer ticket sellers than members. With the money for the tickets you are fortified against loss on any overguarantee.

Check Experience. The luncheon club that meets every week can tell you how many they will have at meetings each week. This may vary by months, for instance it may drop off in the summer vacation months and pick up in the winter, but a study of past attendance can give you a fairly accurate count. In figuring these you might check other events that can cut your attendance—holidays, vacation season, and such. That record of what has happened in the past can be a guide to you.

The Wife or Secretary. In Chapter 4 there was a suggestion that you might write the wife or secretary to help get out the crowd. The wife or secretary can be a help in getting back that acceptance. The wife wants to know if you'll be home for dinner, perhaps if you will have a good lunch, so that she can go light on the budget that evening. I know one club that sent the secretary of each member an orchid. "That's for sending in those postcards for the boss," the card read. Do you think that that girl is going to let the boss lose or forget that card? I know another club that sent the secretary and wife a schedule of the meeting dates so that the girl could remind him when he started to make dates that conflicted with the meeting times. If you can use these best girls in helping you get that count, put them to work. They like to boss things, and they love the recognition. And if you have a ladies' night, appoint one of the brothers to thank the girls for their cooperation.

DON'T FORGET THE SELL

In getting out the crowd I suggested that you sell, sell, sell. If you are serving food, work out some plan to sell the group on responding to that notice. Show the member some reason why it's to his advantage to send in that card. One club charges fifty cents more for the meal if the man has not sent in his card. That's what I mean by an advantage to the member. He'll never send in that card because he feels sorry for the poor secretary. He will do it only because it has some advantage to him. One club put its worst offenders on a "Check Attendance" committee for a year. Perhaps you can't do that, but there must be some appeal. Find it and use it. You'll get the acceptances better if you do.

FOOD BUILDS ATTENDANCE

Food helps in bringing out the crowd. The luncheon-club member says, "You have to eat anyway." And while food does bring many headaches, the meeting manager is stuck with it. Perhaps some of the suggestions given here can help make it less work.

Much of the material up to now has been given over to the type of meeting that has the guest speaker as the main attraction. Now let's talk some about the other types of sessions. What kind? Well, let's start with the Quiz Session.

15 / The Quiz Session

Recently I was in a meeting and listened to a speaker who was not at all brilliant. I'm certain that during his discourse some of his listeners dozed. When he finished and the chairman asked for questions, he got one, and immediately the lecturer became a different person. He was alive, alert, his command of facts and figures on his subject had the group sitting on the edges of the chairs. As we came out of the room, the man next to me said, "Boy, wasn't that a live session?" I agreed that it was. "I thought the guy was a dope when he was speaking," the other went on. "But does he know his stuff!"

You no doubt can remember similar instances. The meeting was about to flop when the chairman opened it for questions. Then it came alive. So whenever possible open the meeting for questions, give the speaker a second chance to make good. A quiz session seldom fails to make the meeting better. That's assuming that the quiz is managed properly.

What are some of the procedures for a good quiz session?

WHEN YOU ARE THE CHAIRMAN

1. *Don't Ask for Questions Unless You Want Them.* Show that you want questions. Your attitude is important in getting questions from any group. If you act as if the questions are not important, you won't get them.

2. *Keep after the Group.* If the speaker wants questions and the questions don't come at first, keep asking until you get some questions. Most groups have questions but they don't want to show their ignorance. Let them see that you want questions, that you're going to get them, and they'll ask the ones they have thought of.

3. *Ask the Listeners to Answer Questions.* This usually will start questions coming. If they won't ask questions, you say, "This group seems to know all the answers. If you don't want me to answer questions, I'll ask you some." After you have asked one or two questions, the group will start asking questions. They would rather have you or the speaker on the spot.

4. *Don't Promise Something Afterwards.* If you tell the group, "After these questions we'll go eat," you're not going to get many questions. They are thinking about that eating.

5. *Use Shill Questions.* Give certain questions to members of the group before the lecturer starts. Instruct them that when the lecturer is finished, each man is to ask the question you have given him. After a few of these planted questions the audience will start to ask questions on its own.

6. *Instruct the Shills.* Tell the shills not to read the questions you give them but to ask them in their own words.

7. *Repeat the Question.* When a listener asks a question, repeat it. This gives the questioner a chance to agree that you have stated the question properly, and it gives the lecturer a few seconds to organize his answer. It also makes

sure that the audience hears the question. You have been in meetings where a man in the front row asks a question. The lecturer starts to answer it, and you have not heard what the question was. By repeating for the lecturer, you make sure that the question is repeated and is heard by everybody.

8. *Don't Mention Time.* Don't say, "We have time for two or three questions," or "After three or four questions, we'll close the meeting." Such statements tend to discour-

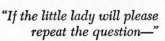

"If the little lady will please repeat the question—"

age questions. If you announce you have time for only two or three questions, you show you don't feel that the questions are important.

9. *Don't Make Fun.* One sure way to discourage questions from a group is to make fun of a question a man asked. If you make any remark that belittles a man's question, you'll not get questions from the other people.

10. *Protect the Speaker.* This has been mentioned before, but you have seen the need for it in quiz sessions. If one of the group asks a question that you feel is not fair, explain to the questioner that you feel it is unfair. If one of the group wants to argue with the speaker on a point, break in and stop the argument. The speaker is your guest, you have to treat him as one.

WHEN YOU HAVE TO ANSWER THE QUESTIONS

11. *Follow a Procedure.* You will find that your quiz session will go over better if you follow a tested procedure

in answering questions. Experienced speakers have found that the following procedure helps them to better quiz sessions. Here is the formula:

First, listen. Look at the person who is asking the question, not down at your notes. Even though the first words tell you what the question is, hear it out. Don't act as if you want to break in. The questioner is getting this chance to speak out in the meeting. Let him talk.

Second, repeat the question. Do this to make sure that all of the group hear and to give the questioner a chance to agree that you have understood the question.

Third, compliment the questioner. Say, "That's a good question" or "I'm glad you brought that one up."

Fourth, answer the question.

Fifth, ask if you have answered. You may think that you have answered, but have not. If he agrees you have, you are off the hook.

In training meetings, when I want the group to re-member the answer, I have added a sixth step to this plan. I ask one of the listeners to repeat the answer. This gives the trainer a chance to repeat and correct. But if you follow the five steps you will find that your quiz sessions will be much improved.

12. *Answer, Don't Lecture.* Answer the question. Don't let the question start you off on a repeat lecture. Remember the story about the small boy who asked his dad a question. The dad said, "Go ask your mother." The young lad said, "I don't want to know that much about it." If you give out too much information in the answer to a question, the class may take that attitude toward you; it doesn't want to know that much.

13. *Don't Dodge Answers.* If you don't know the an-swer, say that you don't. Don't try to appear the wise guy

knowing all the answers. Promise to get the answer for the man. You might use this same plan on a question that is controversial and might start a rhubarb. Say you don't know but will get the answer.

14. *Don't Argue.* If a man asks a question that is embarrassing, don't lecture him for it. Don't get into an argument with any of the group. If you start an argument on any question you're not going to get many more questions.

15. *Don't Let One Person Hog the Questions.* Take questions from all parts of the room. If one man persists in asking the questions, say, "You had one, didn't you? Let's have a question from one of the others."

16. *Watch Your Attitude.* Watch that you are not the wise all-knowing being trying to parade what you know. Your attitude should be one of helpfulness. You are trying to help them understand your subject. If a man has not understood your answer, it is not because he is dumb, it's perhaps because you have not made yourself clear. The speaker has the right attitude when he says, "Oh, I guess I didn't make myself clear on that." Let the group know that you can answer some of their questions, but not all of them. But no matter what they ask, show that you are trying to help.

HOW TO GET THE QUESTION REPEATED

Meeting managers have found that the most difficult job in a quiz session is to get the chairman or the speaker to repeat the question. I know it is difficult, for I have slipped up at times. I have been working as chairman, with no job but to listen to the question and to repeat it. Yet there are times when I allowed the speaker to answer without repeating the question. Here are some plans I have seen used by meeting managers to get that question repeated.

(*a*) A sign on a standard with the wording, "Repeat the Question, Please." This is moved into place in front of the lecturer as he starts the quiz.

(*b*) A flasher sign in the back of the schoolroom that flashes, "Repeat the Question, Please." This flashes as the question is being asked.

(*c*) A buzzer that buzzes when the speaker forgets to repeat.

(*d*) A small sign on the lectern to remind the speaker he is supposed to repeat the question.

(*e*) One member of the group assigned to call out, "Repeat the Question, Please," when the speaker forgets.

(*f*) A class trained to chant, "Repeat the Question, Please," when the speaker forgets.

(*g*) Have a member of the audience take the questions and repeat them.

Some of these devices may seem mighty rough, but they show the importance meeting managers put on getting that question repeated so that all can hear.

THE QUIZ AS THE MEETING

You can build a number of meeting ideas around the quiz. Let's say you tell the group, "Next session we are going to devote the entire meeting to a quiz on the local government. A representative from City Hall will be here to check the answers, but we'll have a list of questions, easy questions, that every voter should be able to answer. We're going to have a chairman ask those questions and you, the club members, will answer them."

Would that make a good meeting? You know that it would. With the difficulty in getting good speakers, you

wonder why more of such ideas aren't used. But suppose
that the meeting is one to be based on questions. Here are
a number of methods of distributing the questions.

> Have a list of questions which the leader uses; he
> asks the questions, a member answers.
>
> Type the questions on cards and pass out the cards;
> each man asks or answers the question he draws.
>
> Let the member draw the cards, and each answers
> the question he draws. He might ask the question
> of another.
>
> Let the man who answers one question correctly
> draw the next question and assign the answer to
> a man he chooses.
>
> Use the team idea. If one man can't answer, another
> on his team answers.

Your own imagination should think up many variations
on these ideas to fit your group.

In running such a quiz session:

17. *Try for a Fair Distribution.* Pass the questions
around. Watch that you don't give two difficult questions
to the same man. If the draw gives one man two toughies
in a row, say, "Pete, your last one was tough, let's give this
to Bill."

18. *Don't Let One Man Answer All.* You'll have certain
eager beavers who will want to answer all questions. Say
to them, "You had one, Charley, this time I'll ask Joe here."

19. *Dodge "Yes" and "No."* Have the men give a full an-

"Well, yes and no—"

swer. Don't let a man answer a question "yes" or "no." If
he gives that kind of an answer, ask him why. If he says,
"I agree with Joe," ask why.

20. *Be Specific.* Don't use questions that are too general
for the listener to understand. Let him know what you are
trying to find out from him.

THE WRITTEN QUIZ

You may want to give a written quiz. It is usually a better check on how well the subject has been understood.
Two popular types of written quizzes that can be used
with the general audience, because they are not too difficult, are the "true and false" and the "multiple choice."
Here are some suggestions on these forms.

True-and-False Quizzes. These are probably the easiest
form of written quiz. The question suggests the answer.
But the form is useful in starting a discussion. In making
up True-and-False Quizzes:

(a) Try to cover the subject fully.

(b) Don't make the answers too apparent.

(c) State questions clearly.

(d) Make questions short.

(e) Have half true, half false.

(f) Mix up the two, not odd numbers true, even
numbers false.

The Multiple-choice Quiz. This type is easier than one
that calls for much writing on the listener's part. But the
group does have help in selecting the correct answer. Used
to start a discussion it is a good tool. For instance:

(a) Pass out the sheets, let the men check them.
Then ask, "How many made this decision?"
Now ask, "Why?"

(b) Ask individuals how they answered certain

questions. Even if the answer is correct, ask "Why?"

THE QUIZ LECTURE

This is a plan I have used when an expert on a subject turns down an invitation to make a speech by saying, "I don't have time to write a speech."

"All right," I come back. "Will you run a quiz session for us on the subject?"

That sounds like a way out, so he asks, "What do you mean, a quiz session?"

"You come before the club," I explain, "and we'll ask you questions about the subject."

"What questions?" he asks.

"You give me a list of about ten or twelve," I explain. "We'll start with those, then the boys will think of others."

The man produces his ten questions. The chairman assigns them to men who will ask in a loud voice. The speaker has not been forced to write a speech, he usually does better than he would if he wrote a speech. Not so many funny stories, perhaps, but he passes out more information. Try this idea on your club sometimes. It makes for a most interesting meeting.

QUIZ CONTESTS

You can arouse real interest in the meeting that is built around a quiz contest. You might stage a quiz bee similar to the spelling bees that you had as a kid at school. For such a session you need:

A judge.

A set of questions and answers.

A scheme of drawing questions that is fair to all.

Members or teams of members to compete.

Perhaps prizes for the winners. These can be dime store trophies of small value; any small prize helps.

PROCEDURE

Divide the group into teams, have two captains choose sides. This will help make the teams about even. Now one team competes against the other.

When a contestant misses, have him go to the foot of the class.

When a question is missed, have members of the other team chant, "Go to the foot of the class."

Stage the contest between officers and members, age vs. youth, women vs. men, husbands vs. wives.

Make sure that contestants understand the rules and scoring system.

Keep things moving, rule out squabbles and too much horseplay.

Have the correct answers written out to settle any squabbles.

VARIETY IN QUIZ CONTESTS

There are almost endless possibilities in any question contests that you can stage. For instance:

One team against another.

A member of one team asks a question, a member of the other answers.

Set up the teams with one, two, three, and four men, as golf teams are organized. Then put one man against one man, two men against two men, etc.

One department against another.

Bosses against the men, or bosses against other bosses.

Newcomers against elder statesmen.

Put your imagination to work on combinations for these contests and you will develop ideas that will work well for your group. You have two sure-fire factors working for you. We all like the quiz program, and we all like contests.

REWARDS

You can add more variety to the quiz session if you work out some form of reward. I've seen sessions run with the rule that when a man answers a question he gets an artificial flower for his buttonhole. After a time the leader can then try to pin flowers on those that have not taken part, if they will just ask a question. Such rewards cost little, but add interest, and the group enjoys them. Nickels and dimes can be used too. In this matter of rewards, don't go overboard. The contestant will work just as hard for a nickel or dime as he will for a more valuable prize. Work out rewards that do not take much time to pass out. The small coin is good in this because, when the man answers, you can toss the coin to him and almost no time has been used.

RADIO AND TV PROGRAM IDEAS

For years there have been a number of quiz-type contests running on the radio and TV and meeting managers have staged meetings patterned after the program. The use of the name of the program tells the group that the meeting will be different. The names of some of the pro-

"Are you serious?"

grams past and present will give you ideas. For instance—
Information Please, Ask-it Basket, Professor Quiz, Doctor
I.Q., the Quiz Kids—any of those names should give you
ideas. There are also local programs that might offer possibilities. The panel shows offer ideas, too—What's My
Line?, I've Got A Secret, Twenty Questions. Use the title,
build your program around the title, and you'll attract attendance. In using these titles, you don't have to follow
the plan of the show. I've seen meetings using the name of
a program that had no resemblance to what happened on
the program. The name had appeal and so the meeting
manager used it to bring out the group. The good meeting
manager is alert for any idea that will add variety to the
programs of his club. These radio and TV ideas can help.

WHEN YOU WANT TO GRADE THE QUIZZES

In some meetings you might want to give written quizzes
and grade each member of the group. You might want to
give the quiz

> After each talk.
> At the end of the morning session.
> At the end of the day's session.

Let's say that you have called this meeting in the office
to explain a procedure. You explain the procedure, and then
you give the group a written quiz to check on whether or
not they understand the procedure. They might be asked
to write out the answers or it might be a true-or-false or
multiple-choice quiz. In any of these types you have to
grade the papers. Before you give any such quiz, ask yourself, "Is the information the quiz gives me worth enough
to spend the time grading the papers?"

Here are two simple ways of checking on the written
quiz.

The Leader Checks. Under this plan the leader asks the question. One of the group answers it. If the answer is correct, the leader asks, "Who has a different answer?" In the end he confirms and asks the group to write the correct answer.

Neighbor Grading. When the group has finished with the quiz, each member of the group passes his paper to the man next to him. Now the leader reads the correct answers and the neighbor grades the paper.

YOUR BIGGEST HELPER

In my book *Making Your Sales Meetings Sell,* I told the meeting managers, "The question is your biggest helper." It can be that for almost anyone who runs meetings. If your speaker has been a flop, perhaps you can liven up things by getting a lively quiz session going. Since this comes after the speech, the members will remember the quiz and forget the indifferent speech. But to be good, the quiz has to be planned. I do a speech that seldom brings any questions. I have done this speech many times and for some reason nobody seems to want to ask questions. Recently a chairman asked me, "If you have a few questions that you would like to have asked, give them to me and I will get them asked."

I explained to him my past experience. "Let's see what we can do," he proposed. "You give me five questions, I'll get them asked, and we'll see what happens."

I wrote out the five questions, he passed them out, and after that talk we had one of the liveliest quiz sessions that I remember.

That's what I mean by planning the quiz session. I'm convinced there would have been no response if that chairman had said, "Does anyone want to ask Mr. Hegarty a question?" But by getting the questions from me, and planting them, he had a lively session.

IT ISN'T EASY, MR. MANAGER

The quiz session may look easy, but if you are to have good participation, you have to prepare. Now it isn't much work to get five questions from your guest speaker and plant them. But you have to get the five questions. Most chairmen will not take the trouble to do that. And most will not take the time to plan the sessions so that they are as good as they can be made.

The question session is good because it gets the audience into the meeting. It's popular because, as the quiz sessions on the radio and TV prove, audiences like them. You'll be able to run many good sessions built around the quiz idea.

Now, let's discuss that ever popular meeting form—the discussion.

16 / The Discussion Session

Last year I made a survey of meeting managers who put on meetings every week in the year and asked this question, "What is the most popular type of meeting you put on?" Well over half of the group said, "The discussion session."

When I asked why, I got these answers:

1. The members like it because they get into the act. They get to speak, and they hear other members express their ideas.

2. They learn more about the subject. If ten men express their ideas on a subject there are certainly more ideas brought out than if you have one guest speaker.

3. They get to sound off about their ideas. Every one of us has a pet idea and we like to expound on that idea.

4. The discussion gives the member a feeling that he belongs to the group, that his ideas are important to the others. They listen to him, don't they?

5. It builds morale. If my club lets me speak out and encourages me to speak out, I feel that it is a better club.

6. It comes closer to being a club meeting. The club members run it, they bring out the ideas, it's theirs.

7. It isn't as tiring as the guest speaker type of meeting. No one man gets to speak long enough to put the group to sleep. If I don't like to hear Joe speak, Pete will be on in a minute, and I like Pete.

8. The member feels, because he takes part, that he is getting more out of the session.

Clubs have run a variety of types of discussions and have given them different names. Those names make the group feel that every meeting is not just more of the same.

SOME NEGATIVES TOO

The discussion is not all on the plus side.

1. It usually takes more time. The group takes this well for the meeting managers say that it is easier to sit through a two-hour discussion than it is to listen to a one-hour speech.

2. You have to prepare for a discussion, and in most cases you have to prepare more than one person. I met with a group recently that was planning a discussion session for its club. The leader and four men were in this group. Each offered ideas, each took notes and assignments. When the session was staged the audience saw only one of the five, the leader. They felt that he was running a fine discussion, but his four helpers were in there pitching, too. As a rule the four sat back and let the others carry on the discussion, but if the discussion lagged, one of them was in with an idea that started it off again.

3. The subject under discussion may be Greek to many of the group, and those men would have to sit silently while others spoke. Usually it doesn't work this way. The inexperienced mix with the experienced. All have ideas and with a good leader almost everybody in the room gets in before the session is finished.

4. The discussion is better for the small group. "What can you do when you have more than thirty in a group?" meeting managers ask me. One method is to stage a "buzz" session, similar to that described later in this chapter. Another is to select ten or more of the group as the discussers. Of course, with the large group it is difficult to get all to take part as much as you would like, but it is possible to stage the discussion with most clubs, and if you have not tried it, you will find that it is a popular innovation.

SETTING UP FOR A DISCUSSION SESSION

If this discussion idea is such a good thing, how do you set up to run one? Here are some suggestions:

Blackboard or Easel Pad. You need a blackboard or easel pad, something to write the ideas on so that the group can see them. The easel pad with white paper and black crayon can be seen more easily, but if you need space for writing, you better have the larger board. I have seen leaders use colored crayons, colored chalk, or the large soft lecturer's chalk on the blackboard. Any bit of showmanship helps.

Notebooks. A group in a discussion should have something to write on. This, of course, depends on the type of subject you are developing. Let's say you are asking the group to develop a plan to get new members for the club. If they write down the ideas suggested, they will have a better chance of using some of them.

Seating and Tables. If you want the group to write, it is well to have tables. For a small group a large table with a group around it is good. If you have the long cafeteria-type table you might arrange it in a "V" with the leader and the blackboard in the open part of the "V." If possible, arrange your chairs so that each member of the group can see the others. Keep the members close together so that no one has to raise his voice to be heard. If a brother has to raise his voice you might have some speechmaking, and you want the session to carry on in a conversational tone if possible. If you can get the group at one table, a round table is best. The long narrow table puts the men on the sides too close together and the ones on the ends too far apart. You might make a "U" out of these long tables with the members on one side of the table only. Or put two of the tables together and get the effect of the round table.

Make It Informal. The spirit of informality helps in the discussion. You might ask the men to take off their coats. The shirt-sleeve idea goes well. I have asked men to take off their neckties. When I have run discussion conferences for a full day, I have asked the group to come in sport clothes. Call everybody in the group by his first name. If you don't know the names, get some 3- by 5-inch file cards and with a soft black crayon letter the man's first name or nickname in large black letters on it. Have him pin this on his shirt.

You are almost certain to get an answer when you ask, "What do you think, Buck?" You want every person to take part.

Your Agenda. I have mentioned preparation before. Let's say that you have selected your subject and as preparation you have written down a list of five or six divisions of that subject. You start your meeting by saying, "This is a broad subject. What parts of it do we want to discuss tonight?" The group gives you its suggestions and you write them on the board. If they fail to suggest one of the points that you feel is important, you might ask, "What about this one?" If the group agrees that it is good, you include it. In working up an agenda for a discussion session I first make up a list of the main points, then I make a list of the minor points that might be discussed under each of the main points. I put these on separate sheets in a three-ring binder. The first page lists my idea of the main points, the second page the minor points under main point number one. With such an agenda I feel I am well prepared. Of course, the group does not always agree with my ideas but as the discussion goes on I change my list to fit the ideas of the group. A group member saw me writing in my notebook and he said, "You're not writing down what we said, are

"I'm glad you asked that question."

you?" I replied, "How do you think I get any ideas out of these discussions?" Because I am the leader I am not supposed to know it all. Your agenda may not need to be as elaborate as the one I have described here, but I work up notes in that order whenever I have to put on one of these discussion sessions.

YOUR JOB AS DISCUSSION LEADER

In running this type of session you are not a lecturer, a guest speaker, or even a teacher giving the group your ideas. You are trying to draw ideas from the group, get those ideas discussed, sift out the good points, and sum up. Your attitude should show that you are there to work as one of the group. To run a discussion session, you—

Start the Meeting. You state the purpose. In your opening talk you develop the idea that you are working together, trying to work out a plan or to develop some ideas that are helpful to all. You may want to set up some limits to govern what you will cover and what you won't. This opening talk should make plain what you are going to discuss and should tell the group why the subject is important to them. You might say, "Let's say you have an idea, Bill; and you, Tom, have an idea. O.K., you each have one idea, right? But if you, Bill, tell Tom your idea; and you, Tom, tell Bill your idea, you both have two ideas, right? Get the point of this kind of session?"

You ask a question that gets the group suggesting points. You write the points on the blackboard.

Since you have a time limit, after the points are listed, you ask the group which of the points they want to cover in this session, you get their agreement on the most important.

Next you start a discussion on that most important point. You do this by listing the minor points that should be covered under this main point. You ask, "Why is this important?" A member says, "It affects the security of the country." You say, "Fine, security" and you write "Security" on the board. Now you ask, "Who'll give me another point?"

When you have all of the points listed, you start the discussion.

You bring up the points in order.
You keep the discussion on the track.
You watch the time.
You check on understanding.
You sum up.
You get agreement on the conclusions.

SOME SUGGESTIONS FOR THE DISCUSSION LEADER

Don't Talk, Ask. After you get the meeting started, don't make any speeches. Your job now is to ask questions.

Listen, Hear Him Out. Let the man who is speaking know that you are listening to him. Look at him. Don't indicate that you want him to stop or that you want to break in. Hear all he has to say. Perhaps he does have difficulty expressing the idea, and you could speed proceedings if you broke in, but let him know that you want his idea nevertheless. You may know what he is going to say as soon as he starts, but let him go. Never interrupt unless he gets off the subject.

You Are Not Supposed to Know All the Answers. When one of the participants asks you what you think about an idea, ask one of the group to answer, then another. You might then give your idea, but only as one of the group, not as the last word.

Keep on the Subject. A discussion can go from business to baseball in nothing flat. When the discussion has strayed, suggest, "This discussion is getting away from the subject. We're discussing security, remember, let's get back to that, will you?" You might admit that the new subject is important, and that at some other time you might discuss it, but now you have to get back to the one selected.

Watch the Talkers. Some of the group will want to do all of the talking. Let the talkers go until they have shown that they are doing most of the talking, then say, "Pete, let's hear from someone else on that." Do that two or three times and the Petes catch on.

Get Nontalkers In. You want every member to get into the discussion, so watch the men who do not volunteer. Give them any jobs you can assign such as summing up a point. Call on them by name. Ask what they think.

Ask Questions That Can't Be Answered by "Yes" or "No." Don't ask questions such as, "Do you think—?" Ask, "Why do you think—?" When one member says, "I agree with Charlie," ask why.

When Nobody Volunteers. When you ask, "Who wants to start this off?" and the group sits there looking at you as if they all expect Joe to do it, ask an individual. Say, "Charlie, what have you to say on this point?" or, "How about you, Gil?" This gives you an opportunity to bring in the persons who have not been speaking up.

Ask the Same Question of Three or Four. At times it works well to ask the same question of three or four of the group. This is a good device to use when the point is important. Get the views of more than one. All may give the same answer, but each will do it in his words, and the group will be interested in what each says. This repetition works well in the meeting in which you are trying to train the group to solicit funds or to get them to work on prospective members.

Use "How" and "Why" a Lot. These two words will help you get the strong silent ones into the discussion. The fellow says, "I agree with Joe." You ask him why. He says, "I would do it just like Charlie said." You ask him how. Don't let any participant get away with a one-word answer. He isn't contributing when he does.

Ask Debatable Questions. It will help spur discussion if you ask such questions as, "Do you think that the country will be harmed so much if the Democrats get in?" You will have opinions on both sides of such a question. Some will say, "Yes," others, "No." And so the question will spur discussion on the point.

Play Dumb at Times. At times it is good to make out that you don't understand a question or an opinion. Ask the man to repeat or elaborate. By filling in the details he will help make himself clear to the group.

Don't Allow Interruptions. While one man is stating his idea, don't allow another to break in. Say, "Hold it, Wilson;

Pete has the floor." When Pete finishes, ask Wilson a question that has him arguing with you rather than with Pete.

One Man's Peeves. Try to stay clear of one man's pet peeves. The group knows that he is always speaking out on this subject, and you don't want him to ruin your discussion by using your time on the peeve here. You might ask, "Is that a problem for all of us?" or "Do all of you feel we should spend some time on that point?" The group will vote the subject down fast if you give them the opportunity.

Avoid Arguments. Arguments liven any discussion, but don't allow one of the group to argue with another. Say,

"You with the bow tie—you must have a question."

"Hold it, Jim, we're all different and we're all bound to have different ideas. In this country we're allowed to express those ideas." Get the man who wants to argue talking to you, rather than to the one who thinks differently.

Use the Compliment. This encourages the expression of ideas. You say, "That's a good question," or, "That's a good idea." The man who has brought up the idea, or has asked the question, feels good, doesn't he? And the others in the group feel that if they ask questions or throw in ideas, they will get a similar pat on the back.

Keep Reassuring. Keep reminding the group that the questions you ask do not indicate the man's idea is not correct. You are trying to get him to explain it more fully.

Get Everybody In. Check on the ones that are taking part without making it too apparent that you are doing so. Try to get all of the group in. Even if a man has made but one or two comments, he feels that he has taken part. Say, "Art, you haven't commented on this." If he says, "I haven't any ideas on it," you might ask, "Why do you think that is?" If you let Art get by with a short answer, the others will duck out from under, too.

Don't Make Fun. Treat every comment seriously. You might be able to get a laugh with some crack about an idea expressed, but that would stamp you as a poor discussion leader. You know how mad you get when the quiz master on the radio or TV gets a laugh at the expense of the helpless contestant. You're pretty much in the position of that quiz master when you are running a discussion. No matter how dumb the comment or question is, listen to it and curb your tendency to wisecrack.

Conclusions. In some types of discussion you may want to sum up the conclusions of the group. You might do this at the end of the discussion on each point. Let's say you are discussing the membership drive. You have discussed plans for approaching prospective members. Before you go on to the next step, which might be what you'll say to these members, you may want to sum up what has been discussed so far. You say, "Are these the four steps we will use in the approach?" These conclusions give you a repetition that helps clarify the points for the group. By using them at the finish of the discussion of the point, you button up the discussion on that point.

Don't Rule Out Ideas, Let the Group Do It. If an idea

comes up that you feel should not be discussed, let the group rule it out. If it is on an entirely different subject, you might express your opinion, but if you rule it out the group might feel you are too arbitrary. It helps if you say, "Joe, I wonder if that idea fits in here. What do you others think?" If there is a place where it might fit, you might ask, "I wonder if it might not come up better under point number five on the board?" When an idea comes up that is off the subject, you can ask, "Let's hold that until later. Will you all buy that?"

To Get Back on the Track. There will be times when you get off the subject but on an angle that both you and the group want to continue. You might say, "Fellows, this does not come under the subject, but it seems mighty interesting to all of you. What do you say that we schedule it for a session of its own?" Another plan is to say, "This side trip has been mighty interesting, but we haven't finished the other subject; let's get back to that." You might say, "Gus, this subject you brought up has been good for some fine discussion, but what do you say we get back to the subject we should be discussing?" To get back again, you might restate the problem under discussion. You could say, "We're getting pretty far off base here—the problem we should be discussing is—" Recently I heard a leader say, "We surely strayed off the reservation. Who will tell me the subject we should be discussing?" You can ask the man who started you off on the side track to restate the original problem. One of my friends says, "When a discussion group of mine gets all snarled up, I call a recess. When they come back, they are ready to go to work on the main subject again."

Don't Let It Die. When the discussion on a point seems to be about finished, stop and sum up, or go to another subject. You might have to urge the group to take part at the start of a discussion, but don't work to drag it out. When they seem to have had enough, call a change.

Don't Hurry. In running a discussion, don't give the impression that you are in a hurry to cover the subject. A discussion session takes time. If you try to apportion time to each part of a subject, you will have trouble. Some men speak slowly, some need too much time to express themselves, but you have to bear with them. Others want to get their chance to speak. If you show that you are worrying about time, you discourage the ones who want to take part. In most discussions it makes little difference whether you cover two or four points. If the group is satisfied to take the time, why should you worry? The other day a meeting manager said, "Ed, he's going on and on on this one point; we're not going to get the whole subject covered." I said, "What difference does it make? The group is interested, isn't it?" It happened that the group covered only two of four points listed for discussion, but the members were so interested that they voted to come back again and stage another discussion on the two points they didn't discuss. And this was a group that was complaining about the dull meetings the club was having. Don't rush or give the appearance that you would like to rush when you run a discussion session. You'll discourage participation if you do.

SOME IDEAS FOR DISCUSSION SESSIONS

1. *The Group Makes Up the Agenda.* This can be done in the meeting or ahead of the meeting. Ask the ones who are to take part to make up a list of the things they want to discuss. In a club you'll usually select a subject, but you can let them say what they want to discuss about the subject. In business, you can let them say without limiting

them to a subject. I've seen fine discussions run on the peeves of the group. One of the most popular subjects for such a meeting is, "What are the main problems you are facing today?" That question could be asked of any kind of worker, couldn't it? The procedure in such a meeting is to

(*a*) Take the list that is given you. You'll have some duplication. The thoughts may be stated in different words. Get agreement that these are the same.

(*b*) Write the list on a blackboard.

(*c*) Get the group's agreement on which should be discussed first. These may be the most important. If you feel

"You say I won't want to answer your question?"

that one problem is more important than another, get the group to agree that it is. Don't make any decisions against the wishes of the group.

(*d*) Start your discussion on the point voted most important. Cover the point, sum up the conclusions, and then go on to the second point.

2. *You Make Up the Agenda.* You can come to this type of meeting with your list of subjects. You might send this out to the group before the meeting asking them to bring in their ideas on any of the points. You might pass it out at the start of the meeting. Let's say that your discussion was a problem-solving session. You want to discuss getting new members. O.K., you pass out the list, and

(*a*) Ask the group if these are the main problems, and if they can suggest any others.

(*b*) Give the group the opportunity to say which problem they would like to discuss first.

(*c*) Open the discussion on the first point, talk it out, sum up, and go on to point two.

3. *The Testimony Session.* In this type of session the members of the group get to boast about the good job they have done on, let's say, getting new members. You let Joe, who has brought in ten new members, and Bill, who accounted for nine, and Pete, who brought in six, tell how they did it. Now you have others ask questions of these star salesmen. You arrange for the questions. Next you let others tell of ideas they have used. In this type of session I have seen guides passed out to the group, to suggest questions that might be asked. I have seen the leader use a guide, and when Joe finished, he asked, "Do you all understand the appeal he used on these solicitations?" If the group said it did, he asked one of the men to explain it. One of my friends says, "There never was an unsuccessful boasting session." There never was. When Joe tells how he got his ten applications, Art thinks of the clever way he got his one, and he wants to share that with the group.

4. *The Problem-solving Session.* This can be applied to a problem of the club, a problem of the town, the state, or the country. Most towns need more school facilities. Would that make a good discussion subject for your group? You know that there are as many different ideas for solving that problem as there are members of the group. O.K., you ask certain members to prepare on the subject and you stage your discussion. You can do the same with any current civic problem. If you want to build publicity for the club, run the discussion with the school board listening in. With

a little thought you will be able to think of twenty such problems that would make excellent discussion subjects.

5. *The Round Table.* This works for the smaller group. Seat the group at a round table and go around the table letting each person speak in turn. I have seen these run with no preparation. The leader asks, "What do you want to talk about?" As the subjects are suggested, the leader writes them on the board. Then comes the vote as to which should be discussed first. Now the discussion goes on as before, except that the chairman calls on each in the order of seating around the table.

6. *The "Buzz" Session.* When you have a group that is too large for everyone to take part in the discussion, you can break up the group into units of six, appoint one man a leader, another a secretary, then have the small groups discuss the subject. Suppose the subject is the current problems in the town. The small groups are given the assignment of listing the top four problems in ten minutes' time. In ten minutes the group chairmen or the secretaries are asked to report back to the large group. As the secretaries report the leader writes the suggestions on the board and the large group is surprised at how closely the small groups seem to agree. Seldom will more than eight problems be listed.

Now with the eight problems singled out, each group is assigned one of the eight problems. It is to take ten minutes to suggest solutions. When the small groups report back, each man in the meeting has a long list of suggestions as to what can be done about the problems.

The buzz session is useful for most leaders feel that when you have a large group, you must rely on the speech or presentation. This type of discussion gets everybody in, each has his say, and each sees how the judgment of the groups agrees on what should be done about each of the problems.

7. *Building a Story.* Let's say you want to get together a list of reasons why a person should join your group. Who could give you a better list than the ones who are now members? You bring the group together. You ask for reasons. You write the reasons on the board. Let's say you have six good reasons. Now you take reason number one and have the group analyze it, you ask the group to say what that reason means to them. Under this reason you list perhaps six points. You discuss each. Follow the same procedure with each of the reasons and you have a powerful story on why a person should join your group. But remember this, the reasons are not your reasons. They are the reasons of the group. And if the group taking part in the discussion is responsible for getting new members, it will use those reasons on prospects. In business, let's say that you want to install a new system in a department. You know how any group of employees resists change. You call the group together to discuss the advantages of the new system. Through discussion, the group builds up its own enthusiasm for the new system. It leaves the meeting asking, "When can it be installed?" I have seen this plan used to discuss the disadvantages of the old system. The discussion brings out all of the faults that the new system is to correct. In both cases the group talks itself into buying an idea.

8. *The Group-run Session.* Members of the club can be assigned to run a discussion on any subject. You ask two or three members of the group to study up on one of the current problems of the day, and two or three others to work up a list of questions to be asked. The first three make

five- or ten-minute presentations, then the others ask questions to get a general discussion started.

9. *Setting Up a Job.* You might want to work out a plan for soliciting membership to your club, or a plan for handling the meetings. In business it might be a plan for handling any task. What better way than to get together the persons who will do the work and talk about how it will be done? You ask a man who has been successful at getting new members, "How do you do this?" He says, "I just ask them." You say, "Yes, but what do you say first?" As each man tells you what he does, you write the answers on the blackboard. In time you wind up with a list of steps that the man goes through in getting the prospect to join. Next you discuss what he does on each. The result will be a report on how the successful solicitor works.

THE DISCUSSION IS GOOD, BUT—

When you stage your first discussion session you will be surprised at the comments from your group. They will like it and ask, "Why don't we do more of this?" But if you had discussion sessions every time you had a meeting, the group would get tired of discussion, too.

But try some discussion meetings. They are good for building a group spirit in a club, they make the member feel that his opinion is important. Study the discussion and how your group can use it. It may work as a tonic in building interest in your club.

And while we are on that subject of variety, how can you use the panel?

17 / You Might Try a Panel

This is a popular type of meeting. You show the club—not one, but four or five speakers or participants. If the club has been having a string of so-so speakers, the panel can be a welcome relief. If you have four men working on a panel, the chances are that one of them will be good. If you want a good panel meeting, you perhaps have to do much more planning than with the single speaker, but the planning pays off. I was on a panel recently in which the meeting manager had arranged for a rhubarb between two of the panelists. They argued in front of the audience about a point. To say that the group loved it is an understatement. I am not sure that this technique is good, but it does hold interest.

The point illustrates the kind of organization that the panel-type meeting can use. I have been on panels that met two or three times before the meeting and laid out the parts of the subject each would cover, even to a list of the points that each panelist would make. Now those meetings went over well, because they were planned to go over well.

One advantage of the panel is that you can usually find members of the club to make up the panel. If that is not possible, you can recruit the panelists from the town. You don't have to worry about the big names with the panel. Four average Joes can usually put on a good show for you.

SOME PANEL MEETING IDEAS YOU MIGHT USE

The Quiz. This works well in the business meeting. You put the experts on the platform and let the help ask questions. You sell the group on asking questions by saying, "Here's your chance, you got the experts here now, ask them." In the club affair, you might set up the school board, the city officials, or similar groups for this type of session. It will help if you get a few questions planted so that the questioning starts readily.

The Presentation Followed by a Quiz or Discussion. In this form the four panelists speak their pieces, then you open the meeting for questions. Keep the individual speeches to less than ten minutes. Allow an equal time for questions.

The Testimony Session. Let's say you're staging a membership drive. You make up a panel of the most successful solicitors and let them tell how they did it. Again have some of the audience primed with questions. This session is sure-fire. As I have mentioned before, there never was a poor boasting session.

The Argument. You might call this a debate or a discussion. But select two panelists on one side of a question, two on the other. Let them present their points, one for, two against. Then have the group set with questions to ask. The question is asked, one side answers, then the other side.

The Joint Session. I've mentioned before the joint meetings of the Sales Executives and Purchasing Agents. This week I read of our two local clubs staging such a panel show. The P.A.'s told what they liked in S.E.'s, the S.E.'s what they liked in P.A.'s. Then came the discussion. There are a number of such combinations of clubs you might try.

THE SET-UP NEEDED

To set up your panel you need a table long enough to seat your group. You can set name cards in front of each panelist. You can make these of white cardboard with the letters large enough for the audience to see and read. If you have a large audience you may need microphones. If possible, provide more than one mike so that the panelists do not have to pass the microphone from one to the other. If you watch the shows on TV you may borrow other ideas that will add interest to your stage set-up.

THE MODERATOR

You need a leader for the panel session and his job might be described as follows:

1. He starts the meeting with a statement that tells what the session is all about. He explains how the meeting will be handled. He introduces the panelists, keeps the meeting on the subject, keeps it moving.

The panel has just been asked to cut twenty minutes.

2. He repeats questions that are asked by the audience. He asks, "Which member of the panel do you want to answer that question?"

3. He speaks as little as possible. This is the panelists' show.

4. He protects the panelists from unfair questions, and stops any member of the audience who attempts to argue with a panelist.

5. He keeps panelists from arguing with each other, unless the argument is planned beforehand.

6. He doesn't allow one panelist to interrupt another. He says, "Mr. Ajax has the floor." When Mr. Ajax is finished, he has the other panelist direct his remarks to the moderator, rather than to Mr. Ajax.

ORGANIZING A PANEL PROGRAM

Here are some steps that you might follow in organizing a panel program.

1. *Select the Subject.* A subject in the news works out well. You might let the panelists help on this.

2. *Select the Panelists.* Let's say that you plan to use club members. Try to pick men that you can depend on to cooperate. You don't need your best speakers. This might be a chance to bring in those members who do not do too much work for the club. Call these men together and explain the plan. Suggest a subject to them. If they would rather take another subject, it will probably be better to let them have their way. Your main interest is a program.

3. *Outline the Points You Want to Cover.* If you select the subject it will be well for you to have the subject divided into parts and a list of the points that should be covered under each part. One meeting manager handled

my part on his program entirely by mail. He gave me an outline of the complete discussion, he told me what the other men would cover, and suggested the points I cover. With what he gave me, I couldn't go far wrong. His meeting was one of the best I ever sat through.

4. *Assign the Parts to Be Covered.* Give each man his assignment and discuss it with the group so that each knows what the other will cover.

5. *Stage a Rehearsal.* After each man has had time to prepare his presentation, stage a group rehearsal so that all will again go over the material and know the job that is expected of them.

6. *Organize the Questions.* If you want questions, write out the ones the panelists want on cards and pass them out to members of the group to ask. Tell the member to memorize the question and ask it, not to read it from the card. Make up the questions so that there are questions for each panelist. I've been at meetings where all of the questions were directed at one panelist. Spread them around.

After reading these suggestions for organizing, you may say, "It is easier to have a guest speaker." That's true, it is, but the panel gives variety to your programs. For a club that meets once each month, two of these panel meetings per year can help balance your program.

HOW THE PANEL HELPS

The panel-type meeting adds variety to the program.

It helps to get more members on the program.

It appeals to a wider interest. While a member might not be interested in the subject covered by a speaker, he might find some interest in one of the points covered by a panelist.

It offers a wider viewpoint. Four men speaking on the

same subject will tackle the subject from more angles than one speaker would.

It's popular. The panel idea attracts the members. Advertise a panel and your notice makes it appear you have an unusual attraction—four speakers for the price of one. The large audience for TV shows of this type indicates the appeal.

Another type of session you might have use for is the training meeting.

18 / The Training Meeting

You might say, "We run a club, we don't have much use for a training meeting." Maybe that's so. But sometime in the life of every group, you have to go out and look for members, or perhaps you have to put on a fund-raising drive. At that time, wouldn't it be a good idea to give the workers some training on this job you want them to do?

"Oh, we do that," you say. "We get them together and have the officers give them pep talks. That's what you mean, isn't it?"

No, not quite. You may get a group enthused with such a meeting, but you do not train the members to do the job with pep talks. That's why the training meeting is different from the ordinary meeting. You do more than speak about the job and ask the group to please go out and do it. Such a meeting leaves them a bit in the dark as to how. They go away, saying, "I'm willing," but wondering.

The training meeting supplies the answers to that question, "How?" It tells the group how to do it, it shows them how, but it goes even further than that. When you have told a group and have shown them, you have not run a training meeting. For how do you know what they have

270

retained? After your telling and showing, do they know what they are to do and how to do it? So in the training meeting you supply some kind of practice that tells you whether or not the group understands what you want it to do. If their practice demonstrates that they do not understand, you need a fourth part of your meeting that corrects and shows how to do the job right.

In the training meeting you need four steps:

1. Telling
2. Showing
3. Practice
4. Correction

TWO SUGGESTIONS ON TRAINING MEETINGS

THE SMALL GROUP IS BETTER

If you plan to do much training in a meeting it is best to have a small group. The important part of the training meeting is that third step, the practice to check on what they have learned. If you have a group that is too large, you can't let everybody practice. Let's say that you have sixty members who are going to work on this project of soliciting funds. You will do a better training job if you break up the group into three groups of twenty and run three meetings. With the smaller group you will be able to let each member practice. You say, "That means I have to run three meetings instead of one." That's right, but you want to raise this money, don't you?

YOU NEED MORE TIME

You need more time for a training meeting than you do for this "Go out and get 'em" type of meeting. The time is taken up by the practice part of the session. You can't rush that, you want to give each worker some opportunity to practice. He'll tackle the job with more assurance if he has had that time to practice. And he will do his work better. A number of suggestions for giving every worker a chance to practice are given on page 276.

HOW TO PUT ON A TRAINING MEETING

Let's say that your club is putting on a drive to raise funds for a building. Let's further assume that this is tied in with a church so that you know your prospects. You plan to ask your church members to pledge money to this fund. Now how do you run a training meeting for the members who are to go out and solicit funds?

Your Two Needs. You need two things before you get the group together for this meeting. First, you need a story for the group to tell, and second, you need a plan for telling that story. Thus, if your meeting is going to be a success, you have to do some planning before the meeting.

The Meeting Objective. With your sales story, and the plan for telling the story worked out, you have your meeting objective. Your purpose is to teach your workers to tell that story in the way you want it told. You know what you want the worker to say, and you know how you want him to say it. Think back to the meetings for workers on fund-raising drives that you have attended. How many of them have had such an objective? Most were to pep them up, weren't they? But in a training meeting your job is to teach the story, and your meeting format must be arranged to do what you want to do.

YOUR MEETING PATTERN

If I had to run such a meeting tomorrow, I would follow this pattern:

STEP ONE: The Telling: The trainer tells the group about the story and the plan for telling it. He then tells the story to the workers, just as if he were soliciting them.

STEP TWO: The Showing: The trainer has one man from the audience make the solicitation to him. This is a solicitation that the two have rehearsed. It shows the workers how the average man should do the solicitation.

STEP THREE: The Checking: The trainer now drills the group in telling the story. Suggestions for drills are given on page 276.

STEP FOUR: The Correction and Assurance: The trainer makes any corrections that are needed. He assures the group that if they follow this plan, if they tell the story in this way, their work will be easier and they will get larger pledges.

Let's analyze each of these steps more fully.

STEP ONE: THE TELLING

There are four parts to this part of the meeting:

(*a*) The trainer explains the objective of the meeting.

(*b*) He explains there is a sales story to tell and a plan for telling it.

(*c*) He sells the group on wanting to tell the story in the way he wants it told.

(*d*) He demonstrates how to tell the story.

NOTES ON THESE FOUR PARTS

The Objective. The objective of this meeting is to teach the workers to tell a better story.

The Story and Plan for Telling It. Because the story told by the workers is so important, that story has been written out and a plan for telling it has been worked up. The worker is going to get both today, and he is going to get a chance to practice telling that story in the way suggested.

The Sell on Wanting to Tell a Better Story. We all know that a worker won't learn because the trainer wants him to. He has to be shown why it is to his interest to learn. Now why should the average fund worker want to do a better job? Of course he is interested or he wouldn't be working. But his is a general interest. If the quota isn't made, he will not worry too much. He will take the cards you give him, he will try to see the people, he'll get the cards back to you. But enthusiasm for the job? He just doesn't have it. This doesn't describe all of the workers, just most of them. I can see you nodding your head.

But no worker wants to go about a job backwards. If there is an easier way to do it, he would like to know about that way. No worker wants to be thought dumb. Not one of them wants members he solicits to report, "The guy that called on me couldn't give me one reason why I should give more." They want to be thought of as good solicitors, as competent. Don't we all?

So you start your meeting by selling the group on why they should want to do better. Here are some thoughts you might work into this sell part of the meeting. The good story well told—

> Makes the job easier.
>
> Gets more agreement from prospects.
>
> Gives the worker assurance that he is working in the most effective way.
>
> Gives the prospect the impression that the worker is a highly intelligent, competent individual.

As you look over that list you can see that any worker would want any of those things. Perhaps the list might not fit your case exactly, but your appeals can be similar. If you are not sure just what will sell your workers on wanting to do a better job, you might try to get them to tell you. Just recently I saw a trainer run a discussion with the workers to determine and get agreement on why it paid them to work effectively. The leader started his discussion with the question, "Why should it pay a worker to tell a good story?" The trainer had a blackboard and when a reason was given he wrote it on the board. In time he had five or six reasons, all good and all applying to this group. In this case the trainer was allowing the listeners to sell themselves. This sell is important to the trainer. His workers will not try to tell his story unless they can see what doing it his way means to them.

The Trainer's Demonstration. The trainer now tells the story to the group, just as if he is soliciting their pledge. He asks them to note how easy it is to tell this story, he asks them to note how logically it flows from point to point, how it covers all the points. He needs some sell on this story, too. He explains that they do not need to memorize the story, that if they will just follow the outline they will get the results they want.

STEP TWO: THE SHOWING

THE TRAINER DEMONSTRATES HOW ANOTHER CAN TELL THE STORY

This is the showing part of the meeting. The group may not accept the fact that the story is easy to tell when they hear the trainer tell it. He is an expert. He wrote it. Of course, he can tell it. But when one of the group is brought up from the audience and tells the story, the others are inclined to say, "If that fellow can do it, I can too." What do you need for this part of the meeting? You need

(*a*) A worker who is willing. Preferably this should be

a member who is not a sales type or a public speaker. We'll call him the stooge.

(*b*) A three- to five-minute dialogue to be used between the stooge and the trainer. This demonstration will go much better if the dialogue is worked out and rehearsed. I suggest that both speak, because if the stooge does all of the speaking he will be making a speech. You don't want the workers to make a speech. The type of dialogue suggested is illustrated on page 285.

STEP THREE: THE CHECKING

When the stooge has finished his demonstration, the trainer passes out the tools the worker is to use in the solicitation. At this point he can do a number of things to check on how much the workers have learned. Here are some suggestions. He can—

1. *Ask Another to Demonstrate.* The trainer has had a prepared stooge do the demonstration. Now he asks if one of the audience would like to try it. It may require some persuasion to get a worker to come up cold and try the pitch, but it is probably the best check on learning that the trainer can make. He might ask a few men before the meeting, "Watch carefully while Stooge does this demonstration, for I want you to come up after he is finished and do it." Before the volunteer starts, the trainer makes it

"This doesn't show the comparison as well as I'd like."

clear that the first man was prepared, but that this second is not.

2. *The Quiz.* The trainer starts the quiz with the question, "What do you say first?" When he gets an answer, he asks, "Why do you say that?" The same procedure is followed until the entire solicitation is covered.

3. *Drill the Group.* This is similar to the quiz except that the group answers the trainer's questions together. He asks, "What do you say first?" The group answers. He asks them to speak louder, please. They repeat the answer, louder. He checks to see that all are taking part in the answers. If he finds that some are not, he asks one of the silent ones to repeat the answer. A similar drill can be made by getting the group to read the story together. After he has gone through the presentation, he may ask one of the group to volunteer to show how the solicitation should be done. With some coaxing he will usually be able to get one member to try. I have seen trainers take a group through such solicitations three times.

4. *Break into Threes.* While I suggest groups of no more than twenty for the training meeting, when the trainer has a large group he can follow the plan of breaking the group into units of three. He assigns one man to act as a coach, the second to act as the solicitor, the third to be the prospective giver. The solicitor makes his presentation, the coach makes his suggestions. The solicitor tries it again. Again there are suggestions. Now the three change places, the donor becomes the solicitor. Again the suggestions from the coach, again the repeat performance. Next the coach does the solicitation. Again the comments. With this much rehearsal, the trainer can have the best of each group give a demonstration. When the groups have finished the rehearsals, he asks each group to vote on which was the best

of his group at giving the presentation. He can then ask
these best performers to give presentations. There may not
be time for all of them to show off but if he has even three
or four do it, he demonstrates how, with a little work,
all of them can get themselves a polished presentation.

5. *The Contest.* One good way to get the group to study
and rehearse this kind of story is a presentation contest.
Let's say the trainer holds one meeting and explains the
story that is to be told, and the plan for telling. He may
drill the group in the telling of the story. During the meeting he breaks the workers up into groups of three, and assigns them the task of studying and rehearsing the presentation together, and assigning one of the group to entering
the contest. Now he puts on a second meeting, perhaps
one week later. At this meeting he stages a presentation
contest. The rules of the contest specify that the man making the presentation gets two or three minutes and that he
has to cover certain points. Further there are no limits on
what the man can do. After all of the contestants have
made their presentations, the listeners vote on which was
best. A small prize or trophy is then given to the winners.

This contest has a number of advantages. First, you have
a device that gets every one of your workers to study the
story you want them to tell. Second, each of your workers
hears a large number of workers tell the story. This repetition helps every listener remember the points. Third, the
listeners are impressed with the ease with which the story
is learned. The contestants demonstrate what a worker can
do with the story if he will take time to study and rehearse.
Of course, the contest takes time, but all thorough training
takes time. It will pay any group planning such a fund or
membership drive to take the time to train the workers
thoroughly.

THE THIRD STEP IS IMPORTANT

Any effort you make to drill your workers on the story they tell will pay off in the work they do. You have to remember that most of the workers have little training in persuasion. You'll find some persons of the sales type that are good at it, and like to do this type of work. But most of your workers are doing it as a duty that they would rather duck. They don't like to ask friends or strangers for money, or to join clubs. This type welcomes any help you can give them, and the drill on how to do the job is a help that they recognize. One chairman of a drive of this sort told me, "My solicitors are busy people. I can't ask them to spend the time to take this training." He felt that his workers did not have the time. Because he didn't want to impose on the time of these important people, the training meetings were made optional. But they were described and sold in the notice that announced the times. The chairman was surprised at the turnout. "I believe it is better than I get at my other meetings," he told me.

Don't assume that your workers do not want this kind of help. Perhaps they have had enough of the pep-talk type of meeting. Why not try training them next time? But remember that you cannot be sure that you have done any training in your meeting until you have run some sort of check that determines what the group has learned. They must learn or you haven't done any training.

Trainers have a slogan, "If the learner hasn't learned, the trainer hasn't taught." If your fund-raising or membership solicitors are not getting the results, perhaps it's because you haven't taught them how.

STEP FOUR: THE CORRECTION AND ASSURANCE

In the usual training meeting there would be some correction. This may be a bit touchy to handle with workers in a fund-raising drive such as we are discussing. But you will note that most of the devices suggested for checking on how well the worker has learned have some self-correction worked into them. For instance, if I see three or four workers do the presentation correctly, is it not likely that I will see an error that I might be making? Most workers do not resent suggestions for improvement, but they might not like to hear these suggestions in front of a group. A skilled trainer handles such corrections under this formula. He—

First, compliments the worker on something he has done well.

Second, gets the worker to tell the trainer what the worker has done wrong.

Third, gets the worker to do the task correctly.

Fourth, gets the worker's agreement that the right way is the easy way and that the worker will have no trouble in telling the story correctly.

It might be difficult to handle the first three steps in a meeting with workers on a fund drive, but the trainer can bear down on that fourth step. One effective way is to assure the group that if they will try this method of presentation three times, they will see how well it works, and they

"*Let's give the old girl a big hand.*"

will then continue to follow the plan because it is easier, and it gets better results. If the worker has been drilled enough in telling the story, he will see this advantage to him. But in so many training meetings you will not be able to do an adequate correction job. Thus the assurance is important. Once the workers start using your story, they will see how well it works, and they will use the story with all prospects. Thus, if you can get them to agree to use the story on their first contacts, they will go on using it.

HOW TRAINING MEETINGS WERE SET UP FOR A UNITED APPEAL CAMPAIGN

[NOTE: This example is given to show how such a problem was handled. The plan followed the steps outlined earlier in this chapter.]

The local United Appeal Group had to raise its budget because the agencies supported found that rising costs made it impossible to operate on the amounts allotted to them. The chairman of the fund came to the local Sales Executives Club and asked for help. "What can we do to help?" the club people asked.

"Can't you work up a training activity to train our workers so that they will do a better job of soliciting?" the chairman asked.

The club decided to see what could be done. First, a sales story was developed; second, a plan for telling the story. The story and plan were approved by the United Appeal people. Two pieces were printed—one, a simple guide for the worker to use with the prospect; and two, a small card that told the worker how to use the guide. Next a series of meetings was set up to train the workers to tell the story as the plan suggested it should be told.

THE STORY

The story was built on the slogan, "It costs more to do as much." After the introductions, these were the first words the worker was to say to the prospective donor. The slogan was printed on the first page of the solicitor's guide.

His next words were, "You agree to that, don't you? It costs more to run your home. It costs more to run your office, more to run anything."

When the prospect agreed, the worker said, "That's what the agencies supported by U.A. find too. Not to do more or to add frills, but to continue what they are now doing, they need more money. That's why U.A. must ask for more this year. It's why I am asking you to make your pledge for a little more this year."

Now the worker was taught to open the little folder and show the prospect a list of the agencies that were supported by U.A. He said, "Here is the list of agencies that U.A. supports. Probably you're more interested in some of them than in others. Which ones are you most interested in?"

The prospect now told the worker which agencies on the list he had an interest in. This was to get the prospect to talk, and when the prospect started talking he was helping the worker sell a larger contribution.

Next the worker pointed out that there were nineteen agencies, and he said, "If you divide your contribution by nineteen, you will realize how little there is for each agency."

The worker now stated that the agencies were needed, that all did useful work, that this method of giving was the American way, that we agreed we wanted to take care of our own community rather than ask the government to do it.

He then asked, "You agree to that, don't you?"

Then the guide helped him ask for that larger contribution. It said, "Because it costs more to do as much, won't you make your contribution for more this year?"

THE MEETING

The training meeting called for the use of two of the members of the Sales Executives Club—one to act as the trainer, the other to make the presentation to show how it should be done. The trainer used a set of charts. Let's go through the charts with him.

Chart One read: START WITH A PAT ON THE BACK.

As he turned this chart the trainer complimented the group on how well they had handled this solicitation in the past. He asked this question, "If you have done such a good job in the past, why have the powers that be asked the Sales Executives Club to come in and run these training meetings?

"That was the question that the Sales Executives Club asked the Chairman when he approached it about handling these training meetings. The Sales Executives wondered too. But the chairman told them this—"

Chart Two: WHY S.E.C.?

1. Make the Job Easier for the Worker.
2. Get More Money.

The trainer pointed out that no one could quarrel with those two objectives. Then he mentioned a third. While the workers in the meeting might all be top salesmen, there were many workers that needed such training. Now he said, "There's a truism in selling that all a salesman needs to supply is—"

Chart Three: A WILLINGNESS TO WORK.

He said, "You workers have that. You signed up to work on this job. You have come here today. You are willing to work. But there is another part of that sales truism. When the salesman supplies that willingness to work, it is the boss's job to teach him to work right. You are willing to work, but it is the job of the managers of this campaign to teach you to work right. Now, just what is working right?"

Chart Four: IS IT TO GET A PLEDGE CARD SIGNED?

The trainer says, "Is that the job? Well, surely it is a part of it. You have to go see the donor, and you have to get him to sign his card. But the U.A. needs more money. So your job is a little bit more than what you see on this chart. You want him to sign his pledge, yes, but—"

Chart Five: YOU WANT HIM TO SIGN THAT PLEDGE FOR MORE.

The Trainer says, "That's your job in this drive. You want the card signed, but you want him to pledge a little more than he gave last year. We all agree to that, don't we? If everybody signs for what they gave last year, we will not reach the goal we set out to reach. So we must ask for more. Now, how will we do that, and what have your U.A. officers provided for you? Well, if I were sending out a sales

"When the cycle reaches this point, watch out."

force tomorrow to see the people named on your cards, and those salesmen were to ask those people to sign their cards for more, I would want two things for those salesmen."

Chart Six: THE TWO THINGS.

1. A Sales Story.
2. A Plan for Telling That Story.

The Trainer says, "Now, that's what the U.A. and the Sales Executives have worked out for you."

NOTE: The trainer now shows the worker's guide and the plan for telling the story. He then goes through the solicitation, telling the group what to say, what to do, and what to ask the prospect to do.

THE DEMONSTRATION BY THE STOOGE

To show how the job should be done, the trainer asks a member of the audience to come up and solicit him. The two now go through this dialogue:

Stooge–Trainer Dialogue for U.A. Meeting

STOOGE: Hello, Mr. Trainer, I've got your card here on the U.A. drive.

TRAINER: That's fine, Dick. Let me have it and I'll sign it.

STOOGE: I'm glad to know you're willing, Mr. Trainer. But see that headline on this little folder, "It costs more to do as much"? You agree to that, don't you?

TRAINER: Yes, it sure does, Dick.

STOOGE: It costs more to run your office. It costs more to run your home. It costs more to do anything you do. Isn't that right?

TRAINER: Yes, I agree to that.

STOOGE: That is the position the United Appeal agencies find themselves in this year. It costs more to do everything they do. So to do just what they are doing, not to add any frills, or add any help, but just to continue what they are doing, they have to ask for more money this year. That sounds reasonable, doesn't it?

TRAINER: Yes, I guess it does.

STOOGE: [Opens folder.] Just to refresh your memory—here are the nineteen agencies which are helped by your U.A. contribution. Look over that list, Mr. Trainer. Which ones would you say you are most interested in?

TRAINER: Well, I like the Red Cross, of course, and both those Scouts, and those Y's I like. The Friendly House, and St. Vincent de Paul. I can go for every one of those.

STOOGE: Well, that is interesting. This afternoon I was talking to a man who was interested in four of the agencies and he didn't mention the same ones you did. I ran into another today who was interested in just one of them— the Boy Scouts. You know, the nineteen agencies touch the interests of about every person in town. Isn't that so?

TRAINER: I guess it is.

STOOGE: Don't you agree that it is a good idea to have one contribution help all the nineteen agencies?

TRAINER: It's sure a lot better than having nineteen people coming in here and asking for contributions.

STOOGE: I thought you would agree to that. You agree, too, that this is the American way, that we want to do this job ourselves, that we don't want the government to step in and take over these agencies? Isn't that right?

TRAINER: Yes, the government's doing too much now.

STOOGE: Well, since everything costs more, since it costs more to run your home, your office, your store—it stands to reason that it costs more to run these agencies, too, doesn't it?

TRAINER: I guess I could go along with you on that.

STOOGE: Well, then considering that everything costs more, here is your card to sign. Won't you make your pledge for a little more this year?

TRAINER: Well, Dick, what you say is fine, but I have been giving them a hundred bucks each year and I think that's a mighty nice contribution. Don't you?

STOOGE: I certainly do. How long have you been giving that hundred dollars, Mr. Trainer?

TRAINER: Well, I would say for the last three or four years. Whenever they started this U.A. thing.

STOOGE: Well, we just agreed that everything costs more than it did last year or the year before. If a hundred dollars was enough when this U.A. thing started, it wouldn't be quite enough today, would it?

TRAINER: But that's a mighty nice contribution, Dick, don't you think?

STOOGE: [Turns to back page of folder.] Mr. Trainer, you want every kid in the country to have a chance at scouting, don't you?

TRAINER: Yes.

STOOGE: You want every kid to have the fun of camping, don't you?

TRAINER: Yes.

STOOGE: You don't want to say, "Look kids, you can't have a camp, or you can't join the Scouts, because the community can't afford it." You want to tell those kids they can have camps, and scouting, and health agencies, don't you?

TRAINER: Sure, I do.

STOOGE: Now, Mr. Trainer, I know you do. What good American wouldn't? But to keep them going, not to expand nor to add services, the agencies need more help from you. So, put a little more on that pledge card this year, won't you?

TRAINER: O.K., Dick, let me have that card.

The trainer next asks for a hand from the audience for the man who made the presentation. He asks such questions as, "That went well, didn't it?" "Didn't it seem logical?"

He is trying to get agreement from the group that this is a good way to make the solicitation.

THE DRILL AND ASSURANCE

The trainer now drilled the group in what they were to say. He asked one man to tell what he was to say first. Then he asked another what to say next. In this way he went through the entire presentation. When one did not get the answer right, he asked another, then went back to the one that missed and asked him if he now had it right.

At the end of this drill the trainer assured the group that the presentation should make the job easier for all of them. He urged them to try it once, to see how it worked. One may say, "But this donor is a friend of mine; I don't need to go through all of this with him."

The trainer agrees that the worker may feel this way about the friend. "But try it with him anyway, won't you? Tell him that I said you were supposed to do it with him, too. But do it, anyway, will you? You'll find that this sales approach will work with either friend or stranger."

THE FOLLOW-UP

Nine training meetings were held. The pattern described here was followed in each. In all, about three hundred workers attended the meetings. Some of these were supervisors and they were urged to train their workers to use this plan of solicitation. The quota was about $275,000.

This was an increase of about 10 per cent over the preceding year. The workers using the story exceeded the increased quota by about $15,000. Surely some of this increase was due to training the solicitors to ask for a larger donation from each donor.

TRAINED WORKERS DO BETTER

If you hired a boy to paint a fence, you probably would give him complete instructions on how to do it. You would probably watch him as he started, you might take the brush and show him how to run on the paint. You would show him where to start, and how to work. If you hired a man to run an expensive machine you would spend more time on his training. But you'll send a member out to collect funds without any training. You feel, just because he can live and breathe and is half willing, that he can do the job for you. Well, perhaps he can. Many membership drives and fund-raising operations are run like that, and get results. But if you want to do the job right, and get all you can from the drive, stage a number of training meetings. They might help you get more members, or more money, or whatever it is you want. But don't think you can do as well with pep talks. Everybody likes them, but they give little help to the worker. He wants some "how," and the only way you can give him that is to train him.

Now let's discuss meeting follow-up.

19 / Meeting Follow-up

Perhaps you don't feel that you need any follow-up of your meetings. Some clubs don't. But then many of the luncheon clubs send me copies of the club publication they mail out to members reporting on the last meeting and urging members to be sure and attend the next. They tell the absent brethren what they missed by not hearing Hegarty, but they also remind them that this next attraction will be better. Any such activity holds up interest in the club.

In a business meeting you may want that follow-up. Let's say that the meeting was called to explain a plan. O.K., now you want to determine if the group understood the plan. Have they tried to use it? What were the results? Many times, with such a meeting, the best follow-up is another meeting. You told the group about the plan in the first, now a week later you have another meeting to iron out any misunderstandings. It has been using the plan for one week. What questions do the listeners have now?

Well, if you feel that you need follow-up, here are some suggestions:

290

HOW TO FOLLOW UP

1. *What's the Objective?* This is the first step in any follow-up. What are you trying to do? Get publicity for the club that will attract new members? Keep the old members interested? What? Define your objective first, and then lay out your plans to attain the objective.

2. *Article in Newspaper.* That article in the newspaper will be read by most everybody in town. I know that, because every time my name appears in the local *News Journal*, friends mention it to me. When it appears in a paper out of town, some friend will usually clip it out and mail it to me. If it is publicity the club wants, arrange to have that follow-up article in the paper. Some clubs hire a reporter from the local paper to handle this for them. Others have a member who knows how to do it. Others invite the editor or a reporter to the meeting. If you can't afford the reporter and don't have a member who knows how to do the job and can't afford the free meal for the reporter, call on the local editor and ask him how to go about it. Any story in the paper makes the member who didn't attend feel that he missed something.

3. *The Club News.* Some of the club publications write up the speaker's talk at length. Others say that he had them rolling in the aisles. But the club news is a good means of follow-up. Too many of these publications look as though they were done hurriedly by a fellow who wasn't much interested in the job. If you will think of what you want to do in this follow-up and slant the copy in the *News* at that objective, you'll get more results from the publication.

4. *Thanks to the Speaker.* This is a must. You invited this man, and even if you paid him, you should still thank him for his time and effort. I have had as many as three

letters, each from different officers, after I have spoken
to a group. It doesn't hurt your club one bit to set up that
routine. You don't have to tell the speaker that he was the
best so far this year. One club I know has a courtesy committee that handles this thank-you chore. If you assign
four men to thank the speaker, he will get at least two letters showing the club's appreciation. And members of the
club are put to work.

5. *Notes to a Few.* One president I know writes a note
to a few of the members who heard the talk asking for
opinions on the speaker and his subject. In doing this the
chairman is sticking his neck out, but he is using the speech
of the day to build interest in the club.

6. *The Quiz Survey.* Another group sends out a quiz survey twice each year. The member is asked to answer a
number of questions about the latest speakers and to give

"Just two things to remember."

any suggestions for subjects that he would like to have
covered by future speakers. This gives the membership a
feeling that they are helping run the program of the club.

7. *The Review.* You might assign one member to take
three minutes and review the speech of the last speaker.
This will give the members who did not attend an idea
of the kind of meeting they missed. Another type of review might bring all of the officers of the club together

to review the past four or five programs. Each officer might be given the job of talking to a number of members before the meeting so that their discussion would reflect the thinking of a larger segment of the club membership.

8. *The Discussion.* I attended a club meeting recently and the speaker did not show up. When the time came for the speaker the chairman explained the dilemma and then led a discussion on the programs that the club had put on in the past few months. A lively discussion went on for much longer than the speaker would have taken. The chairman had prepared for the discussion and he came up with some good ideas on what he might do to produce programs that his members liked.

9. *Take-home Material.* This could be a folder or a few mimeographed sheets that explain the plan the meeting discussed. Let's say you made up a questionnaire that was given to each listener. You asked him to take it home, to read the questions, and after a night's sleep check to find out how many he felt he could answer. A second follow-up might furnish the correct answers for the questions.

10. *The Testimony Session.* Let's say that in your meeting you explained an idea. In your next you ask one or more of the members to explain how they used the idea. This will work in the fund-raising meeting. The meeting explained how they were to approach a prospect. Now let some members who have used the plan explain how they used the idea. You might select any idea expressed by a speaker for this testimony. In one of my speeches I tell the group how they can loosen the muscles of their faces to bring sparkle to their smiles. One president wrote me not long ago, "Ed, I used that idea of yours and at our meeting last week, I asked if any of the other club members had. Three hands went up, and I asked those men to explain

how they had used the idea. They did, and we had a
lively few minutes." Remember, you can't miss when you
let the listeners brag about something they have done. I
spoke to a management group not long ago, and the top
executive offered a prize for the best letter by one of the
supervisors on the use of an idea I presented to them.

11. *The Notes Taken.* Recently a club president sent
me a club publication and the story on my remarks was
headed, "Here are the notes Charlie Whosis took on Ed
Hegarty's speech." He had done a good job, and the story
was quite complete. In the training session you might offer
a prize for the best set of notes taken. If you want notes,
though, you had better provide a notebook and a writing
surface. You'll have to give the group enough time to write
the notes, and it is a good idea to check to see that they
are writing. You might stop and ask, "What have you written on that, Joe?" It's helpful, too, to call attention to points.
When I am explaining a plan to a group, I say at times, "Be
sure to write this down." Most of the listeners obey. Why,
I don't know. It's a good idea, too, to sell the group on why
they should take notes. If you want the listeners to take
notes, here are some suggestions to pass on to the group:

(*a*) Write so you can read it.

(*b*) Write enough so you know what you mean.

(*c*) Look at the notes before too long.

(*d*) Write out fully later.

12. *Set Up a Committee.* You might form a committee
to follow up on the meetings. This group could analyze
each program and see what could be done on follow-up.
Every group has objectives and this committee could work
up plans to make the follow-up help do what your club
wanted to do.

13. *Try a Quiz.* If you are explaining a plan, you might

have a quiz at the end of the meeting. The answers will tell you whether or not the meeting explained the plan.

14. *The Second Meeting.* This is of course the best follow-up. If you are trying to train a group to do anything, you are not going to do the job in one meeting, no matter how simple the task. Training is a continuous job. Most of the suggestions given here could be aided by a follow-up meeting discussing the same subject. Explain the plan today, then bring the group back in a week and let them tell you how the plan is working.

15. *Check the Supervisors.* This works in the business meeting. Ask what the supervisors thought, or have them check the workers who attended the meeting. Perhaps the subject matter was of little interest to either group. It may be that you did not explain why the matter was important to them.

IT PAYS TO CHECK

Your club may seem to be running beautifully. The meetings start on time, they end on time, you get out a full attendance. But there's a reason why it is running well. Wouldn't it be a good idea to check on why? Then when you find out, do more of the same.

If the group is creaking along, and attendance is falling off, you might be more inclined to check on why. But check and check and check. Use all of the means you know. You have known clubs that were the liveliest organizations in town one year, and then a year or two later were struggling to keep going. Yes, it can happen to your group. You can get better, and you can get worse. So check constantly. It pays.

20 / Some Meeting "Don'ts"

Most of these "Don'ts" have been mentioned at least once in this book. Still, if you are putting on a meeting tomorrow and don't have time to read the entire book, you might run through these cautions, and have yourself a better meeting. You might think of these "Don'ts" as a fast course in running meetings.

PLANNING

1. DON'T start without a plan. Get something down on paper. A list of what is going to happen is a start, an outline is better, a synopsis best. The more you have written down, the better meeting you will have.

2. DON'T fail to check. If something goes wrong—the projector isn't ready, there's no electricity to run it—it is not the other fellow's fault. It's yours. Check every detail before you start.

3. DON'T fail to inform the speaker. Don't let a speaker get up on his feet to start talking without telling him how long he has. If you have a special adjournment time, tell him.

296

4. DON'T fail to cover off everybody. Tell everyone on the program what his job is, how much time there is, and give him any other help he needs to do a good performance for you.

5. DON'T fail to make a list of speakers. When you hear that a speaker has appeared before a club and that he is good, write down his name and his address and get some data on how you go about getting him for your club.

6. DON'T neglect your own club as a source of speaking talent. Check through that membership list and see what possibilities you have.

PROMOTING THE MEETING

7. DON'T fail to mail out notices on time. Too often the club notice gets to the member the day of the meeting. He doesn't have time to make arrangements to be there. Give him time. If you have a system of sending two notices, you are much better off.

8. DON'T neglect to telephone. This is a grand way to help get out the crowd. Put some of your members to work on the telephone and you will build up your attendance every time.

9. DON'T neglect the personal. A special personal mail follow-up can do a lot to bring out people for you. If you write just a short personal note on the regular notice, that too will help.

THE MEETING ROOM

10. DON'T take just any room. If your meeting is to be held in the hotel, check to see what rooms they have. Don't pick a poor room if there is a better one available.

11. DON'T set up so that the audience can see the door. Put the door behind the audience.

12. DON'T neglect the platform. Don't stand the speaker on the floor even if he is seven feet tall. Put him on a platform and he will do a better speaking job for you.

13. DON'T fail to check the speaker's aids. If the speaker is using some visual aids, check to see that they can be seen.

14. DON'T use hard chairs. Try to get the best chairs the hotel has available.

15. DON'T crowd the seating. Think of a man's width and move the chairs far enough apart so the men can sit comfortably next to one another.

"I can hear you, but I can't see you."

16. DON'T fail to check the P.A. system. Such a system out of order can foul up any meeting.

17. DON'T try to set up a projector and screen while the meeting is going on. Call a recess while you do it.

18. DON'T place the screen for slides or movies too low. The heads in the front will shut off the view. Check the set-up.

19. DON'T let listeners sit with wraps on their laps. Give them a place to check.

20. DON'T try to show exhibits in a room that is too dark. Use spotlights.

21. DON'T forget fresh air. Some ventilation is needed. Try to see what you can do.

22. DON'T hunt for the light switch when the speaker wants the room darkened. Know where it is. Assign someone to turn it on and turn it off.

23. DON'T blow fuses. Don't let the speaker try to use

electrical aids that won't work in the room you are using. Know the voltage and the current available. Tell him what you have.

24. DON'T fight noise. Keep out of a room in a noisy corner if you can get anything better. Try for quiet.

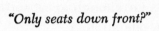

"Only seats down front?"

25. DON'T allow the front seats to be empty. Rope off the back. Use ushers. But fill the front seats.

PROGRAMMING

26. DON'T let the meeting end on a low note. Wind it up with a bang, even if you have to ask the brothers to sing the old club song.

27. DON'T follow a hot-shot speaker with one not so hot.

28. DON'T forget the idea of build-up. Start with the good, then the better, then the best. That's the idea.

29. DON'T follow an inspirational speaker with a number of routine announcements.

30. DON'T forget the sell. Sell the club, the program, everything the club does.

RUNNING THE MEETING

31. DON'T let the club business cut into the speaker's time.

32. DON'T fail to start on time.

33. DON'T run overtime if you can help it.

34. DON'T keep looking at your watch.

35. DON'T give the listeners the impression that you don't know what comes next.

36. DON'T make a meeting wait. Fill in the time.

37. DON'T give the impression that you feel this meeting is in a rush to get finished. Relax.

38. DON'T offer the audience a choice of whether to take a recess now, or skip it; to adjourn now, or go on and finish. You decide.

"What will we do now, girls?"

39. DON'T call a five-minute recess for a large group. It's not enough time.

40. DON'T rush your stretches or recesses. Relax. The rest may be more important than your speakers.

41. DON'T let the audience know you are signaling the speaker that he is running overtime.

42. DON'T set up a disturbance by passing out anything while a speaker is speaking.

43. DON'T let a disturbance bother your guest speaker without doing something about it.

THE GUEST SPEAKER

44. DON'T forget the guest speaker. Keep in touch with him, give him the information he needs, have a brother

meet him at the train, make him welcome, give him whatever assistance he needs, etc., etc., etc.

WHEN YOU'RE THE CHAIRMAN

45. DON'T read all of the speaker's introduction. Read the
vital statistics only. Tell the group something about him in
your own words.

46. DON'T tell stories. Don't tell a funny story about the
speaker.

47. DON'T say, "Without further ado—." It's been said
before, honest.

48. DON'T mention time, ever.

49. DON'T sit behind the speaker soaking up some of his
spotlight.

50. DON'T sound off on your own social or political views.

51. DON'T leave the meeting room after you have introduced the speaker.

52. DON'T call others out, or start a conference where the
group can watch.

53. DON'T give the impression that you are not listening
to the speaker.

54. DON'T try to help the speaker with his speaking aids
unless he asks you.

"Would you rather have a recess now?"

55. DON'T ask, "Are there any questions?" and indicate by your manner that you'll shoot the first man that asks one.

56. DON'T ask for questions without planning what you want. Plant a few with your friends in the audience.

57. DON'T ask for questions and then quickly say, "Mr. Ajax, you must have covered the subject fully for there are no questions."

58. DON'T fail to caution the brothers with whom you have planted questions, "Don't read this."

59. DON'T fail to repeat any question that is asked.

60. DON'T argue with the speaker over anything he says.

61. DON'T fail to thank the speaker, adequately.

WHEN YOU HAVE TO DO SOME SPEAKING

62. DON'T fail to speak loud enough. Speak louder than you feel you need to, and you'll be about right.

63. DON'T let the microphone fool you. Don't whisper into it. Move back a bit and sound off.

64. DON'T hunt for things you want to show.

65. DON'T hunt through your notes for that poem to quote. It isn't that important.

66. DON'T promise to cover something later. The audience wants to go home before that.

"We have to stand on our own two feet."

67. DON'T lean on a lectern, a table, or anything. Stand up and give out.

68. DON'T forget you're supposed to be an expert. That's why you are speaking.

69. DON'T let the chairman sit behind you. Give him a job to do for you, a job he must sit in the audience to do.

70. DON'T have an assistant working behind you, or in the audience while you speak.

71. DON'T have anything moving behind you.

72. DON'T talk from a head table if you can possibly avoid it.

73. DON'T try to compete with any disturbance. Stop while the waiter comes into the room, the fire trucks go by, etc.

74. DON'T worry about your clothes, tug at your necktie, try to button that inside button on your double-breasted coat, heist up your pants. Leave them alone.

75. DON'T carry a large batch of notes up to the lectern. You scare the listeners with them.

76. DON'T make your notes too apparent. You might place them on the lectern before you are called upon.

77. DON'T place your notes behind you so that you have to turn your back to the audience to look at them.

78. DON'T make your notes so complete that you will be tempted to read them.

79. DON'T fail to write your notes large enough for you to see without stooping over.

80. DON'T carry your notes in one hand, shifting from one hand to the other, if you must carry them.

81. DON'T threaten the audience with your notes.

82. DON'T pick up your notes, lay them down, and pick them up again. Make up your mind.

83. DON'T fumble through your notes hunting for that bon mot. Let it lie.

84. DON'T stop speaking to study your notes.

WHEN YOU USE VISUALS

85. DON'T fail to check on whether or not the visuals can be seen. There is little sense in showing anything that the audience can't see.

86. DON'T use a visual with type so small that the listeners can't read.

87. DON'T fail to make any charts large enough so that they can be seen from any part of the room.

"I wish you could see this."

88. DON'T place any visual so low that the heads of those in the front seats will block the view of those in the back.

89. DON'T fail to get enough light on the visual so that it can be seen.

90. DON'T stand in front of the visual when you try to show it. Practice using it so that you do not hide the visual from the audience.

91. DON'T stand so that your shadow falls on the visual when you use a spotlight.

92. DON'T fail to keep the visual covered until you are

ready to show it. No sense having the listeners trying to figure it out.

93. DON'T make so many notes in pencil on your charts that they look untidy.

94. DON'T fail to read everything that is on a chart when you show it. The audience will do that, why not you?

95. DON'T stop to study a chart when you first show it.

96. DON'T fail to practice using any visual you plan to use.

97. DON'T talk to the visual. It can't hear you. Speak to the listeners.

98. DON'T turn back through a set of charts to find some illustration that you missed. Ever see anyone do this gracefully?

99. DON'T fail to tell the group what you want them to see in the visual, or explain the point it is helping you to make. You are explaining points, not visuals.

100. DON'T use a partner to turn a set of charts for you. He must feel like a dummy up there turning charts, mustn't he?

WHEN YOU USE SLIDES TO ILLUSTRATE YOUR TALK

101. DON'T call, "Next slide, please." Work out some signal with the operator. A cricket, a light signal, a word signal does the job smoother. You can give the operator a marked copy of the manuscript, although you'll have trouble if you get off your script.

102. DON'T use an operator with a small group. Run the machine yourself.

103. DON'T assume, because you are using slides, that you need a darkened room. Try showing the slides with the lights on, at least partially.

104. DON'T let the clumsiness of the operator bother you. Carry on as if you expected operators to be all thumbs. Most of them are.

105. DON'T deprecate your slides, apologize for using them, or announce that you are going to run through a number of slides quickly. If you want to run fast, do it without mention. You're running this show.

106. DON'T say, "This is my next to last slide." Sneak up.

WHEN YOU WANT AUDIENCE PARTICIPATION

107. DON'T give up when you ask the audience to do something. Make them do what you want.

108. DON'T allow the audience to do anything halfway. If you want a show of hands, say, "Like this—high—like this."

109. DON'T be vague in your instructions on what you want the listeners to do. Tell them specifically, and demonstrate. Tell them, "Hold the pencil in front of your face, like this."

110. DON'T ask them to do a task without showing them what you want. Demonstrate.

111. DON'T have a member of the audience do a task without explaining what he is doing.

112. DON'T fail to compliment a participant on a job he does well.

113. DON'T forget to thank each participant.

WHEN YOU MUST READ A SPEECH

114. DON'T ever read a speech if you can help it. If you must read, rehearse the reading. Try it on the wife and kids.

115. DON'T apologize for the reading. Act as if it is the thing to do.

116. DON'T try to justify the fact that you are reading this speech. Go ahead and read. The listeners don't like it either.

117. DON'T turn pages—slide them out of the way. Hide the manuscript from the audience if possible.

118. DON'T read fast—read slowly. Write the word "SLOW" in blue pencil about the middle of each page to remind you. Use large letters—you'll need the reminder.

"He's not here?"

119. DON'T read in the same tone. Talk loud now, then louder.

120. DON'T fail to keep eye contact with the audience. Look up now and then. Watch them. They all may be asleep.

121. DON'T read a speech that you don't know. Study what is written, particularly if you used a ghost writer. Study it beforehand, rehearse the words that you might mispronounce or stumble on.

122. DON'T fail to use illustrations. Read the point in the script, then pause to tell the listeners what you mean.

123. DON'T fail to bring in relief. Your reading gets mighty tiresome. Show something now and then, step away from the lectern to explain a point. Keep that audience awake.

124. DON'T fail to stop the reading now and then. Stop and ask a question and wait as though you expected an

answer. When you read a big word, stop and kid it. Keep as human as you can.

125. DON'T fail to change the words in your reading script to speaking words. You are speaking this piece. Try to use words that you might use in conversation.

126. DON'T think of your speech as a script. Don't refer to it as my paper or my manuscript. You are speaking it, aren't you? It's a speech.

127. DON'T forget that the audience will not like the read speech. A man reading a speech is dull. If you are forced to read, try to give the listeners some relief. Show them that you are not a machine reading a speech, that you are a human being.

128. DON'T play with your spectacles, taking them off to speak to the audience, putting them on again to read. Leave them on or off.

LOTS OF DON'TS, AREN'T THERE?

Sounds like a lot, anyway, doesn't it? Of course, no one meeting manager can heed all of them. But the nearer you come to following them, the better meetings you will have.

Index

NOTE: The subjects have been listed in such a way that you can easily find some thought or plan that you want to refer to. For instance, you remember reading something about the leader's attitude in a discussion. O.K., look under *"Attitude"*—there it is, that second item, page 249. What did that author say about personal notes to build attendance? Look under *"Attendance Building,"* down the list now—there it is, page 41. You can save a lot of hunting through the book by using this index.

Meeting

business, 12
ending, 163
follow-up, 291
service club, 1
starting, 151
types of, 144

Members

attitude, 37
mail, 37
microphones, 9

Mistakes

lists of, 9, 23
moderator of panel, 266

noise competition, 27
notes, 9, 24

Notices

letters, 42
personal, 41
plan for, 38
postcards, 40

outline of meeting, 211
outsiders, 45

Panel

ideas, 265
organizing, 267
set-up for, 266
why good, 148, 264

Planning

details, 30
don'ts, 296

Practice

methods, 276
sessions, 276
platform, 25

preparation, 180
presenting the speaker, 189

Program

don'ts, 299
sample, 211
strategy, 66

Promotion

don'ts, 299
ideas, 46

Questions

contests, 242
as ending, 172
fumbling, 11, 21, 29
organizing, 34
repeating, 234, 237
sessions, 233
shill, 234
written, 240

radio and TV ideas, 243
reading a speech, 27
reception of guest speaker, 31
recesses, 27
rehearsal, 219
relaxing the audience, 171
rewards, 243

Room

arrangement, 10, 105, 114
don'ts, 296
in hotel, 121
seating fundamentals, 134
setting up, 124

schedule, 180
screen, 28

Selling

the attraction, 50
an idea to the club, 108